DIALECTICS AND DECONSTRUCTION IN POLITICAL ECONOMY

Also by Robert Albritton

A JAPANESE APPROACH TO POLITICAL ECONOMY
Unoist Variations (*co-editor*)

A JAPANESE APPROACH TO STAGES OF CAPITALIST DEVELOPMENT

A JAPANESE RECONSTRUCTION OF MARXIST THEORY

Dialectics and Deconstruction in Political Economy

Robert Albritton
Professor, Faculty of Arts
York University, Ontario, Canada

First published in Great Britain 1999 by
MACMILLAN PRESS LTD
Houndmills, Basingstoke, Hampshire RG21 6XS and London
Companies and representatives throughout the world

A catalogue record for this book is available from the British Library.

ISBN 0–333–77356–X

First published in the United States of America 1999 by
ST. MARTIN'S PRESS, INC.,
Scholarly and Reference Division,
175 Fifth Avenue, New York, N.Y. 10010

ISBN 0–312–22447–8

Library of Congress Cataloging-in-Publication Data
Albritton, Robert, 1941–
Dialectics and deconstruction in political economy / Robert Albritton.
p. cm.
Includes bibliographical references and index.
ISBN 0–312–22447–8 (cloth)
1. Marxian economics. I. Title.
HB97.5.A443949 1999
335.4—dc21 99–21774
CIP

This book is printed on paper suitable for recycling and made from fully managed and sustained forest sources.

10 9 8 7 6 5 4 3 2 1
08 07 06 05 04 03 02 01 00 99

Printed and bound in Great Britain by
Antony Rowe Ltd, Chippenham, Wiltshire

Contents

Acknowledgements

This book has emerged from years of discussion and thought about Marxian political economy. Given the scope of the book and its gestation period, it would be impossible to trace all the influences on my thought and adequately thank members of classes that I have taught, study groups in which I have participated and participants in the countless conversations I have had. I am thankful to live in such a supportive and stimulating social milieu. But within this milieu there is one person who stands out – Tom Sekine has influenced my thought immensely, and it is through him that I have become acquainted with at least some of the work of Kozo Uno. I also want to thank those who have read parts or all of the manuscript and have offered constructive criticism: John Bell, Colin Duncan, Frank Pearce, Rafael Indart, Stefanos Kourkoulakos, John Simoulidis, Randall Terada, Marc Weinstein, Richard Westra and Alan Zeuge. Finally, grateful acknowledgement is made to Editions Rodopi for permission to print a substantially revised version of 'The Unique Ontology of Capital' (as Chapter 2 of this book), which appeared in Ryszard Panasiuk and Leszek Nowak (eds), *Marx's Theories Today*.

ROBERT ALBRITTON

1 Introduction

Our world is one in which the contradictions of relatively unopposed capitalism are becoming more blatant every day. Neoliberal globalisation is throwing a growing proportion of the world's people into desperate economic insecurity and poverty – providing ever fewer well-paying, secure jobs relative to the world's population. At the same time, irreparable damage to the Earth's environment is accelerating at a truly frightening pace. And one of the great ironies is that because of ideological manipulation, intellectual fashions and fads, and the seeming triumph of neoliberal capitalism, less and less attention is being devoted to the task of refining and improving the theory developed by Marx in *Capital* – the theoretical work that more than any other advances our understanding of capital's deep structures. How ironic that intellectuals would turn away from a theory that sets the explanation of the deep structure of capital on a strong footing precisely at a time when capitalism is the main force wreaking havoc in the world.

Of course there has been and continues to be at least some attention devoted to Marx's *Capital*, but seldom is that attention directed towards refining and improving the theory of capital's inner logic as a *whole* or towards thinking in depth about the most effective use of the theory as a whole to improve our understanding of concrete reality. Typically interpreters have strip-mined *Capital*, extracting only those gems that their intellectual niche market values. Few have attempted to inhabit and reflect upon the world of the theory of capital's deep structure as a whole. Such an effort to dwell on capital's inner logic implies thinking about capitalist dynamics both economically and philosophically in their purest and least dilute forms.[1]

There are a variety of reasons why few have taken this route. Marxian economists have found fault with Marx's theories of value and price, and because they have failed to see the philosophical depth and power of the theory as a whole, they have too easily abandoned it instead of finding ways to rectify its technical flaws.[2] Philosophers have sometimes written about aspects of the philosophical depth of the theory, but because they lack the necessary grounding in economic theory, they too often fail to see the importance of the theory as an economic theory of capital's inner logic as a whole.[3] Finally, some well-meaning Marxian economists have radically reinterpreted *Capital* in order to make it more immediately relevant to the rough and tumble of history, where 'inner logics' seem out of place and disequilibrium is more apparent than equilibrium.[4] Here the internal integrity of a theory of capital's deep structures is sacrificed to the demand for 'relevance' and immediate empirical applicability. The problem, as I see it, is to combine an understanding of the philosophical implications of the theory of capital's deep structure with a rigorous refinement of the theory of capital's economic logic as a whole. This combination of painstaking economic and philosophical analysis is difficult to come by given the division of disciplines in modern academia. It is the work of Japanese political economists Kozo Uno and Tom Sekine that, in my view, most closely approximates this combining of philosophy and economics, and hence it is their work that provides the theoretical basis for this book.[5]

Indeed it is by studying their work that I have become increasingly aware of the unique ontology of capital – an ontology that in its uniqueness requires not only a rethinking of economic theory but also an extensive rethinking of philosophical categories. Above all this book is a rethinking of philosophy from the point of view of Uno and Sekine's approach to political economy, or perhaps a critique of philosophy from the point of view of a particular Marxian philosophical economics.[6] If, as I believe, capital is the most important single determinant of modern history, and if capital has a unique ontology, then it becomes necessary to begin rethinking philosophy from the point of view of capital. A careful analysis of capital's ontology leads us towards challenging and revising nearly every philosophical school, discipline and category. The philosophical economics presented in this book casts doubt on all general philosophical theories of subject–object relations, of language and of knowledge. It does so by insisting that capital's ontology and epistemology are unique, and by showing how this uniqueness fails to be accounted for by the generalising ontologies and epistemologies that are typical of most philosophy. I argue that many fundamental philosophical categories need to be rethought from the point of view of the unique ontology of capital. For example, no general philosophy of subject–object relations will do if it is contradicted by the subject–object relations peculiar to capital. No general theory of language will do if it is contradicted by considerations of how language needs to be understood in relation to the theory of capital. And it will be argued that the science of political economy, which aims to understand capitalism, is not only ontologically, epistemologically and methodologically unique, but is also ontologically differentiated internally between distinct levels of analysis.

According to Uno and Sekine, political economy can be divided into three relatively autonomous levels of analysis: the theory of a purely capitalist society, the theory of stages (no teleology implied) or phases of capitalist development, and the theory of historical change. Their approach is unique in emphasising the distinctiveness of each level and the complex articulations between them. It is an approach that though originating in Uno's work in Japan in the 1950s and 1960s is particularly germaine to today's intellectual milieu, that in being overly sensitive to the pitfalls of essentialism and reductionism has challenged our ability to advance substantive knowledge about the world.

Our age seems increasingly to be one of relativism, cynicism, lack of vision and lack of realistic alternatives. Lack of confidence in our rational capacities has led to timidity when it comes to making knowledge claims. Mainstream economic theory, with its abstract formalism on the one hand and narrow instrumentalism on the other, has not and is not serving us well. Indeed it is too deeply embedded in capitalism itself to achieve the degree of objectivity needed to provide the basis for thinking about the sort of radical structural transformations that are called for by our historical predicament. What is desperately required in this area of intellectual endeavour is theoretical work that is not simply formalistic but instead grasps the substance of the deep structures of capital, and can use this understanding to inform the structural transformations required to achieve democratic socialism.

The need for a science of political economy, by which I mean the same thing as a science of capitalism, derives from our need to understand our past so that we can move towards the future with a sense of who we are and what our possibilities are. Capitalism has been around for such a long time that we have largely become its creatures. Can we rest content to remain so when rampant consumerism threatens the planet and growing inequality threatens the moral fibre of civilised life? And yet, clear and realistic thought about alternatives since the demise of 'actually existing socialism' appears to be undermined by a postmodernism that is all too often morbidly self-indulgent, aestheticist and paralysed by all-encompassing 'undecidability'.

It seems that there is not much to choose between mainstream economic theory that is inherently procapitalist, and postmodernism, which either rejects economic theory or reduces it to radically contingent and contextual rhetoric, and reduces radicalism to a series of hyper-self-conscious cultural posings. Perhaps with most of the ideological weight of the Cold War off our backs, we can now begin to rethink Marxian political economy, taking into account the power of Marx's theory of capital's inner logic as well as the objections of those who would turn away from the seeming essentialism of such a theory. We need a theoretical approach that can both clearly grasp capital's inner logic at the abstract level of pure capitalism, and at more concrete levels of analysis understand the specific articulations of that logic with structures and processes that in their partial autonomy disrupt that logic to some extent, translating a tight inner logic into looser logics that are partial and have some autonomy from each other.

For example, in the theory of a purely capitalist society there is one and only one monetary system that consists of gold and convertible currency. At the level of mid-range stage theory there may be an international monetary system, national (or regional) monetary systems, and even to some extent local monetary systems, that may or may not be based on a gold standard. Furthermore the characteristic degree of autonomy and specific articulations amongst monetary systems may not only differ between stages, but also at the level of historical analysis they may also tend to change in particular directions. Despite this complexity, however, insofar as capital's logic is a force in the world, there will be at least some tendency towards a homogenising effect between monetary systems and at least some tendency for monetary systems to be managed as though they were tied to gold, whether they actually are or not.[7] Thus the 'looser logics' or 'multiple logics' at the levels of stage theory and historical analysis have only relative autonomy, constrained by the force of capital's inner logic insofar as that logic is still operating in the world.

The approach to Marxian political economy that I want to develop in this book is, as stated above, strongly influenced by the work of Japanese political economists Kozo Uno and Tom Sekine. Uno was the founder of a school of thought in Japan based on a rigorous reconceptualisation of Marx's *Capital* coupled with the notion of distinct levels of analysis in political economy. He showed that if we assume a purely capitalist society, it is possible to theorise the inner logic of capital as a self-regulating, commodity-economic logic. At the same time we know that no actual society is purely capitalist, so in order to determine how capital's logic affects the actual course of history it is necessary to consider its articulation with numerous other social forces. To this end Uno proposed the three levels of analysis that I have just introduced.

Sekine has refined and enlarged Uno's work in a number of directions. Most importantly he has brought out the dialectical structure of capital's logic, making explicit parallels between the dialectic of capital and Hegel's *Logic*. Sekine's full and explicit recognition of the dialectical character of capital's inner logic represents an unprecedented theoretical breakthrough in the history of Marxian political economy. The dialectical method not only provides the basis for vastly improving the logical rigor of the theory of a purely capitalist society, it also provides an objective reference to inform Marxian political economy at its more concrete levels.[8] There are in fact strong reasons to believe that the dialectic of capital is the most objective touchstone to be found anywhere within modern social science.

Sekine's reconstruction of Marx's theory of capital's inner logic as a rigorous dialectic also helps to clarify the relations between the theory of pure capitalism, where potential use-value obstacles are overcome by self-expanding value, and more concrete levels where use-value as materiality may resist value and force compromises upon value. Mid-range stage theory, for example, conceptualises historically specific types of use-value constraint the managing of which require specific types of ideological, legal and political support in order for value to constitute a stage-specific type of capital accumulation.

Many theorists have written in passing about levels of analysis or levels of abstraction, but surprisingly few have given this absolutely crucial issue the attention it cries out for.[9] And yet without some such notion in the social sciences, abstract theory is likely to be used in essentialist ways, leading at least some practitioners to react against this, and in their reaction to become antitheory. A more promising way forward is to problematise the relation between abstract theory and more concrete levels of theory, and this would seem to imply some kind of conception of relatively autonomous levels in order to avoid the extremes of crudely empirical history that is presumably uninformed by theory (if this is possible) on the one hand, and history that is reduced to little more than a function of abstract theory on the other. In other words, instead of being entrapped by the tendency to collapse theory into historical analysis or historical analysis into theory, levels of analysis enable us to maintain the integrity of each by insisting on a relative autonomy that problematises their interconnections.

A crucial contribution of a levels of analysis approach is its ability creatively to theorise the social relations between the economic and the non-economic. The nature of the economic in capitalist society becomes crystal clear at the level of the theory of capital's inner logic or the theory of pure capitalism, because at this level we assume that markets are self-regulating, thereby pushing ideological, legal and political forms of regulation into the background. At the level of stage theory, markets are seldom if ever totally self-regulating; hence the accumulation of capital is aided by non-economic structures that take on stage-specific forms. While stage theory is basically structural and synchronic, the historical analysis of capitalism principally concerns itself with change and causality. At this third level of analysis, capitalism is conceived of as a powerful and in some ways unique social force operating in conjunction with other social forces.

Having expressed the need for a greater focus of intellectual energies on levels of analysis, it must be admitted that such a focus raises many daunting problems that this book will identify and begin to grapple with. Perhaps the reason why so many thinkers, after mentioning the need for levels of analysis, pass so quickly on to other issues is precisely the difficulties that arise immediately upon focusing seriously on such a notion. I believe that the avoidance of levels of analysis is currently the most costly avoidance in political economy, an avoidance that this book begins to face up to.

To begin with, let me give a brief sketch of what I see, following the work of Uno and Sekine, as the three levels of political economy. The theory of a purely capitalist society is a theory of the deep structure or inner logic of capital (or the theory of a purely capitalist society) achieved by taking seriously Marx's claim that capital is essentially self-expanding or self-valorising value. If value is to be self-valorising it must be able to operate entirely through self-regulating markets, without outside support, to reproduce and expand itself in ways that are consistent with the viability of social life. Such a situation is a purely capitalist society in the sense the capital reproduces itself and expands while at the same time allowing for the reproduction of social life as a whole. Conceived this way, the logic of capital is a self-determining whole, and all of the fundamental categories of capital can be interconnected in a dialectical logic of value as it is allowed in theory to subsume socioeconomic life in its totality. Such a theory gives us the essence of capitalism by revealing the *modus operandi* of capital when not interfered with by any outside forces. But because of levels of analysis this theory of essence lacks the negative essentialist effects that have driven poststructuralists to distraction.

While one might say that ultimately there is one true essence of capital and that Sekine has correctly identified the starting point, the main categories and their sequence, it does not follow that we will ever reach complete agreement on every detail of its formulation. For even if numerous theorists all take up the same project of using a dialectical method to explore capital's inner logic, there will always be disagreement about how best to formulate the details of this logic. Disagreement, however, will be limited by the shared aim to find the dialectically strongest way to formulate the interconnections between the basic categories of capitalist economic life – value, price, profit, rent, interest, wages and so on – in a purely capitalist society. At this level of analysis we want to know, for example, how in general capitalist profits are related to all other basic economic categories of capitalism. And above all we want to know something about the basic dynamics of capital, or how all the various economic categories move in relation to each other when not interfered with by outside forces. What fundamentally limits the range of disagreement in formulating such a theory is that the dialectical method lets capital's logic emerge in a context of non-interference, so that it is not our logic that we are imposing on capital, but rather the logic that is inherent in capital when left to its own devices, as it is under the assumption of a purely capitalist society, that we are trying by our theorising to allow to emerge.

Stage theory configures capital's logic as it is most characteristically manifested in distinctly different periods of capital accumulation. Such a configuration must include articulations between the dominant economic structures and all other sorts of ideological and political structures that work with them to facilitate capitalist profit making. The challenge at this level is not only to grasp the dominant economic dynamics at work, but also to grasp how these dynamics articulate with all sorts of active and sometimes invasive social forces that are not primarily economic in character. Typically we find that the most dominant and successful mode of capital accumulation characteristic of a whole period is located in particular economically dominant countries (though with international dimensions) from which stage theory with the aid of the theory of capital's logic and historical analysis, abstracts its paradigm of capital accumulation.

There is much greater latitude for disagreement about the construction of stage theory (no teleology implied) than about the construction of the theory of pure capitalism. Stage theory, as I see it, should include the search for a mid-range theory, representing a constellation of the most important social forces as they interact in support of the dominant modes of capital accumulation that are characteristic of an entire period. But even with agreement on this aim, there can be disagreement about the precise level of abstraction at which stage theory should be cast, which breadth and detail of social forces should be included, precisely how more abstract and less abstract theory should be used to inform this level, and even how many stages there should be.

According to Sekine, since the basic contradiction of the dialectic of capital is between value and use-value, and since stage theory basically represents the interaction of the logic of value with historical stage-specific structures (which can be considered a set of use-value constraints), the basic problem of mid-range theory can be formulated as exploring and analysing all the ways that the motion of value must 'compromise' with existing institutions in order to establish a workable mode of capital accumulation. Thus, for example, the organisation of capital is likely to be different when the sorts of use-value produced involve large economies of scale, or when the legal form of the limited-liability, joint-stock company becomes widespread, or when the state actively intervenes to protect industries or promote foreign trade and investment. The result of such an analysis is conversion of the logic of capital into a dynamic of economic, political and ideological institutions that promote a stage-specific mode of capital accumulation or profit making. Stage theory starts, then, with a conception of where capital is located (spatially, temporally and sectorally) and how it operates not on average, but in its most successful and most characteristically capitalist *modus operandi*. Since at the level of basic principles labour power, land and money are the use values that value has the most difficulty managing on its own, it is around these use values that we would particularly centre our analysis of stage-specific institutional supports. The international dimension of capital accumulation and the stage-specific tendencies towards periodic crisis would also be key focal points.

If the key to the use of abstract theory is the value/use-value dialectic, how might historical analysis be most effectively utilised to inform stage theory? For each period there is a 'golden age' when the dominant modes of accumulation are functioning at their best: for mercantilism it is Britain in the 1690–1750 period, for liberalism it is Britain in the 1830–70 period, for imperialism it is Germany and the United States in the 1890–1914 period, and for consumerism it is the United States in the 1950–70 period. No doubt there could be a great deal of dispute over this periodisation.[10] The aim of stage theory, as I see it, is to create a constellation of interrelated structural types informed by the logic of capital and by the historical analysis of each golden age. The historical analysis for stage theory, however, should not simply focus narrowly on, say, Britain for the stage of liberalism because part of the character of capital accumulation in Britain for this period is how it articulates with the rest of the world.

The latitude for disagreement widens as we move from the abstract to the concrete, since at the level of the historical analysis of capitalism all of the disagreements about how to formulate the theory of capital's logic and stage theory are compounded by differences over how to use these more abstract levels of analysis to inform historical analysis. The logic of capital affects all areas of social life and most aspects of our natural world, and may be affected in turn, but these affects are uneven. For example capital continually and directly shapes technological advance and in turn is shaped by it, whereas family structure or particular ideological structures may resist capital's logic and only be reshaped by it gradually over a long period of time. The more that our historical analysis is focused upon long-term structural economic trends, the more directly relevant are the informing powers of both the abstract and mid-range theories of political economy. It is also important to remember that in the context of this book 'historical analysis' always refers to the historical analysis of capitalism. In other words the aim is to determine the specific role of capitalism in history and not to deny the important roles played by other factors.

The strength of the Uno–Sekine approach, with its three levels, rests upon the objective grounding that it receives in the dialectic of capital. The claims to objective knowledge in this case are very similar to those made by Hegel in his *Logic*. Of course there is still great controversy about the relation of Hegel's thought to Marxism. A few examples will illustrate this point. Althusser argues that in the hands of Marx, the Hegelian dialectic is fundamentally transformed. Hegel's centred totality is transformed into a decentred whole. His simple contradiction is transformed into an overdetermined contradiction. His expressive totality is transformed into a structured totality of relatively autonomous practices. His homogeneous time is transformed into heterogeneous times developing unevenly in relation to each other. His developmental, teleological history is transformed into a history with radical breaks and no teleology. According to Althusser, Marx's materialist dialectic does away with Hegelian concepts such as 'aufhebung' (sublation or supersession), negation of the negation, and the transformation of quantity into quality. After the transformations of Althusser's Marx, one might wonder what is left of Hegel's influence on Marx. According to Althusser (1990, p. 216), 'Marx was close to Hegel in his insistence on rejecting every philosophy of the Origin and of the Subject, whether rationalist, empiricist, or transcendental.' But as it turns out Marx is not so close to Hegel even on this issue, according to Althusser (ibid., p. 218), because at the end of Hegel's dialectical process both the origin and subject emerge as incorporated within the process itself. According to Althusser, all that remains of Hegel in Marx's work is the notion of history as a process without a subject.

In sharp contrast to Althusser's veritable exorcism of Hegel from at least Marx's mature works, particularly *Capital*, Postone (1996, p. 75) argues that Marx 'explicitly characterizes capital as the self-moving substance which is Subject.... His analysis suggests that the social relations that characterize capitalism are of a very peculiar sort – they possess the attributes that Hegel accorded the *Geist*.' And in *Late Marxism* Jameson (1990, p. 241) claims that 'any number of straws in the wind point to an impending Hegel revival, of a new kind, likely to draw a revival of Capital-logic along with it.... But the Hegel who emerges from this rereading will be an unfamiliar materialist-mathematical Hegel.' It would seem that the debate on the place of Hegelian dialectics in Marxism is alive and well.

The central aim of this book is to redefine Marxian political economy in a way that is much closer to Postone than to Althusser's structuralism or Derrida's poststructuralism, but that holds a dialogue with Althusser's attempt to ground the scientificity of Marx's *Capital*, and similarly with Derrida's antiessentialism. I intend to do this by appropriating Hegel's dialectic in a new way that avoids the problematic reductionist features of essentialism while maintaining the strength of dialectical logic in bringing to light the necessary inner connections between the categories embedded in the deep structure of capitalism. I shall propose a theory of capital's essence that avoids making historical outcomes a direct or simple function of that essence.

Any serious discussion of dialectics must include Hegel, just as any serious discussion of deconstruction must include Derrida. Hence this book includes a chapter on each. What I am particularly interested to bring out, however, is a particular anti-Hegelian animus that in attempting to escape his essentialism winds up in an epistemological desert where knowledge is reduced to shifting lines (iterations) in the sand blown by the infinite winds of overdetermination. Derrida himself stops short of this desertification of knowledge, but he is so worried about the dangers of theoreticism and essentialism that he carries out extensive slash and burn operations. At the very least these reduce the possibilities of knowledge to groping about a protean and shifting landscape. What is fundamental to anti-essentialism is the total inability to recognise necessity either in being or in thought. But of course anti-essentialism and anti-Hegelianism did not by any means begin with Derrida.

The anti-Hegelian animus that is so widespread in modern thought has particularly aimed at the essentialism of his dialectic coupled with the pronounced religiosity of his thought. In order to clarify and defend my particular appropriation of the Hegelian dialectic for Marxian political economy, I want to discuss a number of anti-essentialist thinkers, the most prominent of which are Althusser and Derrida. But anti-essentialism did not suddenly spring into being with French structuralism and poststructuralism. One of the most influential anti-essentialist social scientists in the modern period is Weber. While he does not seem closely connected in time, space or intellectual framework with Althusser or Derrida, an analysis of the ways in which he theorised the economic and its connections with the non-economic well serve my general project of differentiating the Uno–Sekine approach from other prominent approaches.

In Chapter 2 I explore the unique ontology of capital, an ontology that in my view necessitates levels of analysis. The Uno–Sekine approach that informs my analysis is introduced by discussing a number of basic ontological and epistemological categories that arise when considering the specificities of capital as an object of knowledge. I argue at length that the self-reifying character of capital differentiates it from other social objects of knowledge, making it an object whose deep structure can be grasped by a dialectical logic.

Chapter 3 compares Hegel's dialectic of the deep structure of pure thought with Sekine's dialectic of the deep structure of pure capital. I argue that the dialectic of capital, while being structurally very close to Hegel's dialectic, is different from and superior to Hegel's dialectic of thought in a number of respects; and contrary to Hegel and Colletti, I argue that dialectical thought is most appropriate in the case of the materialist dialectic of capital that necessarily problematises the essentialism of Hegel's idealist dialectic. In that chapter there is also a critical analysis of Adorno's *Negative Dialectics* (1987) and Postone's *Time, Labor, and Social Domination* (1996), since the Frankfurt School tradition that they represent is strongly grounded in a variety of dialogues with Hegel.

Chapter 4 analyses Weber's anti-essentialism, with particular emphasis on how he conceptualised the economic and levels of analysis. I argue that his neo-Kantian ontological and epistemological assumptions did not serve him well in his central project of understanding the uniqueness of modern capitalism, and that in some respects his anti-essentialism produces dogmatism. I believe that dogmatism occurs when definitions and typologies are simply asserted by fiat, or at least tend to be strongly undertheorised.

In Chapter 5 I interrogate Althusser's conceptualisation of capital as an object of knowledge and his pronounced anti-Hegelianism. While Althusser certainly asked many of the right questions about capital as an object of knowledge, his answers are found wanting. And his pronounced anti-Hegelianism leads him to break with some of the most fruitful aspects of Hegel's thought, while ironically he preserves aspects of Hegelianism that are best left behind.

The focus of Chapter 6 is deconstruction and attempts to synthesise it with Marxism, particularly with Marxian political economy. Particular attention is given to Derrida's *Specters of Marx* (1994), his most recent attempt to deal with the extreme strain that results when deconstruction tries to maintain some contact with Marxism. Others who have attempted to go much further in overcoming the strain, such as Ryan (1982) and Gibson–Graham (1996), will also be discussed. Although my analysis is be basically critical of deconstruction as a general approach to social science, it is nonetheless seen as having a limited role in sensitising us to undesirable forms of essentialism. In terms of the approach to political economy that I am advocating, it means that deconstruction offers arguments that can support the necessity for levels of analysis.

2 The Unique Ontology of Capital[1]

The object of knowledge of political economy, as I understand it, is capitalism. It is generally agreed that capitalism has existed for at least 300 years, but in that period it has developed unevenly and taken many different forms, some societies being more capitalist and some less. Despite the multiplicity of forms, there seem to be certain persistent forces or logics at work that tend to homogenise social relations in capitalist societies, even if they fall short of ever achieving full homogenisation. Commodity-economic logics seem to have a certain automaticity about them that, though never total, is discernable, as in the movement of capital from less profitable to more profitable sectors, or in the movement of prices as supply and demand vary. Also, once commodity-economic logics, subsume the labour and production process they are both expansive and invasive, in the sense that in the long run they tend to expand globally and to subsume other forces or shape other social forces more than being shaped by them, as evidenced by the increasing globalisation of capitalism and the impact of capital on all areas of social life. And if we look at capitalist history, it seems as though the tendency towards the domination of economic life by an increasingly self-regulating commodity-economic logic grew until at least the 1870s (some might say to the present day, but today the degree of state intervention and other forms of organised intervention is much greater than in the 1860s in England). These 'common sense' observations suggest that there must be some deep structures that endure through all of capitalism's diverse surface forms. Indeed a history that simply described capitalism's diverse surface forms without theorising deeper structures that might help explain capitalism's continuity and its dynamic directionality would be intellectually irresponsible and bankrupt, especially in the light of Marx's *Capital*, which represents a huge step towards understanding capital's inner logic or deep structure, even if only a first step.

Amongst recent Marxist theorists, Althusser's project was to stress the immense scientific breakthrough represented by Marx's *Capital* (Althusser and Balibar, 1970). To persist with this project in an age of seemingly triumphant capitalism and the correspondingly well-established academic discipline of economic science might strike many as rather perverse. And yet this is precisely what I aim to do. Even if his answers were often not the ones that I would give, Althusser posed interesting questions. The questions in which I am interested are to do with the specificities of the object of knowledge of economic science, or in Althusser's terms, it is my aim to 'problematise' this theoretical object in order to begin to understand its peculiar uniqueness. And as the argument unfolds, it is my hope that the reader will increasingly come to see that Marx's *Capital* does indeed represent an immense breakthrough in economic science, a breakthrough that has been further developed by the work of Uno and Sekine.

I read *Capital* not as a mature work of a well-developed economic science, but as a work that contains language that is not designed fully to recognise the existence of a new way of theorising the deep structure of the economic, language that constrained Marx from fully recognising the potential of his own theory and has constrained commentators to this day. It is understandable, therefore, that someone as astute as Gramsci (1971, p. 400) would claim that *Capital* is a synthesis of Ricardo and Hegel. No doubt there are both Ricardian and Hegelian elements in Marx's theorising of capital, but I argue that these elements can blind us to the novelty of Marx's theory if we fail to consider it as a not altogether successful first attempt to say something quite new. Marx himself was sufficiently caught up in the old language that he could only develop a limited awareness of the potentialities and implications of his formulations. And both disciples and detractors have been so caught up in the political passions that have swirled around *Capital* over the highly charged history of the past century, that clear philosophical thinking about the nature of the economic under capitalism and about the relative success of Marx's *Capital* in theorising it has been almost impossible. Perhaps it is only now that so-called 'socialism' has failed and capitalism has no enemy but itself that we can begin to develop, and perhaps desperately need to develop, the scientific potentialities that have existed in embryonic form in *Capital* and have been waiting to be born for over a century. For it is my contention that *Capital* establishes a basis for theorising the economic under capitalism that has great scientific and critical potential.

In *The Structure of Idealization*, Nowak (1980) extracts from *Capital* a general theory of science. While it is important to explore the similiarities between Marx's *Capital* and other works of science, and there is much that I can agree with in Nowak's work, my emphasis is on highlighting what it is that is different about the science of capitalism, as founded by Marx. It is my contention that Marx's new science of political economy is distinct from other social sciences, particularly from mainstream economic 'science'.

Mainstream economic theory is almost entirely instrumental and technical in the sense that it simply accepts the existence of commodities, money and capital, and then proceeds to convert these 'things' into mathematical variables and abstract models with the aim of helping us better to manipulate these variables in order to enhance profit-making and policy making. There is little concern to problematise the relation between the economic and the non-economic or between abstract model and historical analysis. As a result the theory simply accepts, and in doing so reinforces and accentuates, the subsumption of all social life to economic forces that are placed in the sovereign driver's seat. The disembeddedness of the economic from the social under capitalism is often a normative ideal in mainstream economics, and such disembeddedness is thereby exacerbated in the economic practices that mainstream economics attempts to inform.

And disembeddedness does not simply imply passive conformity to market forces, nor does reembeddedness imply nothing more than central planning. While socialists would want to move away from self-regulating markets towards various forms of democratic planning, the initial steps towards reembedding the economic into the social would require treating economic price as one kind of value amongst other forms of social value. To what extent this alternative way of thinking about the economic would in the long run lead to a dismantling of the market would be determined by a pragmatism aimed at achieving a more egalitarian and democratic society.

These claims may so far not sound very novel, and, – through the use of the term 'disembedded' – perhaps more reminiscent of Polanyi (1944) than Marx. While I think that Polanyi does have some very interesting things to say about the economic, the social and about 'market mentalities', his most significant contributions lie in the areas of structural economic history and economic anthropology and not in economic science *per se*. In my view Marx's scientific breakthrough was made possible by his understanding of reification, or in other words by the sense in which capital is paradoxically both social and antisocial – social in pushing us towards a uniform social order ruled by the commodity, and antisocial in achieving this through progressive atomisation that sets individual against individual and class against class. 'Disembeddedness of the economic', it turns out, is simply a more imagistic, metaphorical and therefore less scientific expression of 'reification'.

Capital is a social relation for Marx, but it is a social relation that once well-established takes on an automaticity and life of its own and uses other social relations for its own self-aggrandisement.[2] Thus, though fundamentally social, the economic becomes both relatively autonomous from and set over and against the rest of social life: it is both social and antisocial. The antisocial character of the economic makes it appear to be a completely separate sphere of social life that can be treated purely quantitatively and technically, as though use-value considerations and non-economic value did not exist. It is this aspect of the economic under capitalism that mainstream economic theory takes as a given, and that the Uno–Sekine approach to political economy problematises.

It is now possible to state the aim of this chapter more concretely. Typically the concepts of ontology, epistemology and methodology have been developed for thought in general, or sometimes more specifically for thought in the social sciences as opposed to thought in the natural sciences.[3] I want to take a different approach. I want at least to start a process of rethinking these categories from the point of view of the specificities of a particular object of knowledge.[4] Thus starting with a discussion of certain basic realities of social relations under capitalism, I shall argue that capital has an inner nature with unique ontological properties requiring very particular ontological, epistemological and methodological categories that by and large do not fit the general philosophical categories handed down to us.[5] Thus from this perspective 'social ontology' is too generalising and hence too homogenising. The uniqueness of the ontology of capital tends to go unrecognised if we start with *social* ontology, and it is this uniqueness that I want to highlight.

Philosophy often addresses questions such as 'What is the nature of science?', 'What is the nature of language?' or 'How does necessity relate to contingency?' While certain intellectual gains may result from asking such questions about the nature of these things in the abstract and in general, preoccupation with them may divert us from asking questions about the specificities of particular objects of knowledge. The discussion of the specific differences between the natural and social sciences goes back as far as the nineteenth century, but little attention has been paid to differences between objects of knowledge within the social sciences, even with the advent of poststructuralism, which is presumably preoccupied with 'difference'.[6] I shall argue below that what gives capital its unique ontology is primarily its reified and self-reifying character.

REIFICATION

Economic reification exists to the extent that social relations among economic actors are mediated by 'things' (the commodity and money), which in turn develop 'social relations' among themselves in markets and come to embody social relations.[7] Or in other words, economic reification implies a market-governed society: a society in which the actions of human economic agents are directed and subsumed by market forces beyond their control. If the economic life of society is completely governed by markets without reliance upon any outside extra-economic force (government intervention or any other kind of organised human intervention), that economy is totally reified.

In *Capital* Marx assumes total reification when he is theorising the law of value, as opposed to when he is discussing history. This is not only made clear by his use of the term 'fetishism', but also by the metaphorical description of humans as mere 'bearers of economic categories' or 'personifications of economic categories'. 'Fetishism of commodities' is used by Marx primarily to accentuate the cognitive confusion produced within political economy by the fact of reification. As I understand it reification refers to the structural logic of capital that converts persons into 'bearers' or '*træger*' of economic forces. Marx uses the metaphors 'bearers' and 'personifications' to emphasise the fact that he is theorising capital as 'self-expanding value', and at the level of abstraction at which he is theorising, humans are viewed simply as members of classes that reproduce themselves by receiving either wages (working class), profits (capitalist class) or rents (landlord class). Indeed the very concept 'self-expanding value' suggests reification as I understand it, since value can only be *self*-expanding to the extent that all inputs and outputs of production are commodified so that the circuit of capital, which in one of its manifestations is *M–C…P…C′–M′* (buying commodities, transforming them in a production process, and selling them at a profit), can expand itself without relying on extra-economic support.[8] Furthermore Marx assumes pure capitalism in the sense that all production is the production of commodities, and all production of commodities is production by commodified labour power employed by capital to maximise profits.[9] Pure capitalism, then, is characterised by total reification (total commodification) and by three and only three economic classes that respectively perform all the productive labour, own and control all the means of production (except monopolisable natural resources, collectively labelled 'land') and own all 'land'. Pure capitalism involves the subsumption of the labour and production process to a system of interlocking markets that are self-regulating in the sense that no extra-economic force (state, monopoly, trade unions and so on) can interfere with the markets.

Since the term 'reification' is particularly associated with the work of Lukács, it is necessary to distinguish my use of the term from his. In his famous essay 'Reification and the Consciousness of the Proletariat', he explicitly states that 'It is beyond the scope of this essay to discuss the central importance of this problem [reification] for economics itself' (Lukács, 1971, pp. 83–4). Instead he claims that 'What is at issue *here*, however, is the question: how far is commodity exchange together with its structural consequences able to influence the *total* outer and inner life of society'? (ibid., p. 84). In short Lukács uses 'reification' to centre a totality that consists of a fragmented and divided consciousness that can only be overthrown and unified by a proletariat that becomes the subject–object of a universal teleology. His totality in the first instance is all of human history, which culminates in a divided consciousness with reification at the centre. And his totality is cultural in the sense that its object is collective consciousness. Lukács is concerned with the impact of the fetishism of commodities on the totality of bourgeois philosophy, an impact that generates a characteristic set of antinomies and dualisms that also permeate hegemonic bourgeois culture.

Contrary to Lukács, I use 'reification' as the most basic category of the economic ontology of capitalism. In my usage, 'fetishism of commodities' only refers to cognitive obstacles (particularly as manifested in bourgeois economic theory) generated by the reified deep structure of capital, whereas for Lukács it often seems that fetishism is the more basic term, with reification being the philosophical outcome of the fact of fetishism. In opposition to Lukács, I believe that it is because capital is a reified reality that it is possible to construct a scientific theory of it, a theory that has some unique properties precisely because capital is the only modern social reality with such powerful reifying and self-reifying tendencies.[10] In my usage reification is a necessary condition for theorising the inner logic of capital, but the extent to which this logic shapes the economic, and the economic shapes other social realms, is made problematic by the fact that reification is only ever partial at the level of concrete history. Reification is always resisted, and the particular ways in which reification and resistance to it is institutionalised in different phases of capitalist development is basic to understanding the character of capital accumulation in those phases (that is, stage theory). Contrary to Lukács I do not view reification as the centre of a divided consciousness that, because of its internal contradictions, can be overthrown by a self-knowing proletariat. For me the reifying force of capital is powerful, but the degree to which it affects various arenas of social life is quite variable and depends upon how those arenas are articulated with the economic and the degree to which the economic is shaped by the logic of capital. Indeed to sort out these issues, it is first necessary to be clear about the logic of capital, and it is in theorising the logic of capital that reification plays a role of fundamental importance. In the Uno–Sekine approach, 'totality' in the first instance refers to a purely capitalist society, a highly restricted totality that can never fully manifest itself empirically, and that therefore only functions to inform more concrete levels of analysis.

In a purely capitalist society where reification is total and all production is capitalist production, each individual worker must sell his or her labour power or be supported by someone who does so in order to survive.[11] Workers are free to sell their labour power to any capitalist who wishes to buy it, and are free to leave one job in the hope of finding a better one. Thus from a purely subjective point of view, each worker is free and may feel free. In reality this freedom is sharply constrained by objective conditions created by the accumulation of capital operating through markets. Because of competition, working conditions and wages amongst unskilled workers in pure capitalism will tend to be equalised, with wages tending towards an individual average based on the cost of reproducing the working class. Thus in a purely capitalist society, working for one capitalist is much the same as working for another, so that 'choice', while present, becomes relatively meaningless. The working class as a whole can either work for capital according to terms over which workers have no control, or starve. What from a subjective point of view appears to be freedom, from an objective point of view is a choice between working on terms dictated by capitalist competition, or death. This is the way in which reification subsumes the agency of workers to the motion of capital. Indeed the agency of workers is nullified insofar as their agency simply fuels the motion of value, which rigidly imposes outcomes upon them and over which they have no control (as long as we assume the existence of pure capitalism). Furthermore capital's fixation on profit means that capital is totally indifferent to workers as human beings, and instead treats labour power as one more commodity input.

The agency of individual capitalists does not fare much better under the regime of total reification that is characteristic of pure capitalism. On the surface it appears that each capitalist is free to produce anything whatsoever in any way he or she pleases, and to shift from producing one thing to another. He or she does not have to sell their labour power because they own productive property outside their person. The individual capitalist may not only feel free, but have this freedom confirmed by gaining great riches. Yet this subjective feeling of freedom is sharply constrained by objective conditions established by the market. Capitalists are only better off than workers from the point of view of freedom in that they are twice removed from death. First they go bankrupt, and only then become workers. Thus a capitalist cannot set wages and working conditions for his workers much above or below those established by the market without losing out to competitors. In order to make a profit, a capitalist must produce what the market dictates and in the manner that it dictates, and even if he or she tries hard to follow market signals, there is still the possibility of bankruptcy in a depression. Capitalists producing in sectors with no profits must shift to sectors with profits or face extinction (as capitalists). Indeed it is the average rate of profit established by market competition that dictates to the capitalist class as a whole what and how it must produce in the long run, in the sense that capitalists producing at below-average profits will shift to sectors producing above-average profits, resulting in a tendency towards the average rate of profit.

Because pure capitalism is based upon the absolute right of private property, some may argue that it cannot be totally reified given its dependence upon an extra-economic system of law. But using Marx's apt phrase, in the context of pure capitalism, law is simply a 'passive reflex' that recognises the separateness of legal persons as property owners engaged in exchange. It is the exchange relations that are fundamental and the concept of legal person is simply a reflex of these relations. Indeed in a sense 'legal person' simply confirms reification because it is a concept that arises from the absolute sovereignty of each individual within the realm of his or her private property, and such sovereign individuals only connect economically through the commodities of exchange.

One might also state that reification cannot be total because the motion of value implies the use of language, and to this extent it must be dependent upon an outside support. I would counter this by claiming that in a purely capitalist society, language, at least insofar as it plays a role in economic transactions, is also a passive reflex of exchange. Indeed very little language is needed for exchange relations. All that need happen is for a seller to place a price tag on a commodity, a buyer to point to the commodity, the seller to hand it over, and the buyer to hand over the amount of money written on the price tag. Of course commodities and money are both 'things' and social forms in the sense that they are things that can only be commodities and money because of a set of social relations. The language embedded in those social relations that enables certain things to be understood as commodities and money, however, is largely determined by reified economic relations. In this context, language is less the instrument of subjects trying to communicate, than a reflex of object-determined social practice.

The above examples are meant to illustrate the sense in which reification is 'total'. Total reification does not mean that human agency disappears, rather that agency is channelled and directed by market forces, and hence loses all autonomy in the sense that all general economic outcomes are determined by the motion of value and not human intentions. There is no economic self-organisation of persons, because direct person-to-person relations are totally replaced by relations mediated by commodities, and because persons are reduced to being simply instrumental to capital's self-expanding motion. Factories, for example, must be theorised as machine-like institutions whose activities are determined by the motion of value, and even the internal relations within factories must be thought of in reified terms. For example workers are simply appendages of machines, and working conditions among factories are equalised by competition that tends to equalise the rate of surplus value. At this level of abstraction we cannot theorise 'factory regimes', which imply, at least to some extent, direct person-to-person power relations.[12] This is an important point because as we move away from the theory of pure capitalism to more concrete levels of analysis, where reification is less than total, agency of varying types and to varying degrees reemerges.

'Reification' is often used loosely in the social sciences to refer to any social institution that develops rigidities and inertia, and resists change by becoming thing-like or machine-like. In this sense it is often used interchangeably with terms such as 'bureaucratisation'. No doubt bureaucracies are reified to some extent, in part because capitalist factories require military-type control, but part of what makes economic reification so powerful is its dynamism and 'creative destruction', which continually threatens bureaucracies that have become too rigid. Economic reification enforces its laws by way of the permanent disruption and insecurity of intense market competition. 'All that is solid melts into air' (Marx, 1978b, p. 476), as the laws of motion of capital feed a continual frenzy of individuals trying to 'make it'.[13]

The two commodities that capital has the most difficulty managing in a purely commodity-economic way are labour power and land, and this is because they are not capitalistically produced. In order to manage labour power purely as a commodity, workers must be assumed to be unorganised and docile, they must be totally divorced from any means of production, they must be legal persons free to sell their labour power, they must receive the product of their necessary labour in order to reproduce themselves, and there must be an 'industrial reserve army', periodically replenished by crises, to keep wages in line with the requirements of industry.

Land is managed commodity-economically through the categories of rent and interest. Rent maintains the average rate of profit by siphoning off surplus profits due to differences in the fertility of land and other monopolisable resource endowments, and through the category 'interest', land can be given a capitalistically rational price by considering what amount of capital would be needed to yield an interest equal to the annual rent of the land.

A purely capitalist society is not only totally reified but also capitalism is historically self-reifying, and this sharply differentiates capital ontologically from other areas of social life. The use of money to make more money through the circuit of capital *M–C–M′* becomes self-expansive once the source of profit falls within its own motion, or, in other words, once *M–C–M′* subsumes the labour and production process, as in *M–C…P…C′–M′*. In this manner reification is reproduced and expanded. At the level of history, this means that once capital sinks its roots into social life there is a tendency for social relations to become more reified, though at the level of the concrete this tendency towards reification always runs into obstacles that prevent it from becoming more than partial. The self-reifying property of capital is particularly important when it comes to understanding such categories as 'totality' and 'abstraction' (see below).

For me, 'reification' brings out most fully the basic ontological properties of capital; I use it strictly as an economic category. For Lukács it is a socio-cultural category that is the centre of a capitalist totality. Contrary to Lukács, I do not see reification as the unifying principle of capitalist culture that permeates the whole; instead it is a characteristic of capital that differentiates it from other social structures even as it may partially reify those structures (such as bureaucracies) by its influence. Furthermore, total reification is a theoretical assumption that we make in order accurately to theorise capital's inner logic. It is not the historical reality of capitalism that with Marcuse and Adorno becomes so totalising that opposition is reduced to aesthetic rebellion. And as a theoretical assumption it is not an arbitrary assumption, supported as it is by the self-reifying tendencies of capital in history. It is 'reification' that helps us to understand how one set of social relations (capital) can develop an inner logic that is set over and against other social relations.

It may seem that my 'reification' means nearly the same thing as Althusser's 'structure', since both concepts are derived from capital's tendency to reduce persons to bearers of economic structures. Despite this similarity, there are some pronounced differences. Althusser reifies 'structure' into a universal category such that all social totalities are unified by a 'structure-in-dominance', and human agency seems always on the brink of being swallowed up by structural determinism. In contrast to Althusser, I see strict structural determinism only in the theoretical context of pure capitalism, or in other words, only at the level of the most abstract economic theory. At more concrete levels of analysis various forms of agency may resist or transform structures. Furthermore the universality of Althusser's 'structure' would emphasise a universal social ontology, whereas my 'reification' emphasises the ontological uniqueness of capital, or of the economic under capitalism.

TOTALITY

More than any other modern thinker, Hegel brings 'totality' from the wings to centre stage. This is because Hegel's dialectical method depends on the existence of totalities governed by necessary inner connections. His dialectical method works best in his *Logic*, because here there nothing is left out of the totality that might form a disruptive outside. The deep structure of pure thought becomes in this case the deep structure of the universe.

Hegel's conception of totality is important for many reasons, but here I shall emphasise three. First, emphasis is placed upon relation rather than entity, and hence his philosophy breaks radically with all forms of atomism (individualism). Second, emphasis is placed on the relation of self to self rather than on self to other. In other words the dialectic unfolds because properties of the self are contradicted by their relations to opposed properties of the self, and not because of relations between a self and another. Third, relations between the basic properties of the self are necessary relations relative to the whole of which they form part. The starting point is a necessary beginning in the sense that it must be the most abstract determination of the totality, which can then be deepened by a self-synthesis that 'fills in' the original emptiness. This 'filling in' is a necessary sequence of categories proceeding through contradiction until closure (a necessary end) is reached and the totality is completely filled in.

It was Lukács who first emphasised the centrality of 'totality' to Marxist theory. According to Lukács 'totality' is the category that most fundamentally distinguishes Marxist theory from bourgeois modes of theorising, and for Lukács the most fundamental totality is universal history, with socialist revolution as its telos. I disagree with Lukács on these formulations. I do not believe that history has a grand teleology (if it does, we do not know what it is), nor do I think that it constitutes a totality, at least not in the strong sense of having some essential principle of unity. I do, however, believe that the inner logic of capital constitutes a totality in the strong sense. It constitutes a totality because once we assume pure capitalism, the totality of economic life becomes reproducible through a commodity-economic logic. Or to put it another way, the commodity becomes a 'cell form' through whose permutations and combinations it is possible to comprehend the material reproduction of an entire society. The theory of capital's logic starts with the commodity form and ends with all of economic life being subsumed to this form as the theory turns full circle, completing itself when capital itself becomes commodified in the form of interest. As a result of closing the circle, a totality is constituted whereby economic life is subsumed to self-regulating markets. The resulting totality is an economic system that governs the material reproduction of social life. This totality, however, only emerges at the most abstract level of theory, the theory of capital's inner logic or pure capitalism. At more concrete levels of analysis there is no totality (at least not in the same sense) because capital's logic is disrupted and resisted, with the consequence that its hold on history is only partial. Thus although capital's logic is always a totalising force in modern history, to the extent that it runs up against resistances, it can never consummate a totality that is unified around an essence at the level of history. This is fortunate because if it could, contrary to Lukács' dream of a proletarian subject–object, reification would become total, and with it humans would become permanently subject to capital's reifying force (Marcuse's nightmare).[14]

Of course, even at the level of concrete history, political economy tries to understand as fully as possible how capital's logic articulates with all other social forces, and in this sense we strive towards completeness (totality?) in our theorising, but at this level of analysis we cannot assume a totality unified by capital's logic. In other words it is one thing to try to understand interconnections as widely and deeply as possible, but quite another to assume that historical reality constitutes a unified totality. Capital's logic may be the most determining social force in modern history, but just how determining is an open question, the answer to which may improve only with the effectiveness of the concrete analysis not only of capital but of all other social forces that play important roles in the shifting 'force field' that is history. Also, it may be pointed out that our knowledge of the effectiveness of capital's logic itself depends to some extent on how well we have worked out our theory of capital's inner logic.

It is clear that 'totality' can have a great variety of meanings. Lukács' totality is universal, with the proletariat being the subject–object that realises the telos of socialist revolution. Althusser's history has no teleology, but is instead a sequence of modes of production, each one a complex totality unified by a 'structure in dominance'. For me the only entity that is a totality in the strong Hegelian sense – that is, in the sense of being a unified whole with some primary unifying factor (the motion of value) – is a purely capitalist society, as theorised in the theory of capital's logic. At the level of the analysis of concrete history, however, this totality is converted into a social force that is unique in its reifying force compared with other social forces. Capital's logic is a powerful totalising force in history, but it never manages to totalise all of modern history in accordance with its own logic.

LANGUAGE

Historically the first condition that would later make possible the commodity form appeared in its most primitive form between two communities. While commodity exchange is sharply distinguished from barter in the dialectic of capital, in history we can think of barter very roughly as the precursor of commodity exchange. All that was required for barter to take place was for two communities to produce surplus commodities that each other desired. One can imagine a barter taking place between two communities without any common spoken language (a silent trade) (Sekine, 1986, p. 38). Perhaps if the exchange became regularised some sort of *lingua franca* or trading language might have developed. In any case, it is perhaps worth emphasising that the first condition of commodity exchange (that is, barter) first developed in a silent space in which language played a negligible role, and to the extent that a *lingua franca* developed, it was shaped primarily by the reality of exchange practices and not the other way round. It is also worth emphasising that the reality in this case is relational, but that the social connection is by way of products.

It was a huge step in time from this first primitive barter which only intimates the commodity form, to a fully fledged, capitalistically produced commodity. The logical difference is that not just the surplus is offered for exchange, but the entire social product, and the exchange is not a barter but is always mediated by money. These seemingly minor logical differences are momentous in their social implications. In a purely capitalist society, for example, all shirts are produced as commodities for sale in an impersonal market. As a capitalist I may offer to sell a particular shirt for $50. If my price is too low I will sell all my shirts immediately, but will make less profit than I might have done. If my price is too high, I will not sell any shirts. And if there is a glut of shirts on the market, the price may fall to the point where I go bankrupt. All of this is determined by markets (social relations between things), so that the outcome depends upon a large number of independent decisions coordinated by an impersonal market. And all such buying and selling transactions can be conducted with little or no verbal communication. The capitalist puts a price tag on the shirt. I point to it indicating that I want to buy it. The capitalist hands me the shirt and I hand him the money. We do not need to touch one another or speak to one another. Our transaction has been mediated by a commodity, money, pointing and a transcultural understanding of buying and selling.

The exchange relation as a relation between 'sharply delimited, separate areas of property' is an inherently solipsistic relation (Sohn-Rethel, 1978, p. 42). 'Accordingly commodity exchange does not depend on language, on what we communicate to each other.... Some semantics for "yes" and "no", for pointing to this or that, and to indicate quantity, is sufficient to the essentials of a transaction exchange' (ibid., p. 41). It is as if the commodities conspire among themselves such that we become mere personifications of their independent action. We do not do the abstracting, rather the commodity form is self-abstracting. It abstracts by ignoring qualitative difference in favour of quantity. Things only differ as prices.

No doubt there is a certain reifying force associated with language, but it lacks the dynamism and brutal enforcement of the self-reproduction that is associated with the reifying force of capital. A 'linguistic turn' that would convert capitalism into nothing but one language game or one discursive practice amongst others must totally fail to understand capital's unique ontology. Capital's unique reifying force suggests that economic language is shaped more by capital's logic than the other way round.

Basic economic categories such as 'commodity' and 'money' are both referential and relational, being rooted in the simplest practical economic transactions.[15] Both concepts refer to readily identifiable things and have the meaning they do in part because of their difference from other concepts. They trail behind them centuries of trading activity. Buying and selling commodities with the use of money is structurally similar across the most diverse cultures located in the most diverse times and spaces. As long as both buyer and seller freely enter the transaction and each transaction is considered an independent event, it might seem quite unproblematic and not give rise to any need for theory. The need for theory is felt when unified markets add up independent transactions, resulting in prices that may have widespread social effects that can be unsettling if not traumatic.

The first political economists only rise slightly above the commonsense, everyday language of buying and selling. They may, as did the early mercantilists, think a little more systematically about how a nation might buy cheap and sell dear in order to enrich itself. What has to be understood is how, in political economy, theoretical languages increasingly distance themselves from the simple transactional language of everyday life, until with Marx's concept of 'capital' we have a systemic relational concept that only achieves complete clarity when we theorise it as the necessary inner connections of self-expanding value.

Concepts such as 'money', 'price' and 'profit' are both deeply rooted in everyday life and transcultural across a good deal of the time and space of Western and non-Western civilisation. As a merchant in Ancient Greece I may make a profit or as a craftsperson in the Middle

Ages I may sell my products for a price, but these concepts and the activities associated with them do not elicit a need for theory until markets become sufficiently well-developed to affect significantly the internal life of society. It is only then that it becomes possible to trace interconnections between various sorts of value categories. At first the connections may seem to be relatively external and we may think that profit is nothing more than buying cheap in one market and selling dear in another, and that the progress of theory is largely a process of deepening our understanding of more or less observational interconnections. Why do prices rise and fall? How is it possible to make profits? Why do crises occur? Why is there so much poverty? The common-sense meanings of value categories (that is, wages, interest, rent, price, profit and so on) are increasingly altered as they become integrated into theoretical languages that attempt to grapple with the above questions.

Theories of political economy attempt to be totalising by understanding the interconnections between the basic categories of economic life, and in doing so they may introduce new concepts such as 'surplus value' that are not found in everyday economic discourse, or they may radically alter everyday concepts by deepening them, as Marx does with 'commodity' and 'capital'. 'Surplus value' is a concept that deepens our understanding of the interconnections between 'wage', 'profit', 'interest' and 'rent'. 'Commodity' as 'cell form' of the commodity-economic logic of capitalism is made more precise and radically deepened, as is 'capital' in Marx's theory. In *Capital* Marx's concept of 'capital' is successively a circulation form, a production relation and a set of distribution relations as the theory moves from the abstract-in-thought to the concrete-in-thought within the theory of pure capitalism.

Marx's theory of capital represents a huge advance on Ricardo's in many important respects, but what is being particularly emphasised here is Marx's understanding of reification. A very major difference between his theory and Ricardo's is a deep sensitivity to the social consequences and historical uniqueness of capital as self-expanding value. Marx had the theoretical greatness to let capital have its way in theory in order to expose its essential alienness from humanity. He was able to do this both because of his profoundly dialectical mind, which was able thoroughly to enter into the objectivity of capital, and because his proletarian standpoint gave him the necessary critical distance from the same objectivity. Commonsense, everyday economic language may provide the raw material for the science of political economy, but in another sense, breaking with such language is a prerequisite to constituting political economy as a science.

ABSTRACTION

Althusser argues strongly against viewing knowledge as a relation between a pregiven knowing subject and a pregiven to-be-known object involving a process of abstraction. He believes that such a model generates 'mirror myths', with the knowing subject trying to mirror the known object. In order to break with all copy theories of knowledge, he argues that knowledge involves a process of production that starts with ideological abstractions and ends with knowledge. In his framework, abstractions that constitute the raw material of knowledge, or what he prefers to call 'generalities I', are pregiven: knowledge is not a process that starts with sensations or perceptions and ends with abstractions. For Althusser knowledge is achieved by a process of production that starts with concepts that are always/already abstract and are governed by structures that assign subjects their places.

A science emerges when a determinant theoretical practice effects an epistemological break with previous 'scientific' ideologies (generalities I). The new science produces an object of knowledge that is in some sense adequate (or at least more adequate) to the real object. Althusser does not really explore the issue of 'adequacy', presumably because what counts as adequate is internal to each science and cannot be generalised. It is clear, however, that given Althusser's epistemological commitments, adequacy cannot involve any notion of mirroring or copying. Indeed the force of the metaphor 'production' is aimed precisely at denying any theory of knowledge in which a knowing subject directly abstracts (copies) knowledge from a known object.

According to Althusser (1969, pp. 198–9), there are structures that govern 'both the development of the object and the development of the theoretical practice which produces knowledge of it'. I would argue that in the case of capitalism, these governing structures are the deep structures of capital or capital's inner logic. As capitalism develops in history, it increasingly develops a logic that cannot be directly read from this history, but can only be grasped by theory. At the same time capital's logic plays an important role in the evolution of modern history, and because that logic is active in history, it is possible to grasp it theoretically. It would seem, then, that Althusser's 'production' metaphor could be misleading, unless we understand the sense in which the production of the object of knowledge is aided by the deep structure of the real object. It is only because capital is the kind of object that it is, that we can theorise its inner logic. Acting within the theoretical practice of political economy, Marx produces an epistemological break, but he is aided in this by the evolution of both political economy (particulary Smith and Ricardo) and the real object (capitalism).

Althusser's animus against the process of abstraction is its seeming connection with a human subject as prime mover. What he does not consider are the sort of arguments made by Sohn-Rethel to the effect that abstraction is not only a mental exercise of subjects but also something that takes place through economic exchange relations. Sohn-Rethel argues, in fact, that in history the 'real abstraction' induced by exchange relations is more fundamental than mental abstraction. Every time an exchange takes place, qualitative differences are suppressed in order to arrive at a quantitative identity. This abstracting from differences through exchange is referred to by Sohn-Rethel as 'real abstraction'.

While I do not agree with the essentialism implied by Sohn-Rethel's claims that the basic cause of all abstractness in history is the commodity form and exchange, the one-sided exaggerations of his arguments give us food for thought about abstractness in history as well as the inner logic of capital. For example he writes that, 'While the concepts of natural science are thought abstractions, the economic concept of value is a real one' (Sohn-Rethel, 1978, p. 20). What he means by this is that through the commodity form and exchange relations all qualitative differentiation is overcome, as value in the form of money comes to identify all things with each other in purely quantitative terms with complete indifference to qualitative differences. The resulting abstraction is not achieved by thought but through action of a peculiar sort. In contrast the abstractions of natural science are not made by the subject matter, but by scientists trying to understand it. This is one of the basic ontological differences that is a necessary condition for the success of the dialectical method in theorising capital.

The real abstractions arising from exchange and from capitalist production processes are the basis for the abstractions of political economy.[16] We should not take this to mean that theoretical practice does not involve mental abstraction as well, rather that mental abstractions are helped along by the real abstractions and the real abstractions are helped along by the mental ones.[17] Thus the abstractions are not simply always/already given, but arise with the rise of exchange processes, and particularly with the rise of capitalistic economic practices. Even the earliest political economists started with concepts already made abstract by real exchange processes. But in another sense the process of self-abstraction that is characteristic of capital in history never completes itself in the commonsense thought of any historical capitalist society, but only in the theory of pure capitalism, for which Marx laid the foundations.

While Sohn-Rethel's emphasis on the complete abstractness of the commodity form demonstrates great acumen, it should be recognised that this abstractness is only fully realised in the theoretical context of a purely capitalist society. It is only in the theory of a purely capitalist society that 'the act of exchange has to be described as abstract movement through abstract (homogeneous, continuous, empty) space and time of abstract substances (materially real but bare of sense-qualities)' (ibid., p. 53). Thus the theoretical practice of Marxian political economy starts with theoretical abstractions that have been purified by previous political economy and ultimately produced by the real abstractions of exchange and production processes in history. Marx the theorist plays a role in reorganising previous abstractions in ways that break decisively with previous economic theory. He also conceptualises new, more abstract abstractions such as 'surplus value' that lie behind the various forms of profit making. Though surplus value is an example of a real abstraction, it can only be arrived at through a process of theoretical production, because the commonsense categories of capitalism do not divide along the lines of surplus value. While an effort of theoretical production is necessary to arrive at the concept, I would argue that it is not like the mental abstractions of, say, physics, which attempts to understand basic natural forces through a process of mental abstraction that focuses on properties that all things have in common, for example mass. There is a difference between doing the theoretical work necessary to recognise the real abstraction, surplus value, and mentally abstracting from all differences between things to determine properties they all have. If the latter is typical of natural science, then the dialectical method will not be effective in this region of cognitive endeavour.

The basis for Marxian political economy is real abstraction, but real abstractions are not always recognisable without a theoretical effort that gets to the necessary inner connections of their deep structure.

'Real abstraction' implies that it is fundamentally capital itself that does the abstracting, and it is we who discover its inner logic, a logic that it certainly does not wear on its sleeve.

What is not seen by many poststructuralists who react against what they perceive as the abstract essentialism of the law of value is that the abstractness of economic law is a product of capital, and that the way to challenge it is not to turn away from abstractness, but rather to determine precisely what the abstractness of capital consists of so that we can better transform it.

Given the above considerations, it is possible to translate Althusser's production metaphor into the language of subject and object. And it is worth making this translation because I believe that we can learn something from it. Capital only becomes an object of knowledge as part of an historical process that at least partially objectifies social life. This process of objectification creates the conditions and the needs for the processes of abstraction of political economy. In a sense social reality itself becomes more abstract because the logic of capital expansion breaks down the 'Chinese walls' of localism and particularism, such that markets become increasingly impersonal and objective, thus approaching their theoretical ideal image as universal, self-regulating systems. In this case the object homogenises, systematises and globalises itself making itself more abstract; or, taking a little liberty, we might say that in a sense capital abstracts itself by manifesting more of its logic in history (at least up to a point) and by influencing the theoretical practice through which humans derive the abstractions that attempt to grasp that logic. As the theorist becomes a participant in a more objectified social reality and becomes him- or herself more objectified (commodified), it becomes more possible to theorise accurately the object that is objectifying the subject. One of the peculiarities of capital is that it is a subjectivised object that objectifies subjects. It is an object that, as self-expanding value, takes on the properties of SUBJECT writ large, and in the process converts human subjects into commodities or mere objects used by value to expand itself.[18] Hence any theory of knowing that involves a simple originating subject abstracting from a simple given object would seem highly inappropriate in this case. Yet the subject–object distinction is useful when considering both the subject–object inversion that is characteristic of capital and the complex character of the subject–object relation that is peculiar to capital as that object we attempt to know as we dance to its tune.

It would seem, then, that Althusser's production metaphor does not easily tell the whole story of capital's ontology and epistemology. It does not underline the fact that capital possesses a distinctive inner logic, nor that the subject–object dualism is undermined by inversions that produce an object of knowledge with subject-like characteristics and knowing subjects with object-like characteristics. While it is certainly true that both capitalism and knowledge of it are socially constructed, what is more interesting is that socially constructed capitalism possesses a dialectical logic that plays a crucial role in its own further development and our knowledge of it. Thus in agreement with Althusser, I claim that knowing in this case does not depend on a direct bridge between sensation and abstraction and that the theory of capital's logic does not simply mirror some historical/empirical reality. But 'production' as a metaphor has its own problems, suggesting that knowledge may be entirely manufactured and that there may be no determinate relation between object of knowledge and real object. Like Althusser I think that the abstractions of Marxian political economy are made possible by a previous political economy from which they break, but in contrast to Althusser I also think that these abstractions are made possible by a capitalist reality that is self-abstracting and hence strongly supports the evolution of political economy.

OBJECTIVITY–SUBJECTIVITY

Within postmodern orthodoxy, claims to objectivity are sometimes seen to be the oppressive delusions of phallocentric thinking. Contrary to this perspective, I argue that there is a kind of objectivity associated with the theory of capital's inner logic. It is not an objectivity achieved by somehow getting outside subjectivity, rather it is an objectified subjectivity, an historically specific objectivity constituted by our being objectified as a result of the reifying forces of capital. To the extent that we resist capital's logic, its objectifying power is attenuated, but in a purely capitalist society we assume this logic to be triumphant. At this abstract level of theory, then, socioeconomic relations are absorbed into capital's logic. Persons are simply bearers of economic categories, and are hence reduced to being actors whose economic script is written by capital's need for self-expansion. It would seem, then, that the only real economic subject left is capital, but if capital is a subject, this is not because it has agency in a human creative sense, but because all such agency is stifled by its inexorable machine-like logic. It is precisely this automatism of capital that constitutes its objectivity and its subjectivity. And while capital has an objective logic that is theorisable, this logic is only partially effective at the level of concrete history. And while this may be so, the objective logic of capital retains its objectivity for all time. Even if three hundred years from now capitalism is a distant memory, the objective logic of that memory will remain – it may not shed much light on economic life in 2300 AD, but it will always shed a great deal of light on how capitalism actually attempted to organise material economic life from its earliest beginnings to its last dying gasps.

If capital is a strange sort of object with subject-like characteristics (it is self-abstracting, self-reifying, self-determining, self-regulating, self-expanding, self-reproducing and self-aggrandising), human individuals in a purely capitalist society are radically subjectified only to be better objectified. Because direct person-to-person relations disappear in the economic relations of a purely capitalist society, there is no personal domination of some persons over other persons.[19] Since there would be no personal dependencies (at least insofar as we theorise society as an *economic* society), individuals might feel like totally free subjects (totally self-made), constrained only by the impersonal forces of the market. Each individual is a sovereign legal subject who is totally free to buy and sell anything, including his or her labour power. But this extreme subjectification is strictly ordered by the necessity for workers to sell their labour power in accordance with terms and conditions over which they have no control, and for capitalists to conduct their activities of buying, producing and selling in accordance with terms and conditions over which they have no control (assuming pure capitalism). Thus, whereas capital consists of a set of objectified social relations, and by using persons for its own self-expansion it takes on subject-like characteristics, individuals become subjectified so that in pursuing 'their interests' (as determined by capital) they can the better add to the dynamism of capital's self-expansion. It follows that in a purely capitalist society the distinction between subject and object is complex, with subjects being objectified and objects being subjectified. Personal subjectivity, considered from an economic point of view, is constituted by a formal legal subjecthood that attaches to private property (including labour power) and gives each individual the right to buy and sell at will, but this is overlaid by a self-expanding value that totally subsumes this will to its own motion.

In the theory of pure capitalism, capital becomes a collective subject with a one-track mind: self-expansion through the maximisation of profit. And the single-mindedness of this subject–object converts individual subjects into mere instruments, or if you like, objects of its overriding value expansion. Objective knowledge is possible in this case precisely because by letting capital get its way in theory, it is as though it tells its own story without our interference. But this story is not told to us directly and immediately, but must be deciphered by theoretical practice. We can carry out this theoretical practice because we are objectified by capital but still have the potential cognitively to become knowing subjects capable of theoretically grasping what is happening to us. We can know capital as a subjectified object because we are objectified subjects. Saying this is quite different from saying that knowledge of capital is self-knowledge in any simple and direct sense. Capital's logic is only our logic insofar as we let it impress its reason upon us. A great deal of capitalist history consists of struggles to resist capital's logic or to carry out damage-control operations to limit its cruel indifference to human suffering. Indeed fully recognising the otherness of a capitalism that is too much with us is a prerequisite to replacing its logic with our democratically organised social life.

Understanding capital's logic in the above sense may help to explain why a certain voluntaristic and possessive individualism seems to have been such a powerful and persistent ideology throughout capitalist history. If capital's logic constructs the individual as a wilful, intensely competitive and centred legal subject, then given the power of this logic in modern history, we would expect that this particular identity would play an important and continuing role even if it vies with numerous other identities as it 'interpellates' individuals as subjects.[20] Whether Freudian, Lacanian, Deleuzian, Foucauldian or other theories of subject construction are utilised, Marxian political economy needs to be included because of the undeniable impact of capital's logic on modern social life. Indeed, compared with the speculative, Freudian-based theories of the subject, the contribution of the theory of capital to thinking about subject construction seems relatively less controversial and far more straight forward, though of course not the whole picture.

NECESSITY–CONTINGENCY

The tensions between the economic necessities of capital's inner logic and the dense inexhaustible spontaneity of the contingent have been a central dilemma of Marxist theory. In recent years the preponderant weight has been on the side of contingency, particularly with post-structuralist thinkers such as Laclau and Mouffe (1985), who see Luxemburg, Sorel and Gramsci as important forerunners of their concept of hegemony, which they mistakenly believe resolves the necessity–contingency dualism. For them society is an open process of interacting discursive totalities. The identities of elements within totalities are relational, being constituted by their interactions with other elements within the totality, and each totality is relational with respect to other totalities that continually subvert any fixing of the totality's identity. Capital, then, must be one discursive totality among others, and it cannot be theorised in terms of economic necessity because for Laclau and Mouffe the economic is immediately political, and the political is characterised by radical contingency. Furthermore they claim that 'necessity only exists as a partial effort to limit contingency' and 'the contingent only exists within the necessary' (ibid., p. 114). Thus capital, like every other discursive totality, is both necessary and contingent; it consists of necessity thoroughly infiltrated and subverted by contingency, which in turn is constrained by necessity. But this is not a very satisfying solution to a deep and abiding philosophical tension. In order to have meaning, 'necessary' and 'contingent' must have identities that are at least partially distinct, but if all identities are radically contingent upon each other to the extent of being ultimately undecidable, then necessity is always a necessity relative to some contingency and the very distinction between the two is in peril. Indeed the assumption of radical contingency and indeterminacy underlying Laclau and Mouffe's theory means that all distinctions are tenuous, and have a tendency to collapse. The paradoxical result is that a theory that aims to be sensitive to difference ends up producing a stultifying homogeneity precisely because it fails to give enough weight to identity.

The political becomes the base or perhaps it becomes everything, in the sense that the only basis for the fixing of identities becomes the ability of certain discursive totalities temporarily to hegemonise by successfully articulating otherwise floating signifiers around certain nodal points. The struggle over meanings is profoundly political and ever shifting. But if we think of capital as simply one discursive totality among others, we can never understand its unique ontology. And if we consider it to be primarily a political hegemony, we can never understand the reifying force of the economic and its peculiar durability.

Laclau and Mouffe argue, for example, that to think of labour power as a commodity blinds us to the fact that, unlike other commodities, labour power is capable of political action (ibid., p. 78). But this conflates labour power with the owner of labour power. While it is true that at the level of concrete social life workers always resist being reduced to just another commodity input into the production process, this does not prevent us from theorising a situation where a worker's capability for self-organisation is overriden by the self-expansion of value and his or her capacity for labour is reduced to the commodity input labour power. Indeed understanding capital's inner logic is a prerequisite for understanding all the ways in which this logic is resisted and altered by human agency in history, and about all the ways in which human agency is in turn shaped and directed by capital's logic. When we theorise labour power as a commodity, we know very well that at more concrete levels of analysis this commodification is only partial, and that workers are capable of self-organisation and resistance. In the context of pure capitalism, what poses difficulties for capital's logic is not that labour power is capable of agency, but that unlike other commodities it cannot be capitalistically produced.[21] What blinds us is not political economy's theorising labour power as a commodity, but rather Laclau and Mouffe's collapsing of distinctions in such a way that it becomes impossible to think of capital's logic. The economic becomes absorbed into the political and capitalism just happens to be a discursive formation that inexplicably hegemonises nodal points for hundreds of years.

One of the great contributions that the Japanese political economists Kozo Uno and Thomas Sekine have made to Marxian political economy is at least the beginnings of a way of moving from abstract economic theory to concrete analysis through relatively autonomous levels of analysis, each with a different logic and a different way of approaching the necessity–contingency connection. I agree with Laclau and Mouffe's (1985) assessment that the relation between abstract economic logic and historical contingency is at the root of the problems that beset the Marxism of the Second and Third Internationals. But I strongly disagree with their solution, because it destroys any possbility of theorising capital's inner logic in an age when it seems particularly important to do so, given the lack of significant nation-state-based opposition that held capitalism in check during the Cold War.

Implied in Marx's various writings is a distinction between levels of analysis, even though he never theorised such a distinction. On the one hand, in the pure capitalism of *Capital* persons are mere bearers of economic structures and personifications of economic categories; on the other hand, in 'The Eighteenth Brumaire' collectivities are clearly capable of various kinds of agency. Thus at the level of pure capitalism agency is absorbed into structure and at the level of historical analysis it clearly is not. It seems, then, that there are different social ontologies at work that imply different epistemologies and methodologies.[22] And if this is the case, it raises many difficult problems about how these distinct levels are to be related.

Marx did not focus his attention on this problem because he felt that capitalism had reached its apex with liberal capitalism in England in the mid nineteenth century, and that the emerging monopoly capitalism was simply a transitional form leading immediately to socialism. The fact that monopoly capitalism proved to be a relatively stable form of capital accumulation prompted Lenin to use the word 'stage' to refer to this phenomenon, but Lenin gave little thought to the connection between the theory of capital's inner logic and the theory of the stage of imperialism. It is only because of the historical buoyancy of capitalism as it persists into the twenty-first century, and because of the recent powerful critiques of economic determinism and essentialism, that the theoretical need for distinct levels of analysis has come to be strongly felt in Marxian political economy.

The theory of capital's logic may be the only theory in the social sciences where a necessitarian dialectical logic is possible.[23] It is possible because what we are trying to determine is the material reproduction of social life entirely through a commodity-economic logic without any human resistance or intervention of any form of extra-economic force. This logic is necessary because of the assumption of reification, according to which all inputs and outputs of production are fully secured in their commodity form. Reification also implies a victory of value over use-value obstacles. The use-value characteristics of typical capitalistically produced commodities must make them suitable for production in infinite numbers for an impersonal market. If the typical commodity had huge economies of scale or were a space station or an urban transportation system, it might not be so easily managed by a purely competitive commodity-economic logic. Furthermore, as discussed above, the commodification of land and labour power is difficult for capital because they are particularly recalcitrant use values that cannot be capitalistically produced. And yet in the theory of capital's logic, the use-value obstacles in the case of labour power are overcome by divorcing workers from the means of production and managing labour power through the wage form, the industrial reserve army, the tendency to equalise the rate of surplus value, and periodic crises.

Strictly speaking capital is only interested in profits and value expansion and is totally indifferent to use value, but this indifference can only be achieved in pure capitalism if we assume docile workers and material commodities that are easily managed commodity-economically. How do we move from this abstract theory in which we allow capital to get its way, to concrete history where capital is often partially thwarted and is forced to compromise its logic in all sorts of ways? How do we move from a theory of economic necessity to the theory of concrete history where this necessity is continually compromised by contingency?

Moving from the theory of abstract economic necessity to the theory of concrete contingent history is essentially a movement from idealised use-values that value can internalise or subsume, to use values that it can only partially subsume and even then only with the help of extra-economic support in the form of ideology, law and politics. The theoretical move from abstract economic necessity to historical contingency requires a mediating level of theory that Uno calls 'stage theory', but could also be called 'mid-range theory'.[24] The problem with the term 'stage' is that it suggests some kind of teleology, which I choose to reject. The problem with 'mid-range' is that it is associated with functionalist sociologists such as Merton (1957), from whom I wish to distance myself. Whatever label is used, the point of this mediating level of theory is to typify modes of capital accumulation as characteristic of different periods of capitalist history. This means theorising the way in which value most typically expands by subsuming use-values with whatever non-economic aids are required. In order to do this we need to locate the most characteristic mode of capital accumulation in time and space, and we need to theorise the use-value sector or sectors that are most central to capital accumulation and most characteristic of it.

Capitalism only developed gradually and unevenly in history. Circulation forms developed first in international trade and first begin to subsume the labour and production process under a domestic market in Britain. Capitalist social forms developed in British agriculture to some extent, but only really became dynamic with the development of woollen textile manufacturing in the eighteenth century.[25] Thus the first stage or period of capitalism is the mode of accumulation that most characteristed British woollen manufacturing in the first half of the eighteenth century. The necessity of capital's logic now had to compromise with the production of a use value organised in a putting-out system and supported by the ideological, legal and political forms that were characteristic of early eighteenth-century Britain.

That capital accumulation should first become dynamic in the putting-out manufacturing of woollens is of course not a necessity. There are many important contingent reasons why it was woollens and why it was a putting-out system, but there is no reason why capital accumulation should have first appeared in this way. Given that it was the putting-out production of woollens, however, our knowledge of capital's inner logic can help us understand the difficulties in value expansion operating in this specific use-value context, where the labour and production process was only formally subsumed to capital and labour power was only indirectly commodified. Indeed all sorts of extra-economic supports are required to treat workers as though they are commodities in a situation where they are not necessarily fully separated from the means of production, as they would be in factory production.[26] Once the use-value context is given, the theory of capital's logic can help us to understand the problem complex that it generates. The problem complex is necessary, but the solutions are contingent upon the particularities of existing ideological, legal and political institutions.

At the level of stage theory, economic necessity is radically transformed in the sense that causally it does not subsume the contingent to itself. It may help orient our study of the contingent and it may help us to generate a problem complex, but our analysis at this level is fundamentally of the contingent that is only partially shaped and constrained by economic necessity. For example a particular form of the family or of religion may persist across several distinctly different stages of capital accumulation, and in this sense may be more stable and enduring than the mode of accumulation, which in various ways may have to accommodate to them. Hence even at the level of stage theory, the contingent may not be derivative or secondary. It has its own being and persistence, with which abstract economic logic must come to terms. The fact that the family, the state and religion do not seem to have inner logics in the same sense as capital does not mean that they cannot have a certain developmental autonomy that may make them quite stable and resistant in the short term to being altered by the logic of capital, even if in the long term (over centuries) there may be a tendency for the logic of capital to shape other social relations more than it is shaped by them. It seems to me that this follows from capital's reifying force, which as Marx puts it so well in 'The Communist Manifesto' (1978b, p. 477), 'batters down all Chinese walls' both geographically and socially.

At the level of mid-range theory, the theory of capital's inner logic helps to locate the dominant form of capital accumulation in time and space. Having located the use-value context, which is contingently given, the theory of capital's economic necessities can generate a problem complex that is resolved in ways that are consistent with the existing array of institutions. Thus stage theory cannot be simply deduced from the theory of pure capitalism, because we cannot deduce the use-value context and we cannot deduce the non-economic institutions available to support capital accumulation. It follows that even at the level of mid-range theory, which is still quite abstract, the necessitarian logic of capital is seriously compromised by having to work through a use-value context not chosen by itself. As a result it is dependent on all sorts of contingent structures that may be relatively autonomous from capital's logic, and it is only through the thorough study of these structures that mid-range theory can be successfully formulated. The logic of economic necessity orients our study of stage-specific capital accumulation, but the independent study of social forces outside this logic is essential to understanding how economic necessity is compromised and how the resulting problem complex is dealt with institutionally and in policy terms.

At the level of the historical analysis of capitalism, which is an even more concrete level of analysis, economic necessity is yet further compromised.[27] Assuming that our historical analysis is of large scale historical changes and the involvement of capital in these changes, the theory of pure capitalism and stage theory can help orient our analysis, but because both of these higher levels of abstraction study only abstract structural dynamics, their use in the study of actual historical change must proceed with due caution. Mid-range theory only typifies a characteristic mode of accumulation; it does not study how this mode of accumulation articulates with all regions of social life and all regions of the globe in an on-going process of change. Here capitalist economic necessity must not only work through a contingently given use-value context, but must also interact with non-capitalist economic forces and with social forces all of which may co-influence historical outcomes such that the causal efficacy of capital's logic can never be determined with certainty. And yet the clearer we are about capital's logic, about mid-range theory and about all the forces operating on an historical outcome, including capital's economic necessity, the clearer we will be about capital's causal role in that particular outcome.

It should now be evident that in theorising capital across the three levels of abstraction, the relation between necessity and contingency is quite complex. It is not a question of pure necessity and pure contingency facing each other across a battle line that continually moves back and forth, with Kautsky leading the charge for necessity and Sorel or Laclau and Mouffe for contingency. The existence of capitalism in history is contingent, but once it exists it generates a set of necessary inner connections. In this sense necessity is victorious at the highest level of abstraction, only to have to make highly compromising deals with contingency at more concrete levels. As a result the relation between necessity and contingency is different at each of the three levels of abstraction. From the point of view that I have just outlined, it should be apparent that Laclau and Mouffe's (1985) claim that we must theorise all social life in terms of interacting and mutually subverting discursive totalities – each of which involves necessity which is always infiltrated by contingency – is both a highly homogenising claim and one that is vague. Instead of collapsing distinctions into a homogenised horizontality consisting only of discursive formations competing for hegemony, we can make more headway by starting with a theory that fully grasps the unique reified character of the economic under capitalism and proceeds from this assumption through a vertical construction of levels of analysis.

We cannot generalise about the relations between necessity and contingency in Marxian political economy, because different types and degrees of necessity are possible at different levels of theory. A certain kind of necessitarian logic is possible at the highest level of abstraction. At the level of mid-range theory, the necessitarian logic of capital must compromise with a complex of typical stage-specific institutions in constituting a type of capital accumulation. Finally, at the level of historical analysis the complexities of change force even further compromises upon the logic of capital, whose effectiveness at this level must always be understood in accordance with degrees of uncertainty and debatable judgements.

ESSENCE

I have written elsewhere about the sense in which capital has a socially constructed and historically specific 'essence' (or if you like, 'deep structure' or 'generative mechanism').[28] I define the essence of capital as its total inner logic, which becomes theorisable when we assume 'total' reification in the specific sense that I have discussed. Here I want to explore the problems surrounding the essence/appearance distinction that Marx borrows from Western metaphysics and utilises at a number of points in the three volumes of *Capital*.

As I have previously argued, the essence of capital is arrived at by a theoretical practice that gradually deepens our understanding of the interconnections of practical, everyday economic concepts such as 'wage', 'profit', 'interest', and 'rent', until finally the theoretical leap of 'idealisation' can be made that begins to grasp the real abstractions of capitalism.[29] When capitalism develops sufficiently in history, it becomes possible to conceive of total reification, though bourgeois economists such as Ricardo would see nothing problematic about reification and hence would simply accept it without problematising it or even bothering to name it. With the addition of certain new conceptions such as 'surplus value' and 'labour power' and the radical deepening of others such as 'commodity' and 'capital', Marx is able to conceive of a self-expanding economic system, whose essence is the commodity-economic logic or value by which it expands itself. It requires a theory to grasp this essence because everyday economic activity neither produces a conception of the whole nor a deep understanding of all the interconnections between the economic variables that make up this whole. There is nothing particularly difficult about capital having an essence; its essence is simply its automaticity or its logic made rigorously theorisable by letting its self-reifying tendency complete itself in theory. In theory we let capital be itself without outside interference, but if it is possible for capital to be itself, then knowledge of that being is knowledge of capital's essence. The essence, necessity, automaticity or logic of capital operates all the time during the capitalist epoch of modern history, but empirical observation cannot on its own arrive at a systematic understanding of capital's essence.

There was an unfortunate tendency for Kautsky and other Second International thinkers to think that Marx's capital was the essence and modern history was the appearance of that essence. The result was a 'logical-historical method' that made the course of history a function of capital's logic.[30] I have been arguing that although capital has an essence that can be wholly theorised, it is not the essence of modern history. Far from it. Capital has only a partial hold on history, and though it may be the strongest causal force in modern history, determining its actual causal efficacy with regard to particular events or states of affairs requires a complex analysis across levels of abstraction and across all of the major social forces active in modern history. Indeed social forces other than capitalism may have greater causal efficacy with regard to particular states of affair.

It is the Kautsky-type essentialism that poststructuralists rail against because of its extreme economic reductionism. The way to escape this essentialism is not through some radical anti-essentialism that so destabilises identities and causes that everything becomes indeterminate, but instead the escape is to understand the sense in which capital does have an essence, precisely not to become dupes of capital's own metaphysics and thereby to avoid economic reductionism while still being able to theorise the specificity of the economic in modern capitalism. It should be abundantly clear that in my reconstruction of Marxian political economy the relationship between the theory of capital's inner logic and the analysis of capitalist history must be radically misinterpreted if it is reduced to an essence–appearance relation. Indeed many of the 'appearances' at the level of capitalist history may be quite autonomous from capital's logic or may actively resist it, and hence not in any sense be appearances of an essence that is pulling the strings from behind the scene.

I have been using 'essence' to refer to the inner logic of capital as a whole, but there is another influential usage – that adopted by Hegel (1969) in *The Science of Logic*. Here we see that Hegel's logic is divided into three doctrines: 'being', 'essence' and 'notion'. If we use 'essence' in the strictly Hegelian sense, then it is possible to see striking parallels with the logic of capital. In his *An Outline of the Dialectic of Capital*, Sekine (1997) reconstructs Marx's *Capital* as a theory of pure capitalism divided into the three doctrines: circulation, production and distribution. Using this Hegelian interpretation, capital's circulation forms represent the 'being' of capital, its production relations represent capital's 'essence' and its distribution relations represent capital's 'notion'. Using 'essence' in this strictly Hegelian sense, it would follow that 'appearance' is simply the middle term between 'essence as reflection within itself' and 'essence as actuality', and as such is a subdoctrine within the doctrine of essence. Sekine divides the doctrine of production into three subdoctrines: the production process, the circulation process and the reproduction process, with the circulation process corresponding to Hegel's doctrine of appearance. In Sekine's doctrine of production, the circulation-forms that have already been presented as capital's 'being' are revisited, only now as a circulation process (similar to Marx's discussion in the first part of *Capital*, vol. II) that is the necessary appearance of a production process, which cannot do without it. In other words the circulation process as appearance is the necessary appearance of this particular capitalist production process. It is, strictly speaking, only in this theoretical context that the circulation process of capital can be considered the 'appearance' of a 'ground', which is the production process of capital. But 'appearance' in this context does not mean that the circulation process is any less real than the production process, simply that the circulation process constitutes the outer manifestation of an inner production process that is the source of value and surplus value. This point is very important to emphasise given the tendency of many Marxists to get at the 'essence' of capital by simply peeling off the circulation process from the production process. This completely ignores the strong inner dependence between essence and appearance, which in dialectical logic reflect into one another.

The theory of capital's logic as a whole is like an essential definition in that it demonstrates to us what capital is 'in and for itself'. I do not know of any other social realities that have the ontological properties of capital to the same extent as capital has. Capital is a socially constructed institution, and once constructed it takes on a life of its own. It is a peculiar self-objectification, an inverted reality in which we see ourselves as the passive objects of a subject–object we have created. By letting reification become complete at the level of abstract theory, we let capital be fully itself, and we can understand capital not as it is for us, but as it is 'in and for itself', that is, as it essentially is. At the same time capital's essence is not the essence of modern history or modern social life, hence in a sense it is possible to claim that the theory of capital's inner logic is a 'non-essentialist theory of essence' (Albritton, 1993a). It is a theory of essence that does not have automatic essentialist effects at the level of history.

TEMPORALITY, SPATIALITY AND HISTORY

The interpretation of Marx's *Capital* that sees it as primarily a theory of a reified pure capitalism no doubt goes against the grain of those who want to move easily back and forth between capital's logic and history. The levels of analysis approach that I am advocating radically problematises this relationship, requiring entirely new levels and ways of theorising.

The theory of a purely capitalist society is in no sense an *a priori* construction. It is a refinement of Marx's *Capital*, which is rooted in history in the sense that it could not have been written before the nineteenth century. But the theory of a purely capitalist society is not the theory of any actual historical society, but is an abstract society based upon extending to completion in theory capital's own self-reifications in history. Thus it is an abstract society that has no particular location in historical time or space. Spatially, a purely capitalist society is abstractly 'global' in the sense that it has no outside and therefore no 'foreign' dimension in the sense of international trade, international investment or international monetary system.[31] Temporally, a purely capitalist society only includes abstract theoretical time. Thus we can know that such a society will have periodic crises, but we cannot know how often or how long the crises will last. We can know that such a society will have tendencies towards concentration and centralisation, but we cannot know at what rate or when this might result in oligopolies or monopolies. A purely capitalist society has no beginning and no end in an historical sense since it does not 'exist' empirically in history, though its declining rate of profit necessitates that it come to an end abstractly.[32] Because it is a totally reified society with a single-minded profit orientation based upon an exploitation of labour that is indifferent to human needs, we might expect resistance to occur. But it is impossible to say anything at this level of theory about what forms this resistance might take and what the results might be. Again given its character, we might expect that some day capitalism will come to an end due to its falling rate of profit, and that certainly anything approaching pure capitalism would be quite intolerable for any length of time to any sort of civilised human life.[33] Yet in the context of the theory of capital's logic, it is impossible to say anything about when and how capital's partial grip on history may come to an end, only that it must some day.

The theory of pure capitalism and the Marxian political economy based on it breaks sharply with all forms of historicism that emphasise the radical contextuality and cultural relativity of all knowledge. The theory being advocated here is contextual only in the limited sense that it could not be produced prior to the development of capitalism in history and the real abstractions associated with this development. Many of the basic concepts of economics such as price, money and profit are quite stable across diverse cultures and great expanses of space and time. Second, the basic concepts of capitalist economics are stable across great expanses of capitalist space and time. Third, though initially produced by Marx in a particular historical context, the basic grasp of capitalist dynamics outlined by Marx in *Capital* and improved on by Uno and Sekine is true for all time. Even if it is only useful for understanding a particular epoch in human history, it will always be useful for understanding that epoch. Of course Marx was limited by the existing theoretical discourses, so his theory is not without lacunae and infelicitous expressions, but he made a momentous breakthrough in laying the basic groundwork for the theoretical comprehension of capital. No doubt many kinds of knowing are contextual or have strong contextual components, but 'absolute historicism' cannot escape the traps of relativism. If the version of Marxian political economy that I am proposing is accepted, then we must reject the claim that all knowledge is radically contingent on context, unless we use context very widely to say that political economy is contingent upon a context consisting of at least the past three hundred years of world history. Indeed capital is not only transcultural, it is the most powerful force the world has ever seen acting to homogenise cultural differences, even if its success is only partial.

'Time' and 'space' are categories that are sharply problematised by the levels of analysis approach outlined here. Each level theorises them differently. At the highest level of abstraction time and space are purely logical, and hence are divorced from any particular historicity. A purely capitalist society is an imaginary global society, and time within this society is purely an abstract and quantitative, linear, sequential time.

Mid-range theory creates an abstract type of capital accumulation that is characteristic of a particular stage, and it does this by using the theory of capital's logic to locate spatially and temporally that mode of capital accumulation which is most successful and most typically capitalist for that stage. Thus, for example, having located cotton manufacturing in England as the most characteristic mode of capital accumulation for the stage of liberalism, it further employs the theory of pure capitalism to conceputalise and interrelate the key social structures that make this mode of accumulation successful. Social structures that have different temporalities in the sense that they develop unevenly relative to each other, are to some extent synchronised to fit the synchronicity of capital, thus rendering an abstract type of capital accumulation. Thus when I treat Locke as a typical theorist of the stage of mercantilism,[34] it is not to deny that many of his ideas are influential across other stages, but rather to show that even his 'liberalism' can be seen to be permeated with ideas and ideals that are typical of the earlier stage, such as acceptance of a very large degree of natural inequality,[35] the use of terrorist punishments to deter crime (Locke advocated that under certain circumstances beggars should have their ears cut off),[36] the justification of African slavery[37] and the promulgation of anti-idleness ideology.[38] Although Locke may be widely labelled 'the father of liberalism', as a highly influential thinker writing during the stage of mercantilism, we can also find ideas that are characteristic of this stage, and it is these ideas that I emphasise in order to depict Locke's ideas as at least to some extent acting as supports to the ideologies that were most dominant during this stage. But clearly this is a reading of Locke that explicitly aims at synchronising his ideas with the dominant mode of capital accumulation. In this sense there is an intentional synchronisation, in this case of ideology with capital accumulation, in order to underline and bring out how certain social structures support the dominant mode of accumulation. Paradoxically, stage theory is essentially a synchrony of a stage-specific dynamic of capital accumulation.

At the level of the historical analysis of capitalism, we can no longer wilfully synchronise relatively autonomous social structures. Rather we must fully account for the uneven development of social structures. For example Locke's ideas selectively spilled over into the centuries that followed their initial publication, and became a material force in the founding of the American republic and in influencing both theorists and legislators of later liberalism. At this level of analysis we must explore the interactions between capitalism and ideology without assuming that the temporalities of the two are synchronised. If Locke was a principal founder of liberalism, then liberal ideology was founded long before the stage of liberalism, and it has continued in various forms to this day. Because capital does not always have the power to synchronise relatively autonomous social practices at the level of history, processes of history that may involve quite different temporalities articulating with each other become difficult to unravel and comprehend. This difficulty is, however, considerably reduced with the informing power of both capital's logic and mid-range stage theory.

TRUTH

It is profoundly unfashionable to speak of truth these days; hence I take a certain pleasure in doing so. A purely capitalist society is like a machine made up of persons connected by commodities, the workings of which we can accurately theorise once we realise that by letting the machine run us in theory, it is possible to grasp the workings of the machine 'in and for itself' as it uses us for its profit-maximising ends. But how do we know that this machine is not simply an artificial construct, a product of the theorist's feverish brain which constructs one-sided utopias or dystopias in order to highlight some aspect of reality? First we know experientially, because as capitalism deepens and societies become more market governed we directly experience the operations of these markets in our daily lives. But this experiential knowing is deeply prone to error because its focus is on using money to make more money, and hence lacks the motivation to think through all the social relations necessitated by the material reproduction of society operating entirely through a commodity-economic logic. It is also a knowing that is deeply motivated not to think about the exploitation of labour by capital. Yet as I have argued earlier, it is the starting point for the development of the discourse of political economy. Political economy develops in tandem with capitalism. As markets become more self-regulating, political economy becomes more abstract and systematic, finally interrelating all value categories. With Smith and Ricardo we see political economy helping capitalism to become more pure by advocating a degree of *laissez faire*. But neither Smith nor Ricardo manage sufficiently to break with common sense, which fixates on the materiality rather than the sociality of value categories. In this sense their theories are not abstract enough to rise to a level that systematises value categories accurately by coming to fully understanding that they are reified social relations.[39] The social forms that establish the conditions by which the social metabolism of things give rise to commodities, money, wages, profits and prices must be fully grasped in order for value categories to be accurately theorised. Marx made this breakthrough because among other things his critical distance enabled him to break with the experiential knowledge of the business world and penetrate capital's objective inner logic.

While there will always be room for debate over the fine points of the theory of capital's inner logic, insofar as it is a theory that systematically interrelates value categories, arriving at a deep structure of the social forms that create the conditions for such quantitative categories to operate as a self-expanding socioeconomic system, it must be on the right path – the path to truth. The truth achievable in this case is unique in the social sciences precisely because once this machine-like capitalism totally escapes our control, as in pure capitalism, we have become totally objectified. We act wholly as passive representatives of types of property through whose interaction quantitative variables are produced that dictate not only our action but our language. We speak the language of commodities and money, such as 'I'll sell you 20 yards of linen for $100'. If the market price turns out to be

$50, then my words are futile. If I want to sell my linen, the market will dictate that I say 'I'll sell you 20 yards of linen for $50'. In short, if we assume pure capitalism it is in the end capital that determines which words we must use in order to be effective. Our theory of capital's logic is successful to the extent that we do not impose our categories on capital, but instead allow capital 'to speak for itself' by not interfering with its objectifying motions.[40]

It follows that capital is a very peculiar theoretical object. It is both of us and set over and against us. Simply to say that the knowledge of capital is self-knowledge is misleading, because in this case we are speaking of a self that has become objectified in an 'other' as estranged or externalised self to the extent that knowledge of this 'other' only gives knowledge of a collective self subsumed to the logic of that externalised subject–object. Because we are both of the other and the other has a logic that objectifies us, we have the potential to gain knowledge of this objectifying force. In this case objective knowledge does not mean finding some Archimedean point outside history, it means allowing an historically constructed object to reveal its logic by purifying our thought of it to the point where we do not interfere with its logic.[41]

While we can have objective knowledge of capital's logic at the level of pure capitalism, we cannot have the same degree of certainty with respect to the causal efficacy of that logic at more concrete levels of analysis. At more concrete levels we are always in the land of judgment calls, though our judgment calls may improve over time to the extent that we improve our political economy and our understanding of other social forces that articulate with capital.

Philosophers have often held the truth as their highest goal. If only we could arrive at the truth, we would discover the key to unlock the secrets of the universe. I am claiming a kind of truth for a certain level of abstraction in a certain version of political economy, but it turns out that this truth does not radically increase our power or control, nor does it make life more simple. Indeed in this case the truth may increase our labours because it reveals just how difficult it is to theorise how this truth (capital's logic) articulates with the social forces that we need to understand in order to better our everyday lives. It is a truth that indicates we have hardly started to understand the social ontology of capital, much less the social ontologies of other major social objects of knowledge or social practices from the psyche to the political.[42] It is a truth that may also be a little embarrassing, because the persistence of capital's logic in history suggests a failure to think out and bring about more humane alternatives. The truth in this case does not have the power by itself to change the world, but it can set our thoughts in much more productive directions, directions that may enable us in the long run to counter more effectively the reifying forces of capital by thoroughly understanding its alien logic and what this logic has done to us and history, so that in the future it might become to a greater degree a history with which we would want to identify.

CONCLUSIONS

The science of political economy, as outlined here, may have many features in common with other sciences.[43] My aim, however, has been to emphasise the unique characteristics of its object of knowledge. I have tried to indicate ways in which both past and current ways of posing philosophical choices and philosophical categories do not always fit the uniqueness of capital as an object of knowledge. The social ontology of Unoist political economy is in some ways more attuned to difference than is poststructuralism. Its methodology varies with the level of analysis: the theory of pure capitalism employs a dialectical logic; the theory of stages develops a theory of abstract types informed by capital's logic and by historical analysis; and historical analysis is the analysis of the historical processes of capitalism informed by the two more abstract levels of analysis. At the risk of oversimplification, the theory of pure capitalism manifests a dialectical method, mid-range theory, with its synchronicity, a methodology that is primarily structural, and historical analysis, with its focus on change, a method that must equally emphasise process and structure. But this is oversimplified because it is more accurate to say that mid-range theory utilises a structural mode of analysis informed by a dialectical logic and by a process-oriented mode of historical analysis, which is itself informed by both a dialectical logic and a structural mode of analysis. Its truth at the most abstract level is objective but not in any sense Archimedean. It is totalising at all levels, but only manages to form a unified totality at the most abstract level. Methodologically it uses different logics and different orienting concepts at different levels of abstraction.

This approach to political economy does not envision a unified totality at the level of historical analysis, and has no imperialist ambitions *vis-à-vis* other research programmes. Its aim is in the first instance to improve the framework by which we gain clarity on capital and capitalism as historical forces, but this aim is also dependent upon research on other social forces. For example the more light that feminist theory can shed on the nature of gender and gender relations, the better will be our understanding of how capital articulates with gender. And if feminists are centrally focused on gender, still they want to understand how other social forces articulate with gender, including capital.

Mainstream economic theory is very different from the sort of Marxian political economy advocated here. Mainstream economic theory has little need for encouragement, since it will certainly remain mainstream for the foreseeable future. It will remain hegemonic because the discipline is deeply permeated by the instrumental values of the business world, which desperately wants to know how to maximise profits, maintain growth and carry out damage control on the destructive spin offs of capitalism in the here and now and at the level of the firm. This hegemony is likely to continue as long as capitalism is hegemonic. In my view the scientific status of such an instrumental discipline is dubious. In any case a great deal of the mathematical formalisation that is so central to the discipline rests upon acceptance of the disembeddedness of the economic from the social as an unproblematic given – as simply natural and factual. Thus mainstream economic theory has great difficulty thinking about the sociality of the economic, about the articulation between the economic and the social and between economic value and other kinds of social value. This is becoming deeply problematic since policy makers take the advice of economists on such long-term problems as growing global inequality and poverty, environmental degradation and the relative stagnation of global capitalism.

With mainstream economic theory the social is reduced to such categories as 'imperfections' or 'externalities.' Hence to the extent that an effort is made to move from an abstract formal model to concrete history, it is usually done in a single leap that involves bringing back a set of externalities. This is a very different way of proceeding from the one I advocate. By starting with a theory of a reified society, it is clear that the economic is always and only reified social relations. As soon as the assumption of total reification is relaxed, as it is with mid-range theory, we need thoroughly to rethink the economic as a set of relatively autonomous practices that articulate with political, ideological and legal practices, which to varying degrees may also be relatively autonomous. Thus the economic is never separated from the social in the Uno–Sekine approach, rather all sociality is absorbed into the economic in the situation of 'total' reification where social outcomes are determined solely by the motion of value.

I am proposing a new research programme based upon Uno and Sekine's reconstruction of Marx's *Capital*. It emphasises in the first place the importance of theorising the material reproduction of a *total* society through a capitalistic commodity-economic logic. Having theorised the totality of capital's inner logic, it is then necessary to use distinct levels of theory to think about how this logic operates at more concrete levels where reification is not total. This variation of Marxian political economy could also be called 'philosophical economics' because of its self-consciousness about the peculiarities of capital as an object of knowledge, because of its problematising the connection between abstract economic theory and history, and because of its problematising the articulation between the economic and the political, ideological, legal and other arenas of social practice.

Ironically Marx may turn out to be right about capitalism being succeeded by democratic socialism despite the recent demise of 'actually-existing socialism'. What is equally clear, however, is that Marx was wrong about the ease with which capitalism might be replaced by socialism. Socialism is only a forward step to the extent that reification can be replaced by democracy, and this has turned out to be far more difficult than originally thought. The approach to Marxian political economy that I am advocating has the capacity to help us in the long run to think clearly and in detail about ways of infiltrating and subverting capitalism's reifications. It would then be up to us to decide how much markets should hold sway and in what contexts and how much 'economic value' should rule our lives as opposed to other sorts of social value.[44]

3 Hegel's Dialectic and the Dialectic of Capital

> The dialectical form of exposition is only correct when it knows its limits.[1]

> We will never be finished with the reading or rereading of Hegel, and, in a certain way, I do nothing other than attempt to explain myself on this point.[2]

Having sketched some of the reasons for believing capital to be an object with peculiar properties, properties that open the possibility of a rigorously dialectical theory of its inner logic, in this chapter my aim is to explore some of the features of that dialectic, including comparisons with Hegel's (1969) famous dialectic of the deep structures of pure thought in his *Science of Logic*. Hegel must, of course, be the central figure in any analysis of modern dialectical theory, but I shall also briefly consider the work of Adorno and Postone as they variously appropriate Hegelian dialectics. I include them in this chapter because they break less sharply with Hegelian dialectics than Weber, Althusser and Derrida, whose perspectives could be considered 'anti-Hegelian'.

The most complete demonstration of capital's dialectical logic can be found in Sekine's two volume works *The Dialectic of Capital* (1986) and *An Outline of The Dialectic of Capital* (1997).[3] In his writings on capital and dialectics, Sekine has stressed the parallels between Hegel's *Science of Logic* and his own dialectic of capital. While Hegel's achievement in developing the basic structure of dialectical thought in the *Science of Logic* is without parallel and the structural parallels between it and the dialectic of capital are pronounced, I want to go further than Sekine in developing some of the differences. Indeed I shall argue that in some important respects the dialectical method works better when its object is capital's inner logic rather than the deep structure of pure thought.

Hegel's great achievement was to discover a method for tracing the necessary inner connections among the basic concepts of self-determining objects, a method that moves forward by starting with the most abstract and empty determinant of the object, which is gradually filled in by a process of negation that destabilises each category, forcing it beyond itself to include other categories until the starting category is completely filled in and closure is reached. The reaching of closure establishes objective knowledge in the sense that the necessary connections between all essential variables of the object are established and its deep structure or inner logic is completely known. This breaks sharply with scepticism, which always plunges knowing into infinite regresses that deny the possibility of complete knowledge of anything. Hegel refers to infinite regress as the 'bad infinity', in contrast to infinity that circles back on itself, forming a closure.

The fundamental difference between Hegel and Marx on dialectics that has conventionally been emphasised is of course the greater materiality of the Marxian dialectic. In a general sense I agree with this emphasis, but this does not get us far because of radically diverse interpretations of what is implied by 'materialist'. What, then, is my position on this issue that so differentiates interpreters of Marx? Like nearly every thinker discussed in this volume, I believe that Hegel's 'spirit' too easily penetrated, encompassed, unified and directed materiality. I believe that the thinkers discussed in this book would, with minor differences, agree with what I consider to be most problematic in Hegel's thought.

First, the deep structure of thought and the deep structure of the material universe are, for Hegel, ultimately one and the same. In other words the material universe is spiritual in the sense that thought is always embedded in matter. Even nature, for example, is simply 'Spirit estranged from itself' (Hegel, 1956, p. 14) such that 'the very stones cry out and raise themselves to spirit' (ibid., p. 15). Despite such statements, it is a mistake to too easily dismiss Hegel on this point since in some sense it may be true that 'the highest level to which Nature attains is life' (ibid., p. 17), and for Hegel life as self-regulating and self-developing matter is essentially 'spirit'. Further, anticipating some of modern science's great discoveries, Hegel claims that 'evolution is thus also involution, in that matter interiorizes itself to become life'(ibid., p. 26). Still, it does not follow that 'divine reason' so permeates nature that it becomes thought-like to the extent that even stones would 'raise themselves to spirit'. Thought may always be embedded in matter, but not all matter is equally thought-like or equally accessible to thought. Despite our desire to feel at home in the universe, matter is often quite resistant to thought and seems to be only partially knowable even after the expenditure of great effort. It may be reassuring to project human qualities onto a God who is supposed to manage the universe according to the best that is in us, but surely this is an anthropocentric delusion. Matter in general is far too inscrutable and recalcitrant to be subsumed to a 'divine reason' that is simply a projection of our reason onto a godhead. This of course does not preclude a 'local' materialist dialectic as in the dialectic of capital.

Second, Hegel claims that the necessary development of the structure of thought and the development of philosophy in history are strictly parallel. All revolutions in history involve the movement of Spirit 'comprehending itself more truly, more deeply, more intimately, and more in unity with itself' (ibid., p. 11). Moreover, 'the history of philosophy shows that there is only One philosophy at diverse stages of its formation' (Hegel, 1991, p. 38), and the sequence of categories in the *Logic* parallel the historical sequence. Thus Hegel (ibid., p. 144) claims that the philosophy of Heraclitus, with its focus on change and becoming, is situated early in the history of philosophy, just as the concept of 'Becoming' is located early in the *Logic*. The sequence of categories in the deep structure of pure thought parallel their sequential appearance in history.

This understanding of Spirit as it permeates both history and philosophy fails to understand the real diversity and specificity of philosophical thought in history, and hence the possibility that there may be more than 'One philosophy at diverse stages of its formation'. Hegel's perspective here leads to a terrible simplification of history as the unfolding of the Idea. Indeed for Hegel peoples only have historical existence insofar as they participate in the unfolding of the Idea; hence entire peoples (Indian or African for example), according to Hegel, have no history. Furthermore history is periodised under the hegemony of the Idea, thus overlooking other possible principles of periodisation, or, what is worse, concealing the diversity of history with a stultifying totalising uniformity.

Third, Hegel gives Spirit the power to lead matter towards an unfolding of its potentialities that ends in complete harmony. This implies a teleological conception of history in which an end is reached where the Idea has realised all its potentialities in a world that has become comfortable, homelike and transparent for human reason. In light of the developments in twentieth-century history, no end of history appears to be in sight – certainly not an harmonious end. The future is always full of surprises as human reason struggles in what often seem to be losing battles with its self-deceptive and self-destructive impulses in order to survive on a planet that has been made progressively less habitable as the capitalist era, drunk on overconsumption, staggers towards the gutter of ecological collapse.

The three basic problems or errors that I have outlined are (1) a tendency to overspiritualise materiality, (2) a tendency to conflate the logical and historical, and (3) a tendency towards positing an harmonious end to history. Hegel's thought attempts to achieve a synthesis between rationalistic and humanistic Christianity on the one hand and philosophy on the other. Religiosity permeates his thought as divine reason eventually achieves the reign of reason on Earth.

The three errors that I have outlined all stem from a failure to appreciate the extent to which materiality may possess a degree of autonomy from thought, and as a result resist it or remain opaque or relatively impenetrable to it. There is a deep religiosity to Hegel's spiritualism that brilliantly fulfils a wish, while avoiding facing up to the real recalcitrance of materiality. This avoidance takes on the character of a symptom when it comes to dealing with contingency, as Hegel struggles with inadequate compromises between giving the contingent some truly autonomous contingency and reducing it to always being an expression of necessity.[4]

A strict Hegelian rendering of the dialectic of capital would spiritualise capital, thus giving it the power to penetrate and subsume all materiality to its own self-expanding motion. It would therefore not recognise any need for distinct levels of analysis since even at the level of history, value would ultimately subsume all use-value obstacles. Furthermore, such a rendering would hold to a parallel between the sequence of categories in history and their sequence within the dialectic of capital. Finally, the inner logic of capital would represent the teleology of history realised, suggesting that capitalism is the end of history.

The Uno–Sekine appropriation of the dialectic breaks sharply with all of these positions precisely because it fully appreciates the obstinate materiality of use-value obstacles to self-expanding value (the 'spiritual' side of the commodity). It is only in theory that value can expand itself through a commodity-economic logic without outside help. The controlled reactivation of use-values at the level of mid-range theory forces compromises upon capital's logic, resulting in qualitatively distinct stage-specific forms of capitalism. And as long as capitalism continues to exist in history we can assume capital's logic is active to some extent in that history, but short of actual historical investigation we cannot determine its role in particular historical outcomes. Furthermore, following Marx's (1973, p. 107) position in the

'Introduction' to the *Grundrisse*, the sequence of categories in the theory of capital's logic does not follow the sequence of their historical unfolding.[5] Finally, far from being the end of history, capitalism must itself come to an end, because its own dialectical logic indicates a falling rate of profit that cannot be reversed and will result in an extreme contradiction between the necessity to maintain the commodification of labour power while at the same time not needing many workers (huge underemployment and unemployment).[6]

In *An Outline of the Dialectic of Capital*, Sekine (1997) shows that there is a close structural similarity between Hegel's *Logic* and his own dialectic, but he does not analyse in any depth the differences between the two dialectics. There are bound to be important differences between a dialectic of the deep structure of pure thought, which begins with a contradiction between 'Being' and 'nothing', and a dialectic of the deep structure of pure capitalism,, which begins with the commodity and the contradiction between 'value' and 'use- value'.

ONTOLOGY

In a statement that could just as well have been written in our historical present, Hegel (1991, p. 54) writes: 'The sickness of our time, which has arrived at the point of dispair, is the assumption that our cognition is only subjective and that this is the last word about it.' In sharp contrast to subjectivism or relativism, Hegel believed that many objects of thought are more or less concept-determined, that concepts are therefore neither purely mental nor physical, and that there is not always a sharp distinction between concepts and the objects that they grasp.[7] This implies that philosophical thought must think of concepts in their complex interconnections with each other as they interconnect in turn with subjects and objects.

Hegel believed that by immersing ourselves in the object of thought and thought of the object, and by thinking dialectically, we could in principle gain objective knowledge of the necessary inner connections among the categories central to that object.[8] To immerse oneself in an object means thoroughly to familiarise oneself with all the categories and theories used to understand the object in question, and to become a passively thinking abstract ego capable of letting the object speak for itself and of hearing what is said. Furthermore, to think dialectically means to think relationally about the movement and interconnections amongst all the central categories, and to think both postively and negatively, including thinking about the positive within the negative so that in negation there is a forward movement towards a new positive.[9]

Sekine makes very similar claims with regard to our thought about capital. As much as possible, we need to listen to capital as it 'speaks' for itself, and to facilitate this we must assume a purely capitalist society in which a commodity-economic logic is self-expanding. Our aim should not be to impose a theory of our own fashioning upon capital, but to let the necessary inner connections among the economic categories of capital's deep structure emerge theoretically without our interference. Just as we assume that in a purely capitalist society the economy is reproduced without human resistance, so in our theory we need to let the categories find their necessary interconnections without our interference.

This is not to imply that there is no work involved in theorising. For Hegel the automatic, imagistic thinking of everyday life takes place largely in what he calls 'representations'. But philosophy cannot 'presuppose its objects as given immediately by representation' (Hegel 1991, p. 24). It is the task of philosophy to put '*thoughts* and *categories*, but more precisely *concepts*, in the place of representations. Representations in general [or 'notions'] can be regarded as *metaphors* of thoughts and concepts' (ibid., pp. 26–7). The common way of thinking about metaphor is to think that abstract concepts are worn-down metaphors, but here Hegel seems to be suggesting something close to the opposite: concrete images and representations are metaphors of abstract concepts.[10] That is, priority is given to the concept and not the 'representations' that may loosely connect with it as its stable of metaphors. Similarly, in the dialectic of capital it is not the rough and tumble, imagistic language of the business world that gives us our object, but rather the fundamental economic concepts in their purity and their interconnections.

Hegel is sensitive to the pressure on philosophy always to connect its pure concepts with representational thinking, but he urges us to resist this pressure. We need to work on thinking abstractly: 'to hold to pure thoughts and to move about in them' (ibid., p. 27). We need to resist the temptations of 'writers, preachers, orators etc., who tell their readers or listeners things that they already knew by heart' (ibid.), and instead discipline ourselves to work in the pure concepts that have the potential to give us real knowledge. Thus it is not at all easy to get the concepts to 'tell their own story' or to get ourselves into a frame of mind where we can hear such a story, which is nothing like the narratives of representational thinking that are so familiar to us.

Hegel (1969, p. 43) begins the 'Introduction' to his *Science of Logic* with the claim that:

> In no science is the need to begin with the subject matter itself, without preliminary reflections, felt more strongly than in the science of logic. In every other science the subject matter and the scientific method are distinguished from each other; also the content does not make an absolute beginning but is dependent on other concepts and is connected on all sides with other material. These other sciences are, therefore, permitted to speak of their ground and its context and also of their method, only as premises…

It would seem to follow from this quotation that political economy cannot start without preliminary reflections. And while this is true, a sharp distinction needs to be made between an empirical science such as physics and a potentially dialectical science such as political economy. The simplest category of the theory of a purely capitalist society is the 'commodity', and it is only this category that can successfully generate the dialectic of capital. Thus while the 'commodity' may not be an 'absolute beginning' without presuppositions, assuming that we want to theorise capital's inner logic, it is a necessary beginning.

Sciences such as physics (Newtonian) are not dialectical at all, according to Hegel. A universal category in physics is only formal: 'its determination is not immanent in it and it does not pass over into particularity. The determinate content falls for that very reason outside the universal; and so is split into fragments ... devoid of necessary connection' (Hegel, 1970, p. 11). What Hegel does not consider here is the possibility of a science such as political economy, where its determination *is* immanent in it, but only partially passes over into particularity in the sense the capital's logic at the level of particularity is partially refracted through human institutions that it does not completely control, is artificially supported by outside forces, is disrupted by 'externalities', and is resisted and supported from both inside and out. Despite all these disruptions, as long as capitalism lasts we would expect some considerable 'signs' of its logic operating at the level of history. Thus with political economy its determinations are immanent, but they only partially 'pass over into particularity'.

Because of its ontology, nature presents a real challenge to dialectics. A dialectic of nature is possible only on the assumption that nature is really just spirit alienated from itself. For Hegel, nature is like 'a Bacchic God unrestrained and unmindful of itself' (ibid., p. 14). 'Not only is the play of forms a prey to boundless and unchecked contingency, but each separate entity is without the notion of itself' (ibid., p. 17). Furthermore, 'It is precisely externality which is characteristic of Nature ... differences are allowed to fall apart and to appear as indifferent to each other' (ibid., p. 20). What Hegel has set up here is a sharp contradiction between the raw, helter-skelter contingency of nature and the necessity of spirit. If nature is characterised by such chaotic radical contingency, then spirit's tasks become all the greater.

Thus while it is perhaps to be expected that an empirical science such as physics can only achieve formal universals, a dialectic of nature is still possible for Hegel, and this is because nature attains to life, and as a result nature can be conceived as an organic whole serving the self-development of life. Once again Hegel's divine reason and spirituality triumph over the falling apart of things in their 'boundless and unchecked contingency'. At times Hegel seems to want to give contingency considerable line to play, only to reel it in later around the revolving circles of necessity.

The problematic tension between necessity and contingency emerges in a particularly sharp fashion in the following quotation from Hegel (1991, p. 40):

> The implicitly rational beginning of the sciences passes over into what is contingent, because they have to bring the universal down to *empirical singularity* and *actuality*. In this field of alterability and contingency, it is not the *Concept* that can be made to count but only *grounds* ... they leave a latitude for their determination – which can be grasped in one way upon one ground, and in another way on another ground, and which admits of no certain and ultimate ground. In the same way the Idea of *nature* loses itself in its dispersion of isolated contingencies; and *natural history, geography, medicine,* etc., that are determined externally by chance and by a play [of circumstances], not by reason. *History*, too, belongs here, inasmuch as, although the Idea is its essence, the appearing of this Idea takes place in contingency and in the field of freedom of choice.

There is much to ponder in this quotation, starting with the question: with what kinds of object of knowledge can we rely on 'the Concept' as opposed to various uncertain grounds? If the Idea is the essence of history, to what extent does this essence lose 'itself in its dispersion of isolated contingencies', or to what extent is history 'determined externally by chance' or by the contingencies associated with 'the field of freedom of choice'? Is the Idea only the essence of history in the last instance, and if so, how much autonomy is allotted to chance, contingency and freedom of choice?

Hegel does not give clear and determinate answers to these questions because his spiritualism enables him to avoid facing up to the possible relative autonomy of various material contingencies. In the end, the resistances of materiality are always tethered to the necessity of the Idea. And while the 'origin and formation of the philosophy of nature presupposes and is conditioned by empirical physics' (Hegel, 1970, p. 6), empirical physics itself cannot be governed by the concept, only by shifting and uncertain grounds and formal universals. At times Hegel seems to recognise, at least to some extent, the recalcitrance of materiality and contingency and the relative autonomy of agency, but the Idea always trumps them in the end and subsumes them to its necessity.

If Hegel had not been such a spiritualist, with the need for everything in the end to come under the governance of divine reason, he might have recognised the usefulness of the conception of levels of analysis in dealing with these issues. 'Levels of analysis' might have enabled him to maintain his rigorous dialectic at the level of thought, while accepting the relative autonomy of other levels of analysis, depending on their particular forms of materiality. Instead of bouncing back and forth between 'boundless and unchecked contingency' on the one hand and 'necessity' on the other, he might have been able to think of history as an unfolding of social forms, partially informed by the evolution of 'the Idea' as well as by other relatively autonomous historical forces. History, then, would not tend to fall apart into chance externalities and dispersed contingencies or be subject to 'boundless and unchecked contingency' on the one hand, or simply be the externalisation of the Idea on the other, rather it would be determined by a complex of structures and processes, some more enduring and some less, some more contingent and some less. In this case 'the Idea' would not necessarily be the essence of history, but would simply be a dialectic that would inform our study of history.

It should be apparent from the above, that for Hegel not all objects are equally receptive to dialectical thought. He claims (1969, p. 40) that 'No subject matter is so absolutely capable of being expounded with a strictly immanent plasticity as is thought in its own necessary development'. Apparently this is because 'thinking is at home with itself, it relates itself to itself, and is its own object' (Hegel 1991, p. 66). Hegel believes that the object of logic, which is the deep structure of pure thought, can be shown to emerge with strict necessity from the nature of the object itself. Thus thought about thought is self-determining, such that all categories are interconnected in a necessary unfolding that completes itself as a larger circle enclosing smaller circles.

Hegel does not consider that the very plasticity of thought might to some extent defeat efforts to demonstrate a necessary unfolding of its fundamental categories. In some senses thought may be too plastic an object for the successful rendering of a rigorous inner logic. Thought thinking about thought may be too much with itself, producing delusions of spiritual perfection and omnipotence. Thought may to some extent benefit from recalcitrant otherness in order to bring it to its senses and induce some humility.

This point aside, it seems that for Hegel the more self-determining or self-actualising an object is the more it can be expounded in accordance with a necessary inner logic. Elsewhere he uses the term 'organic' to refer to such objects (Hegel, 1969, p. 48). And it is not only that some objects are more organic than others, but also the 'same' object may be understood in a more or less organic fashion depending upon whether we approach it with understanding or with reason. It is the understanding that proceeds by a method of abstracting and 'hence as separating and remaining fixed in its separations' (ibid., p. 45), and when applied to logic this approach arrives at the conclusion that logic is purely formal. But when the logical forms 'are taken as fixed determinations and consequently in their separation from each other and not held together in an organic unity, then they are dead forms and spirit which is their living, concrete unity does not dwell in them' (ibid., p. 48).

Objects are organic for Hegel when they are self-sustaining entities that absorb the conditions of their emergence (Inwood, 1992, p. 198), absorb objects in their environments to foster their own growth (ibid., p. 34) or take themselves as their own end (Johnson, 1988, p. 218). Also characteristic of organic objects is an internal logic of concept-determination that directs the object's self-development. Genuine cognition, then, is possible with objects that determine themselves from within themselves, and this cognition is most feasible when the object is 'ripe' or in its most developed form, or in other words, when its concept-determinations are most self-revealing. According to Hegel (1991, p. 17), 'thinking affirms the stubborn determination only to be reconciled with the solid content so far as that content has, at the same time, been able to give itself the shape that is most worthy of it'. By letting the object perfect itself in thought the 'dialectic gives things enough rope to hang themselves, and is thus the "universal irony of the world"'. (cited in Inwood, 1992, p. 147).

It is precisely in this sense that the dialectic of capital gives capital enough rope to hang itself. By letting capital perfect itself and have everything its own way, the theory of a purely capitalist society exposes capital for what it really is, with all its indifference to humans and nature. Furthermore, it would appear that capital in its perfected form has all the properties of a self-developing organic object. While Marx did not have the explicit concept of 'a purely capitalist society', he uses many expressions that indicate that he was groping for such a concept, and he certainly treated capital as an 'organic' object in Hegel's sense.[11]

Marx (1967, pp. 108–9) refers to capital as 'self-valorising value' or 'self-expanding value'. Apparently capital can be thought of as a self that is autonomous in the sense that it has its own inner dynamic that is self-regulating in relation to an environment – that it can valorise and expand itself without outside support or direction of any sort. But this seems to fly in the face of historical reality, which presents overwhelming evidence that capital always has all sorts of outside support. At best capital would seem to be only quasi self-regulating at the level of history as humans intervene in all sorts of ways to support or undermine its reproduction. And yet even if it is only quasi self-regulating in history, we can remove all human intervention in theory and imagine a society that is economically reproduced strictly in accordance with the motion of value. To a large extent this is exactly what Marx did in *Capital*.

The category 'value' runs through the basic economic categories, uniting what might first appear to be entirely separate categories such as 'wages', 'profits', 'rents', 'prices' or 'interest' into an organic object of interdependent categories that have certain necessary interconnections. Furthermore all these categories are connected through markets, which at least in the context of pure capitalism can be considered as self-regulating. It follows that capital can be considered an organic object in the sense that in principle it is self-determining. But is it not peculiar to say that a non-human social self determines human selves, which it subsumes? If capital is a 'self' it must only be in the sense of a complex corporate entity combining persons and things into social relations that somehow determine the actions of the persons who enter them. In other words, it assumes reified social relations.

We tend to think that the paradigm case of a 'self' is an individual human being, and this makes it difficult to conceive of an impersonal self such as capital. This is all the more insidious given the effectiveness of the practical norms that capital enforces. Usually the norms of everyday life stem from some identifiable authority such as the authority of legislation, but the norms of market competition are experienced much more like natural laws – we prosper or perish much as we swim or sink. The impersonality of the complex self 'capital' is part of its tremendous power to take over our lives in a way that leads us to believe we are free.

Saying that capital is an organic object implies that capital is in possession of a certain kind of rationality. Capitalistic rationality is simply behaviour that accords with the impersonal norms that capital dictates. It follows that the more capitalist the society, the more the tendency to identify rationality in general with capitalist rationality. If this is the case, it becomes all the more necessary to clarify the deep structure of capitalistic rationality if we ever want successfully to develop human rationality as opposed to capitalist rationality. And the dialectic of capital, which aims to clarify the deep structure of capitalist rationality, is potentially a highly useful aid to achieve this distancing by giving capital enough rope to hang itself.

It seems, then, that the organic character of capital as an object of knowledge makes it suitable for dialectical treatment, but how does its greater materiality relative to the deep structure of thought produce differences between the dialectic of capital and Hegel's dialectic of thought? An obvious difference is that the object of the dialectic of capital is an historically specific social dynamic and not a universal object, as is the deep structure of thought. A purely capitalist society is simply a capitalist society that is economically reproduced entirely through the operation of a commodity-economic logic, or in other words, it is the inner logic of capitalism. But capitalism did not always exist in history and will not always exist in the future.

The core of the dialectic of capital is a theory of how the self-expanding motion of value manages the real economic life that must somehow be managed in any viable economic arrangement. In all viable societies a division of labour interacts with nature to produce a product that is distributed in ways that support the continued reproduction of that society. With capitalism these universals are managed by self-expanding value in an historically specific way. At the minimum, then, value must come to grips with natural use-values such as raw materials and land, and with productive labour. In a purely capitalist society, extra-economic forces such as state intervention disappear with the self-regulation of the system, but certain use-value obstacles cannot be done away with because they are the conditions of viability of any society.

Thus the theory of a purely capitalist society does not deal with historically contingent and variable issues such as, economies of scale, oligopoly, trade unions, factory regimes, business law, economic policy or problems associated with the production of particular kinds of commodities. It deals only with the interrelation of fundamental economic categories in the abstract and in general as they articulate with one another in a self-regulating market society. In a purely capitalist society we imagine docile and easily manageable use values. Labour power is securely commodified and workers do not resist this commodification, and typical commodities are things such as shirts and bread, and not space stations, electricity generation and distribution systems, complex weapons systems, or large-scale transportation or communication systems that are not easily managed by a competitive commodity-economic logic on its own.

In theorising a purely capitalist society, then, it is not necessary to specify particular commodity products, but it is assumed that they are of a sort that can be managed by value on its own. Of course the specific materialities associated with labour and land raise particular difficulties because while they become commodified in a purely capitalist society, they are not capitalistically produced commodities. In order to manage land, value generates the complex category 'rent', and in order to manage labour, value generates the category 'wage', a law of surplus population and periodic crises specific to capitalism. In order to manage the materiality of capitals with different techniques, value must generate prices of production and profit (as distinct from surplus value), and in order to make capital itself finally self-managing it must generate the category 'interest'.

Capitalist production typically takes place in factories, which at the level of history always manifest some kind of power regime, but in a purely capitalist society we must assume that workers in factories act as capital would have them act, that is, as appendages of machines. In other words a capitalist factory is typically a machine-centred labour process, and workers are assumed to obey the rhythms of the machines just as they are assumed to sell their labour power docilely in a competitive labour market. In the dialectic of capital, value must manage materialities that are common to all societies, such as land and labour, and it must also manage materialities that are specific to capitalism, such as the machine-centred labour and production process, and must continually conquer time by increasing the productivity and intensity of labour. In the long term this further implies the contradictory need both to exploit labour within the production process and to expel labour from it.[12]

BEGINNINGS

Marx (1976, p. 89) was not the first but was probably the most famous person to note that beginnings are difficult and important when we are concerned to theorise a potential object of knowledge. They are difficult because we want to start with a category or categories that seem to be in some sense fundamental to the object of knowledge and have the fewest presuppositions, and they are important because seemingly slight differences at the start of a theory can grow into very significant differences by the end. Ideally we would like to start with a category that is abstract and empty and yet permeates the whole, as does the category 'cell' in biology. And if the object of knowledge is relatively self-determining, as is capital, we want a category that we can rigorously and clearly move forward until we come to grasp fully the inner logic that enables capital to be self-determining.

'Being' might seem to be a logical starting point when the object in question is the deep structure of thought, but with capitalism a variety of starting points may offer themselves. An obvious possibility might be 'labour', but this category is too universal. We need to start with a category that can unfold the historical specificity of capitalism. We could start with 'capital', but this can only be explained fully when we reach the end of the theory, and the explanation of capital presupposes both commodities and money. The starting point needs to be the most abstract and historically specific element of capital. What about 'money'? Money is certainly an element of capital, but it is not the simplest since 'money' presupposes commodities, one of which can be split off to become the universal equivalent. The most logical starting point, then, for the dialectic of capital would seem to be the category 'commodity'.

The start of a dialectic is always a kind of 'bootstrap operation'. We assume the existence of capitalism, and hence start not with just any conception of the commodity but with a commodity that is 'ripe', or as it eventually becomes in a fully developed capitalist society. In other words we start with a capitalistically produced commodity, because this is the form of the commodity that is most 'ripe', even though we cannot fully understand what this means until we reach the end of the theory. In other words the commodity in which we are interested is one that can become capital. This commodity is always produced by wage labour for sale on an impersonal competitive market. Moreover the commodity form as understood here is the simplest social connector that ties together a purely capitalist society into a totality. We know where we want to go in the theory, but we need to get there in the most logically coherent way, building from the abstract to the concrete-in-thought.

In the first instance we need to bring out the most abstract and simple characteristic of a commodity that makes it a capitalist commodity. This characteristic is its exchangeability – in principle every commodity is exchangeable for every other commodity. The most immediate thought of commodities is that they are products that circulate (That is, exchange) in markets. The social homogeneity of commodities, according to which they differ only quantitatively and hence become exchangeable, we call 'value'. In the first instance, then, value is simply some sort of commonality amongst commodities that makes them exchangeable. As exchangeable products, commodities are indistinguishable from each other except quantitatively, and thus each commodity is simply a fraction of an interrelated social totality of values (Sekine, 1997, p. 26). In other words, value is a measure of the social worth of a commodity measured against all other commodities. As the universal connector of commodities, value constitutes the social dimension of a purely capitalist society – that is, a society that is completely governed by a commodity-economic logic.

Commodities should be sharply differentiated from 'goods'. In economic theory goods are products viewed from the point of view of consumption, a point of view that is ultimately private. In contrast commodities imply a social relation between a seller and a purchaser (ibid., p. 26), and value always emerges from the point of view of the seller who has not yet found a purchaser (ibid., p. 27). At a more advanced stage in the dialectic, it will turn out that this seller is a capitalist. Similarly it will turn out that the social significance of each commodity will emerge as value when each commodity is produced with only socially necessary labour, but at this stage of the dialectic we cannot yet ground such a claim.

The social being of commodities cannot exist in a vacuum. It must inhere in the specific materiality of each commodity. This materiality is the property of the commodity that leads purchasers to want it – it is the Use-value of the commodity. Use-value should be sharply distinguished from utility, which focuses on the subjective satisfaction of the consumer (ibid., p. 30). Use-value refers to the materiality of a commodity that is still in the hands of the seller from the point of view of the potential purchaser (ibid.) Once a product is purchased for final consumption it becomes a non-commodity. A capitalistic commodity must contain the opposition between value and use-value that is expressed most clearly when the seller offers a commodity for exchange and a buyer who is interested in that commodity's use-value considers purchasing it.

It follows from what I have asserted that capitalist commodities must be exchanged, and it is at the moment of exchange that both value and use-value are realised or sublated into price. I do not want to outline the dialectic of the value form that generates the money form from the commodity form, but suffice it to say that capitalist commodities must always be sold for money, and it is the monetary moment that realises the moment of exchange or of price, which is the continual 'becoming' of the opposition between value and use-value.[13] If capitalist commodities must be sold for money, it follows that this also sharply differentiates commodities from 'goods' that may be bartered.

In the capitalist commodity, value and use-value exist only in opposition to each other, and it is an evanescent opposition in which value and use-value disappear into exchange value or price at the moment of sale. The seller has a commodity that has a non-use-value or a potential value for him and the purchaser wants a commodity that has a potential use-value for him. The social quantitative side of the commodity is opposed to the material qualitative side. It is this opposition or contradiction that fundamentally imparts the dynamism to capital, as self-expanding value subsumes real economic life in all its materiality in the theory of capital's inner logic. The restless process of price formation is the 'becoming' of capital as value and use-value sublate themselves into price at the moment of exchange.[14]

In the way that I have outlined Sekine's understanding of the relations between value, use-value and price (or exchange value), I have indicated some general parallels with Hegel's Being, Nothing and Becoming. Theorising the deep structure of an historically specific social dynamic must, however, have important differences from theorising the deep structure of thought. 'Being' is presented by Hegel as an unconditional, unmediated, presuppositionless starting point, whereas value has none of these properties. value is not even the first category, for before the dialectic can take its first step the starting point must be located in the commodity. This is not necessary in Hegel's case since the object of knowledge includes everything and hence does not require a locater category. Once the commodity locates the historically specific object of knowledge, the dialectic can begin with value, which in the first instance constitutes the sociality or social being of a purely capitalist society. In short, value as the basic social connector and ordering principle of capitalist society is equivalent to the 'Being' of that historically specific society. It is of course a much more concrete category than 'Being', and hence can neither be as 'empty' nor as 'presuppositionless'. Yet it is undoubtedly true that 'value' is the simplest category when considering circulation forms, and the simplest circulation form is the commodity.

Use-value is perhaps less like 'Nothing' than value is like 'Being'. This is because use-value is definitely something and not simply the negation of value or non-value. Indeed as a use-value a commodity is a materially specific thing with qualities that make it wanted. The basic contradiction of capital's dialectical logic, then, is between value, which would expand itself infinitely if only it could free itself from use-value constraints, and use-value, which, as the vehicle of self-expanding value, constrains such expansion and even continually brings value's preoccupation with pure numbers down to earth with a crash. In its total preoccupation with and insatiable appetite for pure quantitative expansion, value operates to achieve total indifference to use-value, and hence homogenises social life under the sign of numbers as though use-values were nothing. In history, use-value obstacles continually oppose the totalitarian homogenising force of value, forcing it continually to reconfigure and compromise itself, but under the assumptions of the theory of a purely capitalist society we assume use-values, the resistance of which the cunning of capital can overcome on its own. This allows value to complete the dialectic.

The starting point of the dialectic of capital is less obvious than Hegel's *Logic*, even if there is agreement that the object of knowledge is the deep structure of capital. The necessity of this starting point can only be demonstrated by the totality of the dialectic that can be generated from it. Only then does it become apparent that no other starting point can so successfully generate the inner logic of capital. When the dialectic of capital is complete, the central role of the commodity form and the motion of value in overcoming use-value constraints and in generating a set of necessary inner connections becomes apparent.

The starting point of the dialectic embodies in a social and material form value's first successful attempt to prevail over use-value obstacles. It is only after a careful study of the dialectic of capital as a whole that all other approaches to theorising the deep structure of capital pale in comparison.

THE DIALECTIC AS A WHOLE

While it may be agreed that the commodity and value should be the starting point of the theory of capital's logic, there are of course different ways to understand that logic. If the aim, however, is dialectically to allow the deep structure of capital to emerge in the context of a pure capitalism, then disagreements will be limited to what is the best way to understand the reproduction of a purely capitalist society through a commodity-economic logic operating on its own.

Sekine's reconstruction of Marx's *Capital*, following from the work of Uno, divides the theory of pure capitalism into three doctrines: the forms of circulation, the relations of production and the relations of distribution.[15] Each of these doctrines displays structural parallels with Hegel's doctrines of Being, Essence and Notion.

In the doctrine of circulation we dialectically generate the commodity form, the money form and the capital form as circulation forms. These circulation forms have interestingly close parallels with Hegel's 'quality', 'quantity' and 'measure'. I have discussed some of the parallels between the theory of the commodity form and Hegel's theory of quality, but stopped short of discussing the parallels between Hegel's dialectic of determinant being and Sekine's dialectic of the value form. What is particularly interesting here are the parallels between the dialectic of capital's 'expanded form of value' and Hegel's 'finitude', and between Sekine's 'general form of value' and Hegel's 'infinity'. The latter is particularly interesting because it means that there is a close affinity between 'money' in the dialectic of capital and 'infinity' in the *Logic*. Both bring about the involution of the dialectic, making it an infinite circle.

For Hegel, 'measure' is the sublation of quality and quantity, or 'quantities bound up with the quality or nature of things' (Johnson, 1988, p. 66). The capital form first appears as the use of money to buy a commodity cheaply and then 'sell it dear', symbolically represented by Marx as $M–C–M'$. This formula at first appears to be purely quantitative, with the quantitatively larger second M being the sole purpose of the exchange. But as Marx points out, if everyone tries to buy cheap and sell dear, then on average and in the long run no one will succeed, since your selling dear to me will be cancelled out by my selling dear to you. It follows that in order for *M–C–M′* to be the form of capital, there must be a *C* whose productive consumption can consistently produce more value than it cost. Thus as the primitive form of capital, *M–C–M′* must, like Hegel's 'measure', incorporate quality as a determinant *C* along with quantity in the form of profit.

Hegel claims that 'Absolute indifference is the final determination of being before it becomes essence' (1969, p. 383). Similarly in the dialectic of capital, value can only become 'absolutely indifferent' to use-value when it can expand itself without limit while remaining absolutely indifferent to use-value, as in *M–C–M′*. Of course this formula pushes towards the doctrine of production, where its mystery is totally exposed through the exploitation of workers, but considered abstractly in itself *M–C–M′* does imply the unlimited expansion of *M* through any *C* whatsoever.

Industrial capital as 'measure' already represents a transition to the doctrine of production (Essence), where the exploitation of labour power in the labour and production process becomes the enduring substratum underlying the flux of circulation forms.[16] In the doctrine of circulation (Being) the dialectic moves from one distinct category to another, as from 'commodity' to 'money' to 'capital', in a manner that Hegel calls a 'logic of transition'. As Hegel (1991, p. 173) puts it, 'When something becomes other in the sphere of Being the something has thereby vanished.' Thus 'commodity' vanishes in to 'money' and both vanish into 'capital'. Conversely, in the doctrince of production (Essence) we understand categories as related in a totality that illustrates the dependency between the immediate surface categories of circulation (Being) and the deep structures of production (Essence). Thus in the doctrine of production, instead of a passing from one category to the next, we find a logic of reflection between deep and surface structures within a totality. In a sense we return to being, but now what were initially descriptive categories of immediate appearance are transformed into categories that are explained by their place in a totality with an essence.

Empiricism, which starts with the self-subsistent 'data' of immediate experience and then reflects on this data through processes of abstraction, must consider such processes of thought as always moving further away from the data or 'thing-in-itself'. In sharp contrast, Hegel considers immediate experience as transient and fleeting, such 'that reflection, far from taking us further away from the true nature of the thing, in fact reveals its true nature, which was only partially revealed in the immediate appearance' (Johnson, 1988, p. 96). Furthermore, because empiricists generally conceive of reality in terms of separate events (data), it is difficult for them to ponder the inner connections between events.[17] This is a serious liability if we want to explore questions of relative necessity or possibility in connection with the *reciprocity* among events that are spatially or temporally interconnected (ibid., p. 142).[18] Because the theory of a purely capitalist society lays out the necessary inner connections among capitalist economic categories, this theory can illuminate thought at more concrete levels where the events themselves reveal little about their interconnections.

Furthermore the language of everyday discourse is made up of 'representations', and hence is characterised by imagistic thinking rather than conceptual thinking.

The doctrine of production in the dialectic of capital not only manifests a logic of reflection that is similar to Hegel's doctrine of essence, but it also divides similarly into the production process ('essence as reflection within self'), the circulation process ('appearance') and the reproduction process ('actuality').[19] In the doctrine of production we return to the circulation forms (Being), but now as they are interconnected with and embedded in the production process (as Marx does in *Capital* vol. II). The theory of the reproduction process (actuality) demonstrates that a capitalist production process, combined with a capitalist circulation process, can in principle reproduce itself and expand on the basis of its own principles without outside help as long as periodic crises can maintain the commodification of labour power (Sekine's theory of the reproduction process includes both the theory of accumulation from *Capital*, vol. I and the reproduction schema from *Capital*, vol. II). Hegel's 'actuality' is not to be confused with empirical reality, instead it is the essence as it appears. Similarly the theory of reproduction presents the essence of capital (production) as it appears in a process of ongoing reproduction, not as an empirical reality, but as the abstract possibility of a purely capitalist society.

I believe that an important difference between Hegel's essence/appearance and the dialectic of capital's production/circulation is that for Hegel, appearance, while being perhaps one-sided and 'thin', does not radically mislead about essence, the way that circulation sometimes does in Marx's *Capital*. This difference in turn connects with Hegel's spiritualism, which fails to show any humility in the face of materiality's opaqueness, and with Hegel's conservatism, which is basically the acceptance of things as they are. For Hegel appearances benignly connect to essences; they are not shot through with cognitive 'dirty tricks' that continually threaten us with illusion and delusion.

The dialectic of capital, however, cannot come to an end with the theory of reproduction (actuality), because it is still necessary to return to capital as self-relating and developing out of itself in relation to unavoidable use-value obstacles (that is unavoidable even in the ideal conditions of a purely capitalist society). So far capital has been a simple, homogeneous self, but even in a purely capitalist society it must become complex and yet remain unified.

In the doctrine of distribution, capital develops itself out of itself, and thus parallels Hegel's doctrine of the notion, or the subjective logic. The theory of reproduction is already a transition to the doctrine of distribution because it demonstrates that capital can stand on its own as an integral self. In the doctrine of distribution that self must develop complexity while remaining integrated in the face of a number of use-value challenges.

In the theory of reproduction, capital as a homogeneous 'self' reveals its methods not only of reproducing itself but also of accumulating and expanding itself through its relation to homogeneous labour. Having become a self-actualising homogeneous 'self', capital still has fully to develop its relation to the internal complexities of this self and the external complexities of this self's world. The relation of self to self in the doctrine of distribution parallels a similar relation in Hegel's doctrine of notion. Here capital must relate to the internal complexity of differing techniques (as with 'the subjective notion'), to landed property ('the objective notion') and to commercial profit and interest-bearing capital (the Idea). This internal–external differentiation is ultimately mediated and in a sense unified by a rate of profit and by periodic crises.

The doctrine of distribution divides into three sections: the theory of profit (subjectivity) the theory of rent (objectivity), and the theory of interest (Idea). In the theory of profit, technical diversity leads to the formation of prices of production and market prices, while the average rate of profit maintains the unity of capital. Furthermore, technical progress is dealt with by a falling rate of profit, which suggests the possibility of capital's mortality. The theory of rent arises from capital's need to deal with landed property that it cannot directly control even in pure capitalism. In order to deal with the surplus profits associated with unavoidable qualitative differences between parcels of land or land-like resources, capital must generate the category rent. Finally, with interest-bearing capital, capital itself becomes a commodity. As a result the investment movements of capital are 'fine-tuned' by a commodity-economic logic. A dialectic that started with the commodity comes full circle, ending with the commodification of capital itself.

It is not my aim here to discuss all the differences between Marx, Uno and Sekine. But one of Uno's fundamental differences from Marx is too important to ignore, given recent debates. Uno and Sekine claim that Marx introduced the labour theory of value in a way that makes it indefensible. According to Uno, value must be thoroughly established and understood as a circulation form before its substantive grounding in the production process can be understood. Thus in the doctrine of circulation there is no reference to the substance of value, only to the form of value, and the labour theory of value can only be introduced and rigorously theorised in the doctrine of production. This putting off of the introduction of the labour theory of value has sometimes led interpreters to label Uno's approach 'circulationist' when in fact it is simply rigorously dialectical. Uno and Sekine's way of theorising the labour theory of value might have forestalled the debates that took place in the West in part because of Marx's weak and at times ambiguous presentation of the labour theory of value in the early pages of *Capital*, vol. I.[20] Indeed Sekine's dialectic of capital demonstrates the indispensability of the labour theory of value to capital's logic.

Let me summarise the discussion so far of Hegel's *Logic* and the dialectic of capital. Similar to the doctrine of being, the doctrine of circulation uses a logic of transition. According to Miller (Hegel, 1970, p. ix), the categories of Being are primarily descriptive, whereas the categories of Essence are explanatory, and the categories of Notion are self-explanatory. In the doctrine of circulation there is a 'passing over' from the commodity form to the money form to the capital form and in each passing over the previous category vanishes (for example the commodity form disappears into the money form) so that relatedness remains only implicit. As a result the categories of circulation are descriptive. In the doctrine of production, conversely, relatedness is explicit as the circulation forms become grounded in a substantive production process. Central to this relatedness is the capital–labour relation, which is the basis for the extraction of surplus value. Here the circulation forms become the necessary appearances of an essence. As Hegel (1975, p. 163) puts it, 'There is something more to be done than merely rove from one quality to another ... there is a permanent in things, and that permanent is in the first instance their Essence.' Translated into the language of the dialectic of capital, this means that circulation forms can only achieve a grounding in social life that gives them some durability by becoming the appearances of a capitalistic labour and production process. While capital is not 'permanent', it displays a certain endurance and this depends fundamentally on some durability to a capitalistic labour and production process. The categories of the doctrine of production are explanatory in the sense that the primary deep structure of capital is revealed in the capital–labour relation. In the doctrine of distribution the complexities of capital's self-relations are unravelled, hence the categories of this doctrine are 'self-explanatory'.

CLOSURE

Since a dialectic constitutes a whole for Hegel, it must reach some sort of closure, which for Hegel meant something like completing a circle. For Hegel, then, the deep structure of pure thought as well as various other objects of knowledge constitute organic wholes whose necessary inner connections or inner logic can be totally exposed by a dialectic that turns full circle to complete itself. The ideas of completion or closure are totally out of fashion these days, as almost everyone wants openness without closure. Today 'openness' is the intellectual vogue to such an extent that most modern intellectuals have almost a reflex action against the idea of closure. I would claim that to think at all we have to engage in various degrees of closure. Theories, systems and concepts all display varying degrees of openness or closure. Total openness is chaos and total closure is death – neither seem very appealing.

There is a certain closure to the dialectic of capital, but it is not quite the same as that of Hegel's *Logic.* According to Sekine's reconstruction of Marx's *Capital* as a dialectic of capital, the dialectic reaches closure when capital itself is commodified in the form of interest. The ability to overcome constraints and expand infinitely is certainly the ideal that capital would like to achieve, but we know that the form of interest is simply a converted form of surplus value and can only move within limits set by surplus value, so that *M–M′* can not free itself from the constraints bound up with the necessity to exploit labour (and the likelihood that labour will resist) and from the constraints of the falling rate of profit, and cannot escape the environmental constraints that stem largely from the total indifference to use-value that is characteristic of the self-expansion of value. With *M–M′* capital seems to have achieved immortality, because having freed itself from all use-value constraints it can apparently expand infinitely.

The dialectic of capital is possible only because we assume that value has successfully pacified use-values (particularly the most recalcitrant use-values – labour, land and money) that value can either subsume or convert from being potentially oppositional to being cooperative. The fact that *M–M′* (interest or the form of money automatically expanding itself) is a fetishistic form is one measure of the distance that separates Hegel's *Logic* from the dialectic of capital. On the one hand the category 'Interest', in commodifying capital itself, completes the circle that started with the bare bones commodity, and hence is very much like Hegel's Absolute Idea, which finally completes the long march of Being through the deep structure of thought. On the other hand there is a sense in which our thought can come to rest in the Absolute Idea, in sharp contrast to the category 'Interest'. Capital's thought about itself comes to rest in this category, but not *our* thought. Imagine Hegel declaring that the 'Absolute Idea' was the most fetishized form of spirit. *M–M′* is capital's absolute idea, but at the same time *M–M′* is the most fetishistic form of capital. Hence the equivalent of Hegel's absolute idea in the dialectic of capital is the most mystifying of capital's wish-fulfilments. For Hegel, 'Being', having successfully overcome all opposition, comes to rest in the absolute idea. With Sekine's dialectic of capital, 'value' reaches fulfilment in the category 'interest', which arises when capital itself is subsumed to the commodity form, but in this case value's victory over use-value obstacles is rather pyrrhic because we know that pure capitalism never exists in history and that *M–M′* represents the final effacement of social relations that are only pacified by theoretically assuming total reification. It follows that the dialectic of capital reaches closure with 'interest', but it is not like the Hegelian closure, which achieves total contentment and rest. Rather it highlights the total reification implied by capital's logic, a reification that points beyond itself to a reactivation of human resistance and to the reactivation of relatively autonomous social spheres that become absorbed into the economic only insofar as we assume total reification. In short the reactivation is of an agency and contingency that is not simply an externalisation of a core essence, but has the potential of independent causal efficacity.

With the Uno–Sekine approach to political economy, at the level of theorising the liberal stage of capitalism for example, in 1834 the state increased the commodification of labour power by passing the

New Poor Law, and at the same time increasingly disciplined the 'freed up' workforce by developing the Benthamite system of criminal law and prisons. Clearly, then, even at the rather abstract level of stage theory we need to consider forms or types of agency such as legislation, or forms of discipline and resistance to discipline such as the Victorian prison system and resistance to it.

Dialectical logic is essentially an intellectual 'boot strap operation'. From the commodity form we can derive the money form, but at the same time we discover that the money form is necessary for the commodity form to be completely realised. Indeed, as we proceed through the dialectic of capital we eventually discover that the entire dialectic is necessary for the commodity form to be completely realised.

The overall parallels between Hegel's *The Science of Logic* and the dialectic of capital are intriguing. I find myself unable fully to assess Hegel's success in theorising the deep structure of thought in *The Science of Logic*. And yet it is clear to me that Hegel's development of the structure of dialectical logic is without parallel, and that its most successful employment was *The Science of Logic* as opposed to more concrete applications such as *The Philosophy of Right or The Philosophy of History*. Why is it that the basic structures of the dialectic of the deep structure of thought and of the deep structures of capital are so similar? Was Hegel's *The Science of Logic* a giant displacement of the logic of capital or of the deep structure of capitalistic rationality onto thought in general? Or is it simply that capital as an object of knowledge is, like thought, a highly 'organic' object, such that the structure of the necessary inner connections is similar in the two objects? What is certain is that the structure of the dialectic in Hegel's *The Science of Logic* provides the basis for establishing the objectivity of the dialectic of capital.

DIALECTICS AND LEVELS OF ANALYSIS

As previously argued, Hegel's spiritualism enables him to dispense with relatively autonomous levels of analysis, because even where, in nature, the principle of externality is the strongest, nature remains in the last instance an organic whole that is simply the externalisation of the Idea. In contrast the materiality of the dialectic of capital necessitates some form of levels of analysis, becaUse-value does not run through the materiality of history with anything like the ease with which the spirit runs through Hegel's material universe.

With the dialectic of capital, dialectical logic only works in the context of a purely capitalist society, where self-expanding value can constitute an organic whole. Even at the rather abstract level of mid-range theory, value is far from being self-expanding as it is both supported and opposed by all sorts of stage-specific structures. One way of thinking about this is to consider the ways in which value needs support in managing use-values that are not ideal or ideally docile. Thus, for example, in the stage of mercantilism value must indirectly manage a labour and production process that is typically organised as a putting-out system. Lacking direct control over the production process and thereby the product, capital supports the passing of draconian anti-embezzlement laws in an attempt to prevent cottage producers from pilfering the product in order to market it independently, presumably making themselves more money than they would receive from putting-out merchants in the form of piece wages.

This means that though the logic of capital is in a sense 'present' at more concrete levels of analysis, what goes on at these levels cannot in any sense be understood as a direct expression of capital's logic or in any sense be simply deduced from it. Instead we need to translate the logic of capital into institutional configurations informed by capital's logic while being relatively autonomous from it. For example we know from the dialectic of capital that capital has an abstract tendency to concentrate, but we do not have knowledge of the specific and peculiar institutional arrangements that produced the rapid merger movement in the last quarter of the nineteenth century. These institutional arrangements – for example the limited-liability, joint-stock company, economies of scale associated with heavy industry, growing international competition, a growing financial sector, serious international depression, certain technologies and so on – are relatively autonomous from capital's inner logic. Mid-range theory requires independent research and consideration of stage-specific structural dynamics, the understanding of which is only informed by our knowledge of capital's logic. In short, the object of knowledge of mid-range theory is not organic in the sense of being unified into a totality by self-expanding value. But since our aim at this level is to understand the *modus operandi* of a stage-specific form of capital accumulation, the theory of a purely capitalist society provides guidelines for understanding the interrelations amongst the institutions implicated. The particular forms of materiality and levels of concreteness associated with mid-range theory dictate that we abandon dialectical epistemology at this level of abstraction in favour of dialectically informed structuralism.

The dialectic remains in the background, always informing our theorising of stage-specific types of capital accumulation or of particular historical events or conjunctures. Let us say we want to understand a particular economic crisis in the 1860s in Britain. First the dialectic of capital will outline the dynamics that reproduce periodic crises in a purely capitalist society. Then the stage theory of liberalism will theorise the particular forms crises might take under the stage-specific institutions of liberalism. Finally, historical analysis informed by the more abstract levels will theorise the particular crisis, which may have been triggered by the failure of a railway consortium or a bank, or by balance of payments difficulties, or by the cotton shortage resulting from the American Civil War.

Historical analysis is relatively autonomous from stage theory, which only theorises the abstract tendencies and possibilities associated with a specific type of capital accumulation. With historical analysis the concern is with actual outcomes, and hence the best results will require detailed empirical research plus strong informing theories at more abstract levels. The logic of capital is in a sense still operative at the level of historical analysis, but it is likely to be translated into multiple logics that have a situational character operating in contextual force fields. At this level a dialectically and structurally informed empiricism would seem to be the appropriate epistemology.

NEGATIVE DIALECTICS

I decided to include in this chapter a brief discussion of two works from the Frankfurt School – Adorno's *Negative Dialectics* (1987) and Postone's *Time, Labor, and Social Domination* (1996) – because they both extend and transform Hegel's dialectic, and because they represent a tradition of thought that is enormously rich and influential. I find Postone's work particularly interesting because it takes critical theory in new directions, directions that result in a theoretical paradigm that is much closer to that advocated here.

In *Negative Dialectics*, Adorno articulates a project that in some very general ways has parallels with the project of this book. He seems to want to reinterpret Marx in order to avoid the past errors of economic determinism. In order to do this he engages with Hegel, attacking the imperialism of Hegel's universal concept by siding with materiality, while maintaining the need for theory. Theory in the form of negative dialectics still uses concepts such as 'totality' and 'essence', but in a radically critical way to illuminate the essential alternatives hidden by the leaden weight of the existing totality of appearances that would maintain the existing order of oppression, in part by denying the very possibility of critical thought. It is by helping to subvert the established totality that thought makes contact with essence, in the sense of bringing to light real alternatives that have been suppressed and that expose the established order for what it is – an order of domination and oppression.

Adorno's negative dialectic emerges out of a critique of numerous thinkers, but Hegel, with his 'positive' dialectic, is fundamental as the thinker against whom a 'negative' dialectic can most fully be developed. Hegel's dialectic will not do for Adorno for three main reasons. First, it is an egregious example of 'identitarian' thinking – the great suffocating blanket snuffing out critical thought in the modern period. For Adorno (1987, pp. 5–9), Hegel's universal concepts always seem to 'dictate' over particularity, agency and contingency, thus creating a dialectic where an identitarian spirituality forces difference and materiality back into the shadowy recesses of history. Second, Hegel's dialectic assumes the primacy of the subject and a culmination that unifies subject and object (ibid., p. 7). Negative dialectics, in contrast, is always 'groping for the preponderance of the object' in a subject–object relation that is not symmetrical and does not climax in unity (ibid., p. 183). Third, in opposition to the world-affirming and conserving dialectic of Hegel, which reaches a happy ending when humans find themselves at home in the universe, negative dialectics would never come to rest within itself, since its aim is to break out of a context that makes dialectical thinking necessary. In other words, negative dialectics is an attempt to put philosophy at the service of radical human emancipation, which once achieved would make dialectical philosophy unnecessary.

The approach to Marxian political economy that I am advocating also criticises the imperialism of the universal concept while not devaluing theory, and it criticises both subject-centred epistemologies and dialectics as a teleological homecoming. But what I favour and what I offer as a way forward are very different from those of Adorno. To explore these differences let me start by posing a question: why, given Adorno's intellectual orientation, could he not conceive of a dialectic of capital?

The dialectical theory of capital's logic is arrived at by letting the inner connections of capital be most fully themselves. This means that we, the theorists, attempt to avoid interfering with capital in any way –

our attitude is passive, contemplative and meditative. We let capital, in thought, run the world in accordance with its own inner principles. Then we see what we get; we see what capital really is. Some may like the result (the dominant class may like the fact that there is a dominant class), and some may not. But if we want to develop a critique of capital, this must be our starting point. The dialectic of capital comes first and the critique comes second (in the sense that it is developed out of the dialectic). Where I strongly disagree with critical theory is its assumption that the critical pose must come first. This is one of those differences that may seem small at first but has broad ramifications.

Critical theorists assume that any theory that is not immediately and fundamentally critical and subversive must function to affirm the established order. I strongly disagree with this, since those theories that best understand the existing order in the sense of being the most objectively true, are precisely the theories that can most effectively serve the purpose of transformation. If we can in fact, as I believe, achieve something close to an objective account of capital's inner logic, then this gives us incredible clarity on a set of social relations that we want to change, and because of this clarity will be able to change them more effectively.

Of course I also believe that most people would be critical of capital's inner mechanisms if they fully understood them. But the critique of capitalism would not only be of the mechanisms themselves in the context of pure capitalism, but also of these mechanisms in their multitudinous historical manifestations, which depend on their articulation with other social forces. The critique, in fact, has no inherent limit. For example the fact that pure capitalistic rationality always puts short-term profit ahead of all other considerations may be a source of criticism from the point of view of every conceivable value other than profit, be it health, happiness, beauty, ethics, friendship, community or any other value.

In essence, what I am suggesting is that critical theorists cannot simply let capital be. Instead their understanding of it is always shaped by a rush to judgment, that is, a rush to supersede it. There is no place in Adorno's thought for a 'positive' dialectic of capital, because it is not subversive enough. What I am suggesting is that the strongest subversion may well come from a 'positive' dialectic that gives capital enough rope to hang itself, and not from a negative dialectic based on a paranoid vision that makes identitarian thinking so totalitarian that thought itself must continually think against itself in super-self-conscious ways for fear of feeding the monolith. Given the extent to which all concepts seem to be compromised for Adorno, it is no wonder that out of his pessimism little can come but aesthetic rebellion.

The Uno–Sekine approach to political economy deals with the problem of identitarian thinking quite differently from that of Adorno. Instead of opposing Hegel's general ontology and epistemology with another general ontology and epistemology, as in Adorno's negative dialectics, we oppose Hegel's universality with the historical specificity of the dialectic of capital. The materialism comes from focusing on a particular historical object and not from the vague manoeuvrings of negative dialectics. Adorno attempts to bring back materiality by granting the particular the 'same right' as the universal by finding a 'dialectic in the particular itself' rather than always reducing it to nothing more than a 'mediated universal' (Adorno, 1987, p. 329). Negative dialectics must combat Hegel's 'reduction to general concepts' as 'an advance elimination of the counter-agent to those concepts' (ibid., p. 39). As Jameson (1990, p. 33) eloquently puts it, negative dialectics combats the imperialism of general concepts by 'shifting the positions perpetually between particular and universal, transforming the putative universal without warning into a particular, unmasking the alleged particular as a universal in true sheep's or grandmother's clothing'. This sounds good, but what does all this conceptual acrobatics really mean?

In the dialectic of capital we let the universal lord it over the particular, we let value (identity) lord it over use-value (difference), and potential counteragents are reduced to bearers of economic categories. In other words the dialectic of capital is a total triumph of identitarian thought as an expression of capital's logic. Indeed it is so identitarian that one might say that it truly exposes identitarian thought and being in the form of capital. It would be destructive of the dialectic of capital and nonsensical suddenly to transform universals into particulars or identities into difference, for the dialectic of capital represents the total victory of identity over difference: value (identity) actually achieves absolute indifference towards use-value (difference). Adorno, given his assumptions, cannot conceive of this project of letting a particular form of identitarian thought and the identitarian reality corresponding to it to become as identitarian as it would like precisely in order to eventually subvert it.

Instead of adopting a negative dialectics that would continually introduce particularity, contingency and agency directly into the dialectic of capital, Uno–Sekine political economy adopts the strategy of levels of analysis. Adorno does not grasp a cognitive strategy that would let identitarian logic be victorious at one level of analysis only to bring out use-value variations (logics of difference) at more concrete levels. It is not necessary to subvert the general concepts in the first place, particularly if by so doing we can never arrive at a theory of capital's logic. If every conceivable contingency and agency is introduced into the theory from the start, then of course no dialectic of capital is possible. Capital's identitarian logic is not subverted, only our ability to think about it. This is, of course, rather self-defeating. The theory of capital's logic is possible precisely because we intentionally imagine use-values (difference, particularity, agency, materiality) that are relatively docile and easily managed by value (identity), and levels of analysis are necessary precisely because the reactivation of use-value (difference) requires rethinking value (identity) as it articulates with more disruptive forms of use-value (difference). This is a very different way of proceeding from that of negative dialectics, which would disrupt every concept from the start. Adorno's (1987, p. 329) phraseology about granting the particular the 'same right' as the universal by finding a 'dialectic in the particular itself' may read well, but what exactly does it mean? As I understand 'dialectics', it has to do with inner connections amongst concepts. What would a dialectic of the particular look like and how would we construct it? Adorno has very little that is not vague and elliptical to say about this. In the approach I am advocating, it is very important that particularity, contingency and agency be clearly outside the dialectic, precisely as a check on its pretensions.

Adorno would perhaps have difficulty conceiving a dialectical logic that only has a partial grip on modern history. For him 'positive' dialectics always implies a total subsumption of the particular to the general concept, but for Uno–Sekine political economy this is the situation only in the context of a purely capitalist society – a theoretical context that never exists in history. At more concrete levels of analysis, the logic of capital is only partially determinate, as particularity, contingency and agency disrupt its operation. The approach I am advocating offers a third way between the totalising imperialism of Hegel's dialectic and negative dialectics. This third way, the dialectic of capital, gives the general concept full sway at one level of analysis and gives particularity, in its specificity and difference, full attention at other levels. If the relative autonomy of distinct levels of analysis is really taken seriously, negative dialectics becomes otiose insofar as we are concerned to think about capital as an object of knowledge, because it is through levels of analysis that the imperialism of the universal is constrained. Indeed it is only in the field of art that we can make much sense of Adorno's effort to give equal 'rights' to the universal and the particular. A work of art may be highly unique and particular, and yet strives to express the universal. It cannot be reduced to a general concept, yet it is both highly particularistic and universal at the same time.

The second point of Adorno's critique of Hegel, mentioned above, is that Hegel's dialectic always assumes the primacy of the subject, whereas in negative dialectics we are always 'groping for the preponderance of the object' (Adorno, 1987, p. 183). Since the dialectic of capital is an historically specific logic, it does not need to deal with a universal question about subjects and objects in the abstract and in general, as does negative dialectics. Instead the issue is one of subject–object relations within a purely capitalist society and at more concrete levels of analysis. Also, it is not a question of 'groping for the preponderance of the object', since the 'object' (capital) becomes totally preponderant as its absorbs all subjectivity. In some respects the universal subject–object problematic that Adorno is caught up with is entirely displaced in the dialectic of capital. Like a 'subject', capital is self-moving and self-reproducing, and like an object it is not a human and is potentially knowable by humans. Capital is the subject and object of the dialectic of capital. Furthermore in the theory of the dialectic of capital, we construct a theory that enables capital like a subject, to tell its own story.

According to Adorno (ibid., p. 183), 'An object can be conceived only by a subject but always remains something other than the subject, whereas a subject by its very nature is from the outset an object as well.' The point being made here is that because subject and object are asymetrical, no subject–object synthesis is possible. Rather, for Adorno there is a permanent tension and entwining between subject and object. But as universal claims, are these propositions true? To say that 'an object can be conceived only by a subject but always remains something other than the subject' may seem to be a truism. But in the case of the dialectic of capital a subjectified object is conceived by an objectified subject that is reduced to a mere personification of the object, such that the sense in which the object 'always remains something other' is by no means clear. Capital has definite subject-like properties and yet it is made up of social relations materialised by a commodity-economic logic. In this case there is no pure 'object' conceived by a pure 'subject.' The crux of the matter is that the subject–object problematic, as conceived by Adorno (and most other philosophers who dwell on it), does not fit the dialectic of capital all that well; hence when these concepts are utilised with their conventional meanings and within the context of the dialectic of capital, the result is paradox.

While it is clear that Adorno wants to get away from subject-centred epistemologies, he also is wary of reified objects. To soften up hardened objects, Adorno proposes to use Benjamin's concept of 'constellation'. This metaphor provides a framework for thinking about objects that is decentred and relational. Or, as Adorno (ibid., p. 163) puts it, constellational thinking conceives of an object in its 'historical positional value … in its relation to other objects'. Weber's historical sociology is a good example of constellational thinking because he thinks of constellations of ideal-types that do not swallow up particulars but instead remain heuristic. Like Adorno, Weber is an antisystem thinker who ponders constellations that explore the 'historic positional value' of objects in their interrelations (that is, multicausally).

The dialectic of capital is clearly not a 'constellation' in Adorno's sense, and the concept (or metaphor) seems out of place even at more concrete levels of analysis. For example mid-range theory is not simply a decentred constellation, but an effort to sketch out important differences between forms of capital accumulation that have been dominant during different phases of history, and in its construction of abstract types it is guided by the dialectic of capital.

Again, while much of what Adorno says about subject and object is interesting, within an Uno–Sekine political economy it is not necessary to come to any general conclusions about subjects and objects, since they are considered rather differently at different levels of abstraction. We do not need to think in the abstract and in general about an intertwining that is not symmetrical and is not synthetic. It is not a question of softening or disintegrating hardened objects or concepts, but of letting them show off their hardness to the fullest, precisely so that we can understand what we are up against.

In a purely capitalist society, capital may constitute itself as a subject–object unity, but at more concrete levels, where persons are not simply bearers of economic categories, this unity is partial as efforts are continually made to reconstitute it in the face of disruptions. Individuals think of themselves as autonomous subjects and to some extent they are, particularly when they mobilise themselves to resist the objectifying powers of capital and to ameliorate its fallout. Subjects are always objectified to some extent and objects are to varying extents subjectified – that is transformed by subjects or by collective agency. Thus at these more concrete levels of analysis, some of Adorno's formulations about the relatively autonomous 'entwining' of subject and object are benign but not very interesting, given the variety of subjects and objects and interrelations.

The third major critique of Hegel challenges Hegel's view that the desirable state of affairs is realisation of the dialectic in history. In contrast, for negative dialectics the desirable state of affairs is one in which oppressive domination has been disposed of and hence the need for negative dialectics. This is because Adorno considers the history of thought to be essentially the march of a 'dialectic of enlightenment' (ibid., p. 118). Underlying this grand march is 'the barter principle', which 'imposes on the whole world an obligation to become identical, to become total' (ibid., 146). 'The barter principle' is the source of what Sohn-Rethel (1978) calls 'real abstraction' – the tendency through exchange to displace qualitative difference with quantitative identity. Both Sohn-Rethel and Adorno emphasise the primary role of economic exchange in the processes of homogenisation and abstraction in history. For Adorno, its role in history seems much the same as the Absolute Idea for Hegel – both represent a dominant force in history, the difference being that realisation of the barter principle, far from achieving a kind of final homecoming, represents the coming of hell on earth.

Embedded in such a view is a huge essentialism that cannot be demonstrated. Indeed, like most universal essentialisms it exaggerates one specific causal factor in history. Moreover, as Postone (1996) has forcefully argued, by overemphasising the barter principle Adorno cannot understand the unique ontology of capital, which among other things involves a specific organisation of the labour and production process. Not only does the emphasis on barter produce an overly circulationist view of capital, but also, as I have argued, barter and exchange value are distinct, and fully developed exchange value is specific to capitalism and has nothing to do with barter. Barter is a totally localised exchange of one use-value for another without the benefit of money, and therefore cannot generate a commodity-economic logic.

By placing the entire weight of history behind the coming of his totalitarian society, Adorno has produced a paranoid nightmare, escape from which is nearly impossible. If the barter principle has more or less completed itself, and its completion is totalitarian, then there would appear to be no escape. The culmination of history is an 'iron cage', and there seem to be no contradictions internal to the barter principle that might promise a way out. Adorno's negative dialectics is therefore a counsel of despair in the face of a totalitarian society lacking internal contradictions. The very concepts he uses are already colonised by identitarian thinking.

A look at the way Adorno deals with 'essence' and 'appearance' will give a sense of how he attempts to decolonise such concepts. According to Adorno (1987, p. 167), Hegel hypostatises 'essence' 'as the pure, spiritual being-in-itself' or a 'mere product of the cognitive subject, in which the subject ultimately finds itself confirmed'. In contrast negative dialectics views 'essence' as 'the law of doom thus far obeyed by history, a law the more irresistable the more it will hide beneath the facts, only to be comfortably denied by them' (ibid.). The world conceived by the subject is thus 'not its own but a world hostile to the subject' (ibid.). Similar to the way in which it handles the subject–object relation, negative dialectics redirects 'essence' rather than rejecting it, because 'to deny that there is an essence means to side with appearance, with the total ideology which existence has since become' (ibid., p. 168). Negative dialectics 'can break the spell of identification' that Adorno believes has become so total in our times (ibid., p. 172), but since dialectical theory is always immanent (ibid., p. 197), the aim of negative dialectics is 'to break out of the context from within.... By means of logic, dialectics grasps the coercive character of logic' (ibid., p. 406). Logic that is radically critical and transformative can get at the *essential* potentialities that are hidden by totalising *appearances*.

On the one hand Adorno would not abandon 'essence', since to do so would be to side with appearance and the total functionalist ideology of our time. On the other hand essence is 'the law of doom thus far obeyed by history', and hence negative dialectics must find alternative essences behind appearances that will bring out the potentialities being denied by the fixed, stultifying essences that have so far dominated us.

Adorno gives us precious little guidance on constructing a social science that would give particulars cognitively equal rights with universals. Formulations such as 'thinking against thought' or 'logics of disintegration' are vague, and therefore in a sense mystifying. It follows that his claim that negative dialectics makes dialectics more materialist is not very convincing. If as Adorno claims, 'not only the machineries of production, distribution, and domination, but economic and social relations and ideologies are inextricably interwoven, and in which living people have become bits of ideology' (ibid., p. 267), if the social world has become as total as this, it is not clear how social theory can effectively use the thought of that world to think against it.

If society has become as totalitarian as Adorno believes, then surely it would be helpful to have a theory of the totalitarian logic that dominates us. By theorising capital's inner logic, Sekine's dialectic of capital enables us to understand the tiger on paper as a first step towards converting it to a paper tiger. Letting capital's logic emerge in a dialectic need not produce the identitarian thinking that Adorno so fears. Levels of analysis are designed explicitly to prevent the imperialism of the universal over the particular, by starting with a clear and precise theory of the universal's imperialism.

And it is not a question of granting particulars equal rights by finding a dialectic of the particular. Instead, by constricting the dialectic to a purely capitalist society, at more concrete levels particulars can be granted as much autonomy and explanatory power as they deserve without resorting to a mystical 'dialectic in the particular itself'. In this way the logic of capital is not conceived as omnipotent, nor as necessarily and always achieving totality at the level of history. On the contrary, history may be full of actual or potential particular social forces that may resist capital and ultimately do away with capitalism. Indeed the dialectic of capital demonstrates that capital's logic contains severe contradictions, which indicate that working our way out from capitalism will eventually become life's prime need if not prime want. It is simply not necessary or desirable to go through the conceptual acrobatics required to ensure that every concept is destablised by somehow locating 'counter-agents' within it from the start (ibid., p. 39). It makes far better sense to let the general concepts rule over the particulars and establish their necessary inner connections among themselves, precisely to bring out their exclusionary and dominating character. The result is a theory that gives us the clearest possible identification of capital, which can then serve as a basis for critique and counteragency. The dialectic of capital presents in entirely material and definite terms the nature of the thing we want to criticise in order to work our way out from its continued domination.

Because Uno–Sekine political economy limits dialectics to pure capitalism, it is clear that there would be agreement with Adorno that in a freer society all dialectics would be left behind, but the purpose of dialectics in the here and now differs. Uno–Sekine political economy uses dialectics only to give us a better understanding of the beast we want to oppose, whereas negative dialectics aims to keep alive at least a flicker of critical thought in an otherwise 'one-dimensional' world.[21] The dialectic of capital will always exist as the theory of capital's inner logic, but after the demise of capitalism it will only be used to understand a mode of production that existed in the past, and not a living logic from which we need to extricate ourselves. Negative dialectics would presumably not exist at all in a liberated society, because we would no longer be homogenised and suffocated by identitarian thought generated by the barter principle. Of course it is not at all clear what Adorno's free society would be like, but presumably all domination would come to an end, since otherwise negative dialectics would still have a role to play.

The above arguments will indicate to the reader why I am rather dubious about Jameson's (1990, p. 5) claim 'that Adorno's Marxism … may turn out to be just what we need today'.[22] According to Jameson (ibid., p. 68), 'It is the mimetic component of the individual philosophical sentence – its tendency to narrativize the conceptual – that finally springs the isolated abstract concept out of its bad identity and allows it, as it were, to be thought from the inside and from the outside all at once…' It seems to me that narrativizing the conceptual is precisely what we do not need if we value a political economy based on a theory of capital's deep structure. The dialectic of capital deals not with 'isolated' but with interconnected abstract concepts, and it considers their necessary inner connections fully 'from the inside' before it steps back to consider them 'from the outside'.

CRITICAL POSITIVE DIALECTICS

I turn next to Postone's *Time, Labor, and Social Domination* (1996). This work represents a giant step away from Adorno's rather tortured and often vague or even mystifying poetics towards a far more materialist version of critical theory. Postone achieves this by breaking sharply with negative dialectics in favour of a uniquely Postonian dialectic of capital that is somewhere between Adorno's negative dialectics and Sekine's positive dialectic of capital.

There are a number of important points of agreement between the Uno–Sekine approach and that of Postone. First, he fully recognises the unique social ontology of capital as a particular interrelating of labour, wealth and time (ibid., p. 5). Second, in part this social ontology constitutes the domination of people by abstract social structures that are self-perpetuating and self-expanding (ibid., pp. 3, 30–1, 125–7, 154, 269). Third, he recognises the parallel between Hegel's Absolute and capital and claims that capital has a dialectical logic (ibid., pp. 75–81, 156). Fourth, the inner logic of these social structures has a directional dynamic that is self-contradictory, most blatantly in 'the treadmill effect' – the contradiction between the need to maintain the commodification and exploitation of labour power on the one hand and the expulsion of labour from the production process that results from productivity increases on the other (ibid., pp. 33–9, 290, 346). Fifth, he recognises that political economy requires distinct levels of analysis (ibid., pp. 127, 184, 301, 321, 358, 369).

What makes Postone's work so much more materialist than Adorno's is his effort to rethink *Capital* and capitalism as a set of historically specific social forms and not simply the current manifestation of the primordial barter principle, the source of that 'desubjectifying process that has paralleled the historic subject formation since time immemorial' (Adorno, 1987, p. 124). Postone's giant step forward, however, is undermined to some extent in my view by inadequate attention to the theory of capital's inner logic as a whole. His claim that this logic is dialectical is weakened by his extraction of only a few key points from the dialectic. In addition, although he explicitly claims that he is theorising at the most abstract level of analysis, he never even begins to theorise the relation between this level and the more concrete levels to which he refers. This is unfortunate, for the validity of some of his claims at the abstract level depend upon how he conceptualises the other levels. Finally, I believe that his position is weakened as social science by a long-standing critical theory assumption that abstract theoretical formulations must point in a direction that is directly and radically transformative or else they somehow support the existing repressive order. Let me address each of these three points in more detail.

Postone has some interesting and in many ways accurate things to say about certain key economic variables in Marx's *Capital*, but he never really addresses the theory of capital's logic as a whole. The focus is on the nature of the commodity, of value, of time, and of labour, but not on the logic as a whole. We really never know exactly what kind of theory this is and exactly how it relates to more concrete levels of analysis.

Postone (1996, p. 52) is critical of Lange, in whose view 'the law of value is a theory of equilibrium; as such, it has nothing to do with the developmental dynamics of capitalism'. In opposition to Postone I want to argue that the law of value is, among other things, a theory of equilibrium (dynamic not static equilibrium), and it also has something to do 'with the developmental dynamics of capitalism'. At the abstract level of a purely capitalist society, value tends towards equilibrium in the phase of prosperity before a crisis sets in, but the dynamics at this level of analysis are purely abstract, devoid of historical determinacy. Thus the law of value demonstrates the necessity for periodic crises to occur and for capitalism to come to an end, but it does not directly or fully explain any particular historical crisis, nor does it directly or fully explain in historical terms how or when capitalism may come to an end.

It is not surprising that Marx himself uses the category 'equilibrium' since his entire theory depends on tendencies towards equilibrium.[23] If there were no tendencies towards equilibrium, then capitalism would simply be a situation of chaos instead of a cosmos – prices would be arbitrary, capital would not move from less profitable to more profitable undertakings and wages would be arbitrary. It is fashionable these days to attack the notion of equilibrium because of its static connotations. But equilibrium as Marx used it did not suggest that if capitalism were left to itself it would tend towards static harmony, rather, for Marx, equilibrium was a dynamic concept – it was something that capital always strove for and actually asymptotically approached only in the phase of prosperity before the onset of crisis.

One of the important contributions of Postone's book is his analysis of the abstract time characteristic of capitalism, in contrast to concrete time. Concrete time is event-determined, such as the time it takes from the sowing of seed to harvest; whereas abstract time marches on in a 'uniform, continuous, homogeneous' way, oblivious to events and in a manner that subsumes and disciplines activity under capitalism. Following this, one would expect that a theory of capital's inner logic would manifest abstract time to the fullest extent. Postone, however, argues that 'Marx's law of value grasps as a determinate law of history, the dialectical dynamic of transformation and reconstitution characteristic of capitalist society' (Postone, 1996, p. 300). The question then emerges: in exactly what sense does abstract time articulate with historical time; and hence in what sense is the law of value 'a determinate law of history'?

The levels of analysis approach that I am advocating considers the relation between the logical (abstract theory) and the historical to raise a set of fundamental and pressing issues that have been nearly ignored by political economy and social science generally. How can capital be a 'self-moving substance which is subject' (ibid., p. 75) and hence constitute a 'dialectical logic' (ibid., p. 76) with 'attributes that Hegel accorded to Geist'[24] (ibid., p. 75) on the one hand, and on the other, 'once established, the law of value could also be mediated politically' (ibid., p. 291). Value and capital are either 'self-moving substance' without reliance on political mediation, or if such reliance exists, then of course they are not 'self-moving'. There is apparently a mixing up of levels of analysis here.

In order to break with economism and reductionism and respond creatively to the challenges posed by poststructuralism, it is absolutely essential to realise that the logic of capital never has a total grip on history, and that while it is a totalising force, it never achieves totality except in thought. When Postone claims that value is a 'socially total mediation' without a clear conception of pure capitalism where this statement is definitely true, it is too easy for him to think it is true even at the level of historical concreteness. Postone seems to believe that capital achieves totality at the level of history and that the law of value is the underlying essence of modern history. In so arguing he appears to be falling back into an essentialism that represents in this instance a backward step from Adorno's *Negative Dialectics*.

We need to distinguish sharply between the 'intrinsic developmental logic' at the level of pure capitalism and the presence/absence of that logic at the level of history. At the level of history *there is* a tendency towards a treadmill effect, towards periodic crisis and towards a declining rate of profit, but it is also essential to realise that the presence of capital's logic at the level of history is articulated with numerous other social forces that may deflect or displace capital's logic in ways that make it only partially present and therefore partially absent.

Postone apparently does not see the need to theorise the inner logic of capital as a whole; instead he isolates his own selective 'inner core', which is then specified to be the prime mover of modern history, as well as the source of the fundamental contradictions that will bring down capitalism. The need to have a clear and precise understanding of capital's logic as a whole is sacrificed to the wish to supersede capitalism.

I agree with Postone that the theory of capital's logic reveals contradictions between value expansion and wealth creation, between abstract time and concrete time, and between the capitalist organisation of labour and alternatives. I also believe that a very large number of other contradictions exist within capital's logic, and it is not clear why they should be left out.

Instead of mapping the dialectic of capital as a whole, Postone extracts his own 'core' from this logic and uses it to advocate a particular politics. The result is a tendentious exaggeration of the differences between his approach and 'traditional' Marxism. According to Postone (ibid., p. 13), the 'anachronistic character of traditional Marxism' is 'rooted in its failure to grasp capitalism adequately' And while this may be true, how do we know if Postone has grasped capitalism adequately, if he only selectively appropriates concepts from capital's logic, as opposed to presenting it as a whole, or, if that is asking too much, at least presenting a sketch that would delimit the theory and indicate some of its major necessary inner connections. If it is so important that 'the fundamental core of capitalism must be reconceptualised', then much more attention needs to be devoted to delimiting this core and demonstrating that it is indeed fundamental. For example, precisely what is the role of market competition in capital's inner logic? Can the 'developmental dynamics of capitalism' be understood without markets and tendencies towards equilibrium? Postone often presents his reconceptualisation of capital's core as being true to Marx, but given Marx's emphasis on the market and tendencies towards equilibrium, the extraction of surplus value and class, these claims appear dubious since these are all things that Postone deemphasises. Postone claims that 'in capitalism labour imparts an objective character to itself and social relations' (ibid., p. 172), but why single out labour, when clearly in the dialectic of capital it is the commodity form that is most fundamental in imparting 'an objective character to itself and social relations'? Or again, why refer to 'the domination of the producers by the historically specific mediating dimension of their own labour' (ibid., p. 183), when this can be directly translated to mean simply the domination of labour by capital? Labour, after all, can only be a 'socially mediating activity' because it is subsumed to the market forms of capital that enable it to become the substance of value. If it is true, as Postone claims, that the 'labour process [is] molded by the process of valorisation.' (ibid., p. 346), then it would seem to be rather undialectical to try to separate the labour process so much from market processes.

All of this goes to show that Postone draws too sharp a distinction and perhaps even a false distinction between 'static equilibrium' and 'historical dynamic', between circulationist approaches that emphasise the market and his own productivist approach, which emphasises labour. Indeed at times he seems to want to deemphasise radically, if not to purge altogether the market from the logic of capital.

Instead of getting a dialectic that could demonstrate his claim that the basic contradiction is not capital versus labour but capitalistically organised labour versus alternatives, we get an argument that is forced by a preconceived telos. This weakens his overall argument, which seems to draw sharp boundaries where none need be. For surely these two contradictions are too closely integrated to be separated like this. Any transition to democratic socialism in the twenty-first century will involve a struggle of labour against capital with the aim, among other things, of radically reorganising the labour process. Postone presents no strong arguments to support his claim that class struggle can only 'humanize capitalism' or push us towards 'organized capitalism' (ibid., p. 324). He gives us no strong reasons to believe that 'the historical overcoming of the labour process as shaped by capital' (ibid., p. 334) can be achieved without class struggle, and he does not come up with any alternative agent of change than the working class ('working people'?) broadly understood.

Postone claims that 'the value of a commodity is an individuated moment of a general social mediation' (ibid., p. 191), and so it is, but he fails to mention that the 'general social mediation' is the market where direct relations between persons are replaced by relations always mediated by commodities, money and capital as circulation forms. To displace the market as much as possible from his theory, Postone usually substitutes terms such as 'abstract', 'impersonal' or 'structural' domination for the market, which of course is a large part of the abstract, impersonal and structural domination to which he refers.

According to Postone (ibid., p. 89), 'Revealing the potential in the actual helps action to be socially transformative in a conscious way'. Postone, like other critical theorists, wants to reveal the potential in the actual. This is an admirable goal, but its success, I would argue, depends on first getting the actual very clear without any preconceptions about potentials. It is out of such clarity that potentials will emerge. Otherwise wish-fulfilments will always bend the argument from the start.

CONCLUSIONS

No single philosopher has done more to advance our understanding of dialectical reason than Hegel. Analysing Hegel is thus essential to understanding the nature of the dialectic of capital. Contrary to thinkers such as Colletti (1975), I believe that not only is a materialist dialectics possible, but also that it is where dialectics is most fitting. Hegel's spiritualised dialectics is always redolent with religiosity, and hence too easily sublates all forms of materiality into the forward march of spirit towards totality. Dialectics works best with the dialectic of capital because capital is a peculiar object that is both social and material while being potentially self-determining or organic.

In the remainder of the book I shall deal with thinkers who are to varying extents anti-Hegelian. In analysing their work, I shall further clarify and defend a Hegelian dimension to political economy while also accepting some of their critiques of Hegel. This will help to clarify further the particular approach to Marxian political economy that I am advocating.

I turn next to a discussion of Weber's work, not only because of his enormous influence, but also because of his strong rejection of Hegelian essentialism. Indeed I shall argue that he goes too far in this direction, and as a result fails to grasp the specific organic character of the economic under capitalism.

4 The Anti-Essentialism of Max Weber

It may seem a little strange to include a chapter on Max Weber in a book that is centrally concerned with dialectics and deconstruction. That I do so stems not only from his enormous influence, but also from his anti-essentialism, which has been particularly brought out and emphasised by numerous thinkers reflecting on his relation to deconstructivist thought broadly conceived. Furthermore Weber was concerned with many of the same problems as I am, particularly the reifying and reductionist tendencies associated with abstract general theories in the social sciences. His solutions are different from mine because he did not think that any sort of Hegelian dialectic was consistent with the understanding of the complex interaction of relatively autonomous spheres in the history of our social life. Indeed his neo-Kantian ontology and epistemology would seem to preclude dialectical logics from the social sciences at the outset.

Strong anti-essentialist and postmodernist trends in the social sciences have sparked renewed interest in Weber.[1] The Nietzschean strand in his thought has been reemphasised, and many see his work as anticipating Foucault in a number of important respects.[2] It is perhaps not entirely surprising to find that Weber's stock is rising at the same time as Marx's stock is falling. Thus Holton and Turner (1989, pp. 11–12) take as their mission the defence of 'Weber against many artificial and misguided criticisms from Marxism', emphasising Weber's 'on-going relevance', particularly in the light of Marxism's 'exhaustion and collapse' and 'the interesting revival of interest in liberalism and libertarianism'.

My aim in this chapter is not so much to react to the judgments of Holton and Turner as to show that, even given Weber's sensibility, that theory should not do violence to history, that there are better ways to understand the nature and course of modern capitalism than those chosen by Weber. Still ,Weber makes profound contributions to our understanding of capitalist society and capitalist history, and places us on guard against the dangers of essentialist theory. He believes that the abstractions of theory are in some sense always one-sided and incomplete, so that they are best utilised circumspectly and heuristically.

My concern in this chapter is to compare and contrast the way Weber understands modern capitalism with the Uno–Sekine version of Marxian political economy that I am advocating in this work. The main focus is on how each conceives of the social and the economic and their interrelation, starting with basic ontological and epistemological differences. Both points of view are interested in understanding the uniqueness of capitalism. The philosophical difference that is most fundamental is ontology, and this difference is manifest in Weber's acceptance of marginal utility theory in opposition to Marx's theory of capital's inner logic.[3]

ONTOLOGY AND ITS IMPLICATIONS

According to Weber, reality is an infinite flux, part of which is valued by humans and hence becomes a focus of their attention, or in other words becomes meaningful. Most fundamentally 'we are *cultural beings*, endowed with the capacity and the will to take a deliberate attitude towards the world and to lend it *significance*', and 'Culture' is a finite segment of the meaningless infinity of the world process, a segment on which *human beings* confer meaning and significance' (Weber, 1949, p. 81). It follows that the phenomena studied by social science are always cultural in the sense that they are meaningful to us because we care about them and value them. It is our will that slices and segments phenomena out of 'the meaningless infinity of the world process', and creates concepts that are used as analytical tools to shed light on these phenomena and any problems associated with them that we wish to solve. According to Zaret (1980, p. 1183), 'a basic tenet of the neo-Kantian school to which Weber belonged' is that 'values establish selective points of view that create discrete events out of the infinite flow of history'.

For Weber, we cannot know anything about the nature of reality other than certain appearances that we temporarily and one-sidedly capture in artificially created mental constructs that we call 'concepts.' In the natural sciences it is possible to construct general causal laws to the extent that phenomena such as gravity repeat themselves and appear to be relatively universal. In contrast the social sciences are always concerned to understand unique cultural–historical configurations and their causes. Abstract causal laws can contribute little to this understanding, which requires ideal-types to get at the uniqueness of the causes involved. For only ideal-types, by isolating and focusing on particular unique causes, can get at the kind of causality that is relevant to the social science advocated by Weber. Thus the ideal-type 'Protestant ethic' is hypothesised to be an important cause of the ideal-type 'spirit of capitalism.' In other words, in the genesis of capitalism the stronger the Protestant ethic in a society, the more likely it is to develop a spirit of capitalism.

Given what I have argued in Chapter 2, the reader will be aware that whether or not one thinks it worthwhile to assert or theorise a general ontology, in my view it is important to be alert to the possibility that different arenas or domains of social science might have distinct ontologies, since this is clear by the case with capital as an object of knowledge. Weber, of course, does not consider this possibility, and hence he has a tendency to flatten the ontological landscape of the social compared with the approach that I am advocating. This is largely because Weber adopts a universal 'voluntarist theory of action' (Burger, 1987, p. 172) that emphasises the human will in the shaping of history, and hence he cannot think clearly about variations that may to a large extent involve the determination of agency by structure.

No doubt we do have 'the capacity and the will to take a deliberate attitude towards the world and lend it significance' (Weber, 1949, p. 81). But sometimes the opposite occurs and it is the world that lends significance to us. In a sense only humans can create meaning, but often they are aided by the structure of the world, and once created, meanings may become embedded in the world such that real mechanisms operating in history may constrain the availability of certain meanings and reinforce others, while at the same time such mechanisms may constrain behaviour no matter what meanings are adopted. Indeed in the case of a purely capitalist society, humans are reduced to being mere bearers of economic categories – it is the categories and their dynamic that are ultimately in command, no matter what meanings particular individuals may adopt.[4] In many cases it may be misleading even to use concepts such as 'confer meaning', because meaning may evolve imperceptibly in the practical life of large numbers of people over long periods of time as unconscious solutions to their various coordination problems – problems and solutions that are themselves constrained by the law of value.

Capital, language, the human psyche – these and other domains of human life may have distinct ontologies requiring distinct epistemologies. It could even be considered essentialist to start with the assumption that all social phenomena are cultural in Weber's sense. At the very least such an assumption may tend to blind us to the ontological uniqueness of various regions of social life. Such considerations lead to the surprising conclusion that despite his anti-essentialist stance, Weber still harbours distinctly essentialist assumptions that tend to flatten the social landscape in the sense that the social is viewed as ontologically homogeneous.

According to Burger (1987, p. 214), 'Weber's account of the role of Calvinism in the modernisation of the West thus is an account of the penetration of the concerns and inner logic particular to one specific sphere – the religious – into other spheres of life, and of the reorganisation of action in the latter in accordance with the demands and requirements of the former.' Does this mean that the essential difference between Weber's approach and that of Uno and Sekine is that they focus on the inner logic of capital instead of the inner logic of Calvinism? For Weber, at least according to Burger, we can presumably focus on any social sphere that interests us and do the same thing that he did with Calvinism. Of course Weber is assuming that religion plays a central role in the genesis of capitalism, but he may be overstating his case. He does not consider the possibility that the 'inner logics' of different social spheres may be ontologically different, and that because of this some spheres may have greater long-term causal efficacy than others.[5] He develops some suggestive speculative relations between religion and capitalism, but he does not really establish the causal force of religion. Indeed it is certainly possible that economics played a greater role in the rise of Calvinism than the other way round, and I would argue that religion in general does not have an inner logic anything like that of capital.

Kalberg (1994, p. 84) claims that 'Weber perceives basic social reality as an unending flow of concrete occurrences, unconnected events, and punctuated happenings. Amidst this maze, persons are confronted by a chaos of inexhaustible realities that overwhelm them in an endless stream of both fragmented and interwoven appearances.' Assuming for the sake of argument that there is a 'basic *social* reality', why should we assume it to be made up of 'unconnected events'? Surely social reality is relational such that events are interconnected and have only relative autonomy. Perhaps persons are typically confronted by a small number of oppressive realities (rather than 'an unending flow') that present them with a very small range of choices, centring around survival. Finally, perhaps the 'social' consists of ontologically distinct realities.

In what follows I shall try to show how Weber's ontological assumptions actually undermine his aim to understand capitalism as a unique historical configuration, and how important a theory of capital's inner logic is to this project.

THE ECONOMIC

How can one define the economic? Weber (1949, p. 64) admits that '"economic" phenomena are vague and not easily defined.' According to Weber (1978a, p. 63) 'Action will be said to be "economically oriented" so far as, according to its subjective meaning, it is concerned with the satisfaction of a desire for "utilities" (Nutzleistungen). "Economic action" (Wirtshaften) is any peaceful exercise of an actor's control over resources which is in its main impulse oriented towards economic ends.' The action with which Weber is concerned is always social or cultural action in the sense that it is behaviour oriented to or by socially significant meaning schema. The social consists of meaning schema, the institutions that embody them and individuals who act with some orientation towards them. Economic action for Weber is a type of social action alongside other types of action such as political action, legal action, administrative action and religious action. Yet the basic definition 'concerned with the satisfaction of a desire for utilities' is vague in the extreme.

'By "utilities" (Nutzleistungen) will always be meant the specific and concrete, real or imagined, advantages (Chancen) of opportunities for present or future use as they are estimated and made an object of specific provision by one or more economically acting individuals' (ibid., p. 68). This definition of 'utility' does not help much since according to it nearly anything can be considered a utility, including a public office, a religious ritual, a law or a public policy. It is also possible that in many societies various types of action aimed at satisfying the desire for utilities may not be considered economic by the actors themselves. For example, having a child can be considered an action aimed at satisfying a desire for utilities, as can being seen at church on Sunday, but the actors themselves may not view these as economic actions. Finally, the definitions seem circular since 'economic' was previously defined by 'utility', and now Weber uses 'economically acting individuals' as an important phrase in the definition of 'utility'. Lack of clarity on the distinction between the economic and the non-economic and between capitalism and non-capitalism is a source of difficulty in Weber's texts. Take for example the following quotation from Weber (Andreski, 1983, pp. 40–1):

> It has been argued that capitalist economy did not play a dominant role in Antiquity, and did not in fact exist. However, to accept this view is to limit needlessly the concept of capitalist economy to a single form of valorisation of capital – the exploitation of other people's labour on a contractual basis – and thus to introduce social factors. Instead we should take into account only economic factors.

I shall return to this quotation later when considering his understanding of capitalism, but for now I want to focus on his use of 'economic factors.' Here he wants to separate economic from social factors, but previously he has defined the economic as a form of social action. Once we separate the social from the economic, what is left of the economic? If exploitation is social rather than economic, then presumably it is some kind of social action that does not have to do with the desire for utilities, but this is patently false. Furthermore, even exchange relations and property relations are forms of social action. Given the framework established in *Economy and Society*, the distinctions made in the above quotation make no sense.

How does Marxian political economy avoid the difficulties of circularity and infinite regress to be found in Weber's attempts at universal definitions. Why don't we find Marx struggling as Weber does with universal stipulative definitions of the economic? First, Marx would never separate social and economic factors, since economic relations are simply social relations reified by a commodity-economic logic. Second, for Marxian political economy the delimitation of the economic is best achieved by the theory of a purely capitalist society. It is no simple stipulative definition that delimits the economic but the theory of capital's inner logic as a whole. This is because it is only with the sort of reification that becomes apparent with capitalism that the economic becomes sufficiently autonomous to be theorisable as a dialectical logic. Thus the theory of pure capitalism is a theory of a purely economic society in the sense that social relations become totally dominated by a commodity-economic logic, so that our delimitation of the economic comes from this theory as a whole and not a stipulative definition. We can utilise our understanding of the economic achieved through this theory to understand precapitalist societies in their economic aspects, even though in such societies economic action tended to be so mixed with military, religious and other kinds of social action that the actors involved would seldom have considered their action as primarily economic.

Two basic criticisms of Weber are implied by the above argument. The first is the relative arbitrariness of proceeding by attempting to make universal stipulative definitions of the economic. Weber's universal definitions, because of their stipulative nature, seem to be dogmatic. Indeed it is not any advance at all and it is arguably regressive to replace essentialism with dogmatism, because at least with essentialism there is a theory that can be argued against or refuted. The second criticism concerns the unnecessary analytical restrictions that can attach to Weber's requirement of subjective meaningfulness. Why should our analysis of the economic in precapitalist societies be limited to what the actors involved considered to be economic action, when very few actions would have been viewed as primarily economic? For example we need to be able to analyse actions that the actors believed to be religious, but we believe to have been more economic than religious, or at least to have had strong economic aspects.

Weber's universal definition of the economic is consistent with his universalist, neo-Kantian ontology. According to Kalberg (1994, p. 30), 'For Weber, regular action can result not only from values, but also from affectual, traditional, and even means-end rational action. The manner in which action is *uprooted* from its natural random flow and transformed into regularities anchored in these types of action constitutes one of his most central and basic themes.' Unoist political economy does not start with the assumption that action has a 'natural random flow' from which it must be 'uprooted' and 'transformed into regularities' by wilful action. Rather action is always already structured by social domains that may to some extent be ontologically distinct. It is not necessary to intervene in the 'random flow' with stipulative definitions of the economic because the theory of a purely capitalist society can serve as an objective basis for our understanding of the nature of the economic. Further examples of the problematic nature of Weber's definitional approach will emerge in my analysis of his understanding of capitalism.

CAPITALISM

As with the economic, Weber attempts to construct a universal definition of capitalism. As the quotation on page 102 indicates, capitalism for Weber existed as far back as antiquity, but he does emphasise the uniqueness of modern capitalism as a specific type. In a continuation of the previous quotation in Andreski (1983, p. 41) about capitalism in antiquity, Weber writes: 'Where we find that property is an object of trade and is utilised by individuals for profit-making enterprise in a market economy, there we have capitalism.' Based on this definition, where there are markets and profit making there is capitalism, even if the profit making is from purely merchant activity, from money lending or from the activities of self-employed artisans. Capitalism exists to the extent that there is buying and selling with a view to profit. Or as Weber puts it, 'capital always means wealth used to gain profit in commerce' (ibid., p. 39). With this definition capitalism is nearly universal, as claimed by Weber when he writes: 'capitalism of various forms can be found in all periods of history' (ibid., p. 109). Even slave agriculture is capitalist so long as slaves are traded on the market (ibid., p. 40). Of course slave agriculture can be part of a capitalist society, as it was in the American South, but that does not mean that it should itself be considered capitalist. Rather we should think of slave agriculture as influenced by its capitalist environment.

Weber, however, is primarily concerned to draw out the specificities of modern bourgeois capitalism. He discusses the importance of the separation of business from the household and of rational book-keeping, but then claims that 'all these peculiarities of Western capitalism have derived their significance in the last analysis only from their association with the capitalist organisation of labour' (ibid., p. 26). He then declares that 'Exact calculation – the basis of everything else – is only possible on the basis of free labour' (ibid.) Why should we accept his dogmatic claim that 'exact calculation is the basis of everything else'? If the basis of exact calculation is free labour, why should it not be the basis of everything else, or perhaps there is no single basis?

Indeed in two different contexts Weber lists a number of conditions of 'rational capital accounting'. This list can be seen as a concerted effort by Weber to define the conditions of existence of modern capitalism. In *General Economic History* (Weber, 1987, pp. 276–7) the conditions include:

1. 'the appropriation of all physical means of production ... as disposable property of autonomous private industrial companies'.
2. 'freedom of the market'.
3. 'rational technology ... which implies mechanisation'.
4. 'calculable law'.

5. 'free labour'.
6. 'the commercialisation of economic life'.

In *Economy and Society* (Weber, 1978a, pp. 161–2) the list of conditions for 'a maximum of formal rationality of capital accounting in production enterprises' is:

1. 'appropriation of all material means of production by owners' and 'market freedom'.
2. 'complete autonomy in the selection of management by the owners'.
3. 'free labor, freedom of the labor market, and freedom in the selection of workers'.
4. 'complete absence of substantive regulation of consumption, production, and prices' or 'substantive freedom of contract'.
5. 'complete calculability of the technical conditions of the production process' or 'mechanically rational technology'.
6. 'complete calculability of the functioning of public administration and the legal order'.
7. 'the most complete separation possible of the enterprise and its conditions of success and failure from the household or private budgetary unit'.
8. 'a monetary system with the highest possible degree of formal rationality'.

While it is not necessary for the dialectical theory of capital to make such lists, what strikes me about them is their general compatibility with a Marxian concept of pure capitalism.[6] If Marx or Uno were to make a list of the conditions of existence of a purely capitalist society, it would be formulated somewhat differently and would include some points not formulated by Weber, but what is interesting to me is that none of Weber's formulations are inconsistent with a purely capitalist society, and this is because such a society would among other things, maximise capitalistic rationality.

Thus far in the discussion there are two primary points to which Marx and Uno would take strong exception. First, they would utterly reject Weber's market-based or circulationist definition of capitalism, which makes capitalism universal and thereby reduces its distinctiveness. Second, they would reject Weber's statement that exact calculation is the basis of everything else. Some of the other differences in the formulation of the lists would include the following:

1. Leaving out the owner's right to appoint management, since this follows from the absolute right of private property and would be viewed as less important than other points.
2. Instead of referring to 'free' labour, Marx and Uno would use 'commodification of labour-power'.
3. There would be emphasis on the distinctiveness of the commodity, which is always produced to be exchanged for money, as opposed to mere 'goods', which may be bartered.
4. Profit making based on the exploitation of labour would be prominent on the list.

For political reasons Weber could not base his social economics on Marx's *Capital,* but it seems to me that Marx's theory ties together the conditions in his list in a dynamic theory of the economic in a purely capitalist society much better than the static formalism of marginal utility theory. Indeed, precisely because Marx views economic relations as commodity-economically reified social relations, his theory would connect well with a mid-range economic sociology. Furthermore Marx's theory incorporates the economic uniqueness of capitalism in its emphasis on capitalism as an historically specific mode of production, whereas marginal utility economics is a universalist theory. It could be argued that marginal utility theory, with its subjectivist value theory, dovetails neatly into Weber's emphasis on subjective meaningfulness. While there is no doubt a great deal to this point, I do not think that an emphasis on subjective meaningfulness is necessarily inconsistent with Marxian political economy unless it is made into an essentialist social ontology, as it is by Weber. In addition there is the parallel between marginal utility theory's emphasis on rational economic man and Weber's central focus on rationalisation as the key to understanding modernity. With regard to this point, it might be argued that Weber tends to reify 'rationalisation' and that a stronger, more social and more autonomous economic theory might have enabled him to approach the theme of rationalisation in a less essentialist, less reified and more balanced and materialist way.

Weber is fully aware that Marxian economics offers an alternative, and he never systematically defends his choice of Austrian marginalism. For example Weber (1978a, pp. 97–8) writes:

> Economic theory – which could, however, also be developed along very different lines – might then very well say that this exploitation of the power distribution (which itself is a consequence of the insti-

> tution of private property in goods and the means of production) permits it only to this particular class of economic actors to conduct their operations in accordance with the 'interest' criterion.

On the one hand Weber wants to grasp modern Western capitalism in all its uniqueness as an historical 'individual', and on the other hand he refuses systematically to explore the dynamics of capitalism as unique at the level of economics. This contradiction is a consequence of the peculiar way in which he combines the pseudo-universalist economics of marginalism with his culturalist approach to social science. Capitalism for Weber is not so much an historically specific mode of production, as one among a number of terms that he applies to modern economic life, understood from the point of view of the spread of a particular kind of culture characterised by its formal rationality and protestant discipline.

LEVELS OF ANALYSIS

A case can be made that in Weber's analysis of capitalism there are at least three levels of analysis, which on the face of it seem similar to Unoist political economy. The three levels of abstraction are pure economic theory, social economics or economic sociology, and economic history.[7] Pure economic theory abstracts economic concepts to such a high level that all non-economic impurities are filtered out – the economic can be considered in isolation and in its purity. Mid-level economic sociology reinstates the non-economic, so that the ideal-types at this level consider the political and cultural dimensions of the economic, but still at a high level of generality. Economic history may use mid-level ideal-types, but they must now be situated in the consideration of concrete cultural contexts and concrete historical facts.

Weber (1949, p. 94) recognises the danger of what I call 'the logical-historical method':[8]

> Nothing, however, is more dangerous than the *confusion* of theory and history stemming from naturalistic prejudices. This confusion expresses itself firstly in the belief that the 'true' content and the essence of historical reality is portrayed in such theoretical constructs or secondly, in the use of these constructs as a procrustean bed into which history is to be forced or thirdly, in the hypostatisation of such 'ideas' as real 'forces' and as 'true' reality which

> operates behind the passage of events and which works itself out in history.

There is no doubt that numerous Marxists, including many associated with the Second International and with whom Weber would have been familiar, have used Marx's *Capital* as a source of abstract economic laws to be applied directly to history, and this may have been one reason why Weber rejected the use of Marx's *Capital* at the level of abstract economic theory, though marginal utility theory could in principle also be directly applied to history. In contrast the Unoist approach sees capital's logic as one uniquely strong force amongst others operating in capitalist history; and at the level of history, capital's logic is partially broken down and mixed with numerous supporting and opposing forces. Thus while it is a mistake to reduce history to the working out of capital's logic, that logic is at work in history even though it is translated into a looser partial logic as it operates through the resistances of human institutions.

According to Weber (ibid., pp. 89–90), what he sometimes calls 'pure economic theory', and at other times 'exact economic theory' or 'abstract economic theory', 'offers us an ideal picture of events on the commodity-market under conditions of a society organised on the principles of an exchange economy, free competition, and rigorously rational conduct.' It follows that the market is only one aspect of social reality, but by abstracting and accentuating its main features, we can construct a 'utopia' that never exists but that clarifies market phenomena wherever they do exist to some extent. The understanding of economic action is clarified by the ideal-types of a pure market economy.

Weber left pure economic theory to the economists. He freely extracted concepts from Austrian marginalism, but did not himself attempt to construct a theory of pure economics. For Weber, the ideal-types of pure economic theory are the most 'unreal' ideal-types in the sense that they are the furthest removed from the historical concrete.[9] On the other hand they provide the paradigm case of 'ideal-type' because of the 'rigorous and errorless rational conduct' assumed (ibid., p. 42). As previously quoted, pure economic theory assumes 'an exchange economy, free competition and rigorously rational conduct' (ibid., p. 90), and such assumptions 'scarcely ever correspond completely with reality but … *approximate* it in various degrees' (ibid., p. 44, emphasis added). For example, according to Weber (1978a, p. 92): 'For purposes of economic theory, it is the marginal *consumer* who determines the direction of production. In actual fact, given the actual distribution of power, this is only true in a limited sense for the modern situation.' The theorist of pure economics abstracts purely economic variables, leaving behind considerations of politics and power in order to construct an 'internally consistent system' that is like a utopia (Weber, 1949, p. 90). This internally consistent abstract system may yield quantitative laws such as a theory of price determination, but for Weber such a theory is (ibid., p. 77) only a 'preliminary step' in clarifying the '*general* aspects of exchange and the technique of the market'.[10] This is because his main interest is to explain the uniqueness of modern capitalism, which he finds best pursued at the level of mid-range economic sociology. What matters is not so much the technical aspects of how prices are formed, but instead 'the *cultural significance* of the concrete *historical* fact that today exchange exists on a mass scale' (ibid., p. 77).

There is a pronounced contrast between Weber and Unoist political economy in how they approach 'pure economic theory'. For Weber, abstract economic theory is only a 'preliminary' step already carried out adequately by the marginalists. Abstract economic theory is simply a systematic 'utopia' of ideal-types assuming strictly rational economic action, which he can freely mine for his mid-range sociology. In contrast Unoist political economy claims that the reified automaticity of a purely capitalist society contains inherent dynamics and necessary inner connections that can be theorised dialectically and are crucial to advance our understanding of capitalism.

WEBER AND UNOIST POLITICAL ECONOMY

A purely capitalist society has a utopian (or dystopian) element in the sense that it involves extending to completion in thought tendencies that are only partially manifest in history. For this we must imagine 'idealised' or 'stylised' use-values (materiality) that the motion of value can manage through its own self-expansion. The dialectic of capital makes it clear that pure capitalism could never exist in history. How is this 'utopia' different from marginal utility theory, which 'treats human action as if it ran its course from beginning to end under the control of commercial calculation' (Weber, 1975a, p. 31)? As Weber (ibid., p. 29) puts it, 'It quite *suffices* for economic theory if we can *theoretically conceive* of a relatively large number of people ... each of whom disposes of the available "supplies of commodities" and "labour powers" ... for the sole and exclusive purpose of peaceably achieving an “optimum” of satisfaction of his *various* competing needs.’ It could be said that marginal utility theory is simply completing in theory an historical tendency.

By theorising capitalism as a projection of individual rationality, such an approach fails to come to grips with the reifying force of capitalism that in its unique power is the defining characteristic of capitalism’s uniqueness. Capitalism is theorised not as a commodity-economic logic but as individuals projecting their rational calculations in free markets. Such an approach cannot begin to understand how the logic of capital can run roughshod over other human values. It cannot understand capital’s irrationalities and its crisis tendencies.

Weber does understand capital’s reifying force to some extent, but because he has no theory of capital’s inner logic, this reifying force is understood primarily in cultural terms as the advance of a certain kind of rationality that permeates the whole like a ‘spirit’.[11] Weber analyses this rationality in part by utilising the distinction between formal and substantive rationality. Formal rationality exists to the extent that decision making is expressed in ‘numerical, calculable terms’ (Weber, 1978a, p. 85). Substantive rationality, on the contrary, occurs when decision making is shaped ‘under some criterion (past, present, or potential) of ultimate values’ (ibid.) Weber claims that there is an irresolvable contradiction between formal and substantive rationality in the sense that formal rationality is absolutely indifferent to issues of justice, and substantive rationality may sacrifice the economic efficiency that goes along with formal rationality (ibid., p. 94). For example, ‘Profitability is indeed *formally* a rational category, but for that very reason it is indifferent with respect to *substantive* postulates unless these can make themselves felt in the market in the form of sufficient purchasing power’ (ibid., p. 94). Elsewhere Weber writes: ‘The fact that the maximum of *formal* rationality in capital accounting is possible only where the workers are subjected to domination by entrepreneurs, is a further specific element of *substantive* irrationality in the modern economic order’ (ibid., p. 138).

In the light of these highly suggestive revelations, it is disappointing that Weber does not explore the contradiction between formal and substantive rationality in any depth or with any systematicness. There are no doubt many reasons for his relative neglect of this contradiction. One reason is that had he explored it in depth, it may have led him perilously close to Marx. Another reason is that his primary concern was with formal rationality as the centrepiece of modern rationalisation, and substantive rationality was not only of less interest but also was a kind of Pandora's box for Weber. Finally, there is some evidence that Weber believed that substantive rationality was more often than not in accord (though the accord could never be total) with formal rationality in the context of modern capitalism. Indeed there is more than a hint that any strong assertion of substantive over formal rationality, as in a planned socialist economy, would destroy the economic rationality of modern society. In a planned economy, according to Weber (ibid., pp. 110–11), substantive rationality would seriously undermine formal rationality and the economic growth that goes with it. There is a sense in which this is true. To the extent that substantive rationality involves the reassertion of claims of use-values over value, undermining the demonic drive towards economic growth at all costs might be one of the great attractions of a planned economy.

Weber's neo-Kantian ontological and epistemological commitments make it impossible for him to think that capital could have a theorisable inner logic, even though many of his writings point to that very likelihood. At the level of his mid-range economic sociology, the market is not simply an arena for determining prices, it is 'the most impersonal relationship of practical life into which humans can enter with one another', and 'the reason for the impersonality of the market is its matter-of-factness, its orientation to the commodity and only to that' (ibid., p. 636). Indeed according to Weber, 'consociation through exchange in the *market'* is 'the archetype of all rational social action'. (ibid., p. 635). Furthermore 'the constant expansion of the market' is 'an *inherent* tendency of the market consociation' (ibid., p. 337, emphasis added). Weber argues that the cultural/political significance of the market is that it continually expands and in doing so fosters a peculiar kind of formal rationality that is indifferent to everything but profit maximisation. As he puts it: 'Where complete market freedom is given, the highest degree of formal rationality in capital accounting is *absolutely indifferent* to all the substantive considerations involved' (Weber, 1947, p. 212). This comes very close to the absolute indifference of value to use-value in the dialectic of capital. But the dialectic of capital theorises capital's rationality and not ours, a distinction that Weber utterly fails to recognise. For Weber, capital's rationality is our rationality.

It appears that many of Weber's pronouncements in his economic sociology are heavily influenced by Marx, and yet capitalism for Weber is not so much an historically specific mode of production, as one among a number of labels that he applies to modern society, understood first of all as the spread of a certain kind of rationality.

Capital and capitalism have no particular centrality and are not theorised as a system; instead capitalism is a loose bundle of action orientations and institutional types surrounding 'rational capital accounting'.

In the following passage Weber seems to have a good grasp of the reification associated with capitalist economics:

> The capitalistic economy of the present day is an immense cosmos into which the individual is born, and which presents itself to him, at least as an individual, as an unalterable order of things in which he must live. It forces the individual, in so far as he is involved in the system of market relationships, to conform to capitalist rules of action ... the worker who cannot or will not adapt himself to them will be thrown into the street without a job (Andreski, 1983, p. 115).

Weber fails to mention that even if the worker does conform to capitalist rules of action he or she may end up on the street without a job. But the main point to be made is that Weber never takes the step from statements such as this to theorising capital as a system that can reproduce itself and in so doing reproduces the capitalist rules of social action. Unlike Marx, he never tries to probe the inner logic of capital. As a result he fails to understand the unique ontology of capital and hence the need carefully to consider its distinctiveness when considering its articulation with other social arenas. Instead rationalisation and bureaucratisation become 'spirits' that tend to absorb all into what Althusser would call an 'expressive whole' – an idealist whole without substantial materialist differentiation. While Weber's multicausal approach to historical explanation would suggest relatively autonomous social spheres, in his thinking about capitalism the relative autonomy is compromised by a certain essentialism. Thus Weber's multicausal (or multispeculation) approach to comparative historical sociology so highly touted by Kalberg (1994), is less multicausal than it would be if it recognised the unique ontology of capital, and as a result was forced not only to consider capital's unique economic dynamic but also to focus very carefully on its articulation with social realms that are ontologically distinct from it.

Contrary to Weber's ontological assumptions, when it comes to theorising capital there is a certain logic embedded in concrete reality itself that aids our abstractions. In this sense we might say that capital is to some extent self-reifying and self-abstracting – as it expands itself, it expands and deepens reification and at the same time becomes more 'abstract' in the sense that an economic system becomes more autonomous and identifiable as a self-contained logic. These claims are not far from some of Weber's claims. When we add together his emphasis on the objectifying character of the market and capital and his claim that 'the constant expansion of the market' is 'an inherent tendency', contrary to his ontology, such language implies a logic operating to some extent within concrete reality itself. Presumably with the inherent expansion of the market comes an expansion of reification, and 'inherent expansion' implies an inner logic that would extend and deepen reification. Weber seems to think that to admit such a thing would commit one to the pernicious view that concrete reality is the direct outcome of an economic inner logic. But this does not follow since a single abstract logic may be counteracted by all sorts of other forces that may deflect it, transform it or in particular cases nullify its effectiveness altogether at the level of the concrete. In short, one logic does not empirical reality make.[12]

Of course when 'pure economic theory' is as universal, formal and technical as marginalist economics, social economics becomes something for which there is a crying need. If the economic is associated with the technical, then there is a need to introduce the social at some level of analysis. The Unoist paradigm provides once again a sharp contrast with this situation. In the Unoist case the economic consists of historically specific reified social relations. The technical is never divorced from the social. The move from the theory of capital's dynamics in the abstract and in general to stage theory does not involve reorganising economic concepts according to some external intellectual interest, such as Weber's interest in rationalisation. Instead it involves rethinking capital accumulation in a more concrete context where political and ideological factors play a major role. And this rethinking is facilitated by clarity achieved at the more abstract level on the nature of the economic in a purely capitalist society, so that at the level of stage theory we have some basis for sorting out the specific interactions between the economic and the non-economic.

The economic in a purely capitalist society presents an absolutely unique theoretical object that is at one and the same time a social object and an object that has the automaticity associated with certain natural processes.[13] It is for this reason that Sekine (1997) argues that it is the only object of knowledge capable of being theorised in accordance with a strict dialectical logic. And it is for this reason that I claim that the economic is ontologically distinct from other social realms.

Weber wants to understand modern capitalism as a unique 'historical individual', and yet for him the uniqueness cannot be discovered within pure economic theory (which is formal and technical), but only in the cultural accoutrements of modern capitalism, such as a work ethic, bureaucracy and legal-rational authority. He does not think that capital itself has a logic; he does not see the significance of reification internal to the economic. Instead he extracts from the economic a certain kind of rationality, which produces a variety of quasi-reified cultural configurations. Indeed for Weber modern society as a whole is reified, as suggested by the metaphor 'iron cage'. As a result the uniquely reified character of the economic in contrast to other regions of social life cannot be grasped, and hence there can be no ability to consider the specific articulations between the economic and the non-economic. Furthermore this overstating of a kind of generalised, suffocating reification can only produce a politics of extreme voluntarism that somehow overthrows the reified totality (Lukács), or a politics of extreme pessimism that succumbs to the inevitability of the reified totality (sometimes Weber and sometimes Marcuse and others of the Frankfurt School).

Weber's criticisms of Marxist theory are primarily directed at the crude 'logical-historical method' that is characteristic of the Marxism of the Second International. According to this method, the inner logic of capital was applied more or less directly to history as though history were a direct outcome of capital's logic. On the other hand, with regard to the 'ideal-types' of Marx's texts, Weber (1949, p. 103) writes: 'The eminent, indeed unique, *heuristic* significance of these ideal types when they are used for the *assessment* of reality is known to everyone who has ever employed Marxian concepts and hypotheses.' Characteristically Weber thinks that the choice is between an essentialist economic theory operating behind events to determine the course of history on the one hand, and on the other a rejection of essentialism that sees the economic as simply an aspect of social life that can be artificially isolated for the sake of analysis through the use of ideal-types. But this is not the only choice. Instead I want to theorise capital's logic, and then, through a variety of complex mediations involving levels of theory and interconnections between the economic and non-economic, try to determine the impact of that logic on history, considering it as a particularly powerful and persistent social force articulated with other social forces, but differentiated from them in its reified character and reifying capacity.

The interpretation of Marxian political economy that I am advocating would not employ 'ideal-types' as a central methodological strategy. According to Weber (1949, p. 96), an ideal-type is 'a purely analytical construct created by ourselves.' The categories of the theory of pure capitalism might be more appropriately labelled 'real types' since they are arrived at by letting capital's self-reifying and self-abstracting force complete itself in theory. The categories of stage theory are abstractions from a particular historical context aided by the theory of capital's logic. I prefer to call such concepts 'abstract types' or 'material types' to emphasise that they are not purely mental constructs, but abstractions from a particular material context guided by the theory of capital's logic. Thus the central categories of stage theory are not average types, genetic types, teleological types or extreme types. For example cotton manufacturing, as the most typical form of capital in the stage of liberalism, is a material type abstracted in accordance with knowledge of capital's inner logic. It is not arrived at by some kind of averaging, by imagining an extreme type, or by abstracting from an origin or telos. It is that form of capital which is most capitalist and most successful and typical in its operation, but this can only be determined by referring to a theory that precisely informs us exactly what capital is. Perhaps the categories of stage theory should be called 'dialectical types' since they are abstractions informed by a dialectical logic.

Hekman (1983) advocates Weberian methodology because she thinks that the ideal-type effects a synthesis between structure and agency. Given the approach adopted here, any general solution to the structure–agency problem must be defective, since the relation between structure and agency is conceived differently at different levels of analysis. At the level of the theory of pure capitalism, economic structures absorb or subsume human agency such that humans continue to act but their actions only serve to power the motions of value that determine all outcomes. Human action loses its agency in any meaningful sense because even the possibility of influencing outcomes is nullified. At the level of stage theory we are mainly concerned to characterise forms of abstract structure and abstract collective agency that are typical of stage-specific types of capital accumulation. At this level we are not primarily concerned with trying to explain processes of change, for this kind of analysis belongs to the more concrete level of historical analysis. At the level of historical analysis we need to consider the degree to which various structures are 'agencied' and agencies are structured, as agency and structure interact in processes of change. At the level of historical analysis our thoughts about the evolution of capitalism may be informed and greatly enhanced by the two more abstract levels. It follows that the way we think about structure and agency varies with the level of theory. There is no general solution to the problem.

One of the main lines drawn in modern social science has been between Weberian approaches that emphasise subjective meaningfulness and a sharp distinction between social and natural sciences on the one hand, and positivist approaches that emphasise 'data' and a unified scientific method on the other. I am trying to draw a different line, one that separates those with a homogeneous social ontology, such as positivists and Weber, and those who at least open the door to the possibility of more than one social ontology, such as Marx and Uno.

Unfortunately many Marxist scholars today have adopted a version of the Weberian paradigm, marked either by ignoring the theory of capital's inner logic altogether, or by treating it not as a coherent theory but as a collection of insights that can be freely mined in accordance with each theorist's interests. As a result the specific clarity that Marx was attempting to achieve with regard to the economic under capitalism is lost, and the economic becomes immediately mixed with all manner of political and cultural variables in accordance with the interests of some particular school of thought. The main focus of Marxian political economy, then, becomes a mid-range theory that freely mixes economic variables with other variables without any theoretical basis for clarifying the economic variables to begin with, or for understanding their ontological uniqueness.

THE ECONOMIC AND THE SOCIAL

According to the above analysis the economic is both ontologically distinct from other social realms and has an internally stratified social ontology. This is in marked contrast to Weber's thought, according to which 'the social' emerged as the key category of the human sciences, and with it a certain homogeneity and uniformity with *social* science. The social came to encompass all the ongoing interactions that make up human history to such an extent that all regions of interaction were seen as ontologically the same – they are all arenas of meaningful *social* action. In opposition to Weber, I have argued for a social ontology that is differentiated, and of course this implies a social epistemology that is also differentiated.

The economic, the psychic and the linguistic may all have deep structures, but they are not necessarily ontologically the same. If the social *per se* is not a unified object of knowledge, it can best be known by work aimed at understanding the articulations between various distinct social ontologies. And while the social consists of a good deal more than minds, languages and economic practices, I mention these because they are among the strongest candidates for theorising a deep structure and for having distinct ontologies. While this study is aimed at highlighting the ontological uniqueness of the economic, explorations of the ontological uniquenesses of other social realms would be a prerequisite to fulfilling what I see as the great promise of this approach.

The homogenising influence of the category 'social' in modern social science can not be overstated.[14] Since the 'linguistic turn', the analogy between a language and a society has sometimes been pushed to the point of near identity (Winch, 1958). From this point it is easy to generalise, claiming that the economy is like a language (Baudrillard, 1975) and the psyche is like a language (Lacan, 1977). In this way one area of social life, language and linguistic behaviour, reigns over other areas, blinding us to their ontological uniqueness. In principle the same thing could happen with either the economic or the psychic, using the 'social' as a Trojan horse to obscure other areas of social life. While at certain levels of analysis it may be worthwhile to theorise about language in general or society in general, the danger is a certain homogenisation of the social landscape. Some linguistic phenomena may be very general, but they may also articulate with, say, the economic in a unique way. Perhaps the reifying force peculiar to capital's economic ontology requires us to rethink language as it articulates with the economic, or perhaps the peculiar structure of the unconscious requires us to rethink language as it articulates with the human psyche.

There are strategic reasons for saying that the social does not exist, not because all social identities are radically precarious, as Laclau and Mouffe (1985) would argue, but because the category so easily lulls us into homogenising our ways of thinking. The social is not necessarily a melting pot in which 'social ontology', 'social structure', 'social relation' and 'social interaction' are a univocal.

In much modern economic theory the relation between the economic and the social is not problematised at all, and in most cases if the social enters theorising at all it falls under the category of 'imperfections' or 'externalities', or is in accordance with a market-based 'rational choice' model. This is because positivist economics simply accepts as given, natural and unproblematic, a certain disembeddedness of the economic from the social that is peculiar to capitalism.

Weberian economic sociology is a big improvement over positivist economics because it endeavours to develop a mid-range economic sociology that integrates the economic with the social and the historical. Its strength is the development of an institutional or cultural sociology of economics. Its failure is its inability to develop a philosophical economics that can clearly identify and differentiate those economic and social variables that are specific to capitalism and to interconnect them as capital's logic of value expansion. Lacking a philosophical basis for such clarification, Weberian approaches to economics will tend to combine or to blend categories together in *ad hoc* ways, and to rely only on common sense or on the particular value orientation of the theorist to relate the economic and the social.

CONCLUSIONS

A philosophical economics is needed to clarify (1) the specific ontology of capitalist economics, (2) the reified character of all basic capitalist economic variables, (3) the domain-specific stratification of the economic and (4) how to consider the relation between the economic and the social, both in understanding the past and in dereifying and socialising the economic in the future.

Weber's contribution lies less in the area of methodology than in substantive studies in comparative historical sociology – particularly his *Sociology of Religion* and *The Protestant Ethic and the Spirit of Capitalism (1958)*. In these works he carries out comparative structural analyses that include reference to various forms of collective consciousness. Many of the peculiarities of his work, such as his voluntarist action theory, can best be understood in the historical intellectual context that motivated him to differentiate himself from the German historical school, with its strong Hegelian influences.

While Weber did break with Hegel's essentialism to a large extent, he did not break with Hegel in every respect. For example, compared with positivism,Weber has more similarities with Hegel, even if the similarities do not run deep. For example, like Hegel he is concerned with the big picture of history towards which he adopts an internal point of view. His concern with ideas and 'spirits' as material forces in history, has at least some similarity with Hegel, though Weber's historical analysis is much more materialist than Hegel's. Finally, Weber's fixation with rationalisation gives his thought a certain degree of essentialism, even though he never constructs an essentialist theory that, like Lukacs' 'reification', becomes the centre of a theoretical totality.

Many an interpreter has praised Weber's scepticism, his refusal to construct general theories, and his heuristic use of concepts. There is of course some appeal in an approach that avoids reifying theories and concepts, but I would argue that very often some kind of implicit theory lies behind Weber's generalisations and that had he made these theories more explicit, his thought would have had more purchase on the world and therefore have had more of a basis for acceptance or rejection. There is a combination of anti-essentialism and dogmatism in Weber that may at first seem rather peculiar, but as I shall argue at greater length later in this book, the two nearly always go together. The more anti-essentialist a thinker, the less basis he or she has for making any claims about states of affairs and their interconnections, and the less possibility he or she has for theorising any form of necessity in objects or thoughts about them. This is not a problem as long as that person does not make substantive claims about what exists, but simply criticises those who do. Once such claims are made, however, they are bound to appear dogmatic since to do more than assert such claims would commit the thinker to some kind of theory that would necessarily be 'exclusionary', and to anti-essentialists, essentialism is simply an extreme form of exclusion. Weber's dogmatism is most apparent in *Economy and Society*, with its exhausting but not exhaustive (that would be essentialist) array of stipulative definitions and typologies.

Weber was more interested in the uniqueness of modern Western civilisation than in the uniqueness of capitalism as an economic system. He was also very interested in the causal impact of religion upon history. Perhaps, then, some of my criticisms are a little unfair, but I would point out that even if his main concern was the uniqueness of modern Western civilisation, understanding the uniqueness of capitalism must certainly be central, since nothing so definitively established its uniqueness and contributed to the triumph of the West over other civilisations. But Weber was prevented from doing this by his methodological individualism and voluntarist action theory, which resulted in his displacing reification from the economic to capitalist culture, understood as a particular form of rationalisation.

Others have made a great deal of Weber's methodological individualism. You will note that I have not, and this is because I do not think that it plays a big role in his most successful substantive work. Like Burger (1987), I believe that Weber borrowed much of his epistemology from Rickert, and that it does not stand up well to close inspection. Weber's particular formulation of 'ideal-type' was original, but I think it is best understood as a cover term that embraces a whole sct of issues about the use of concepts in historical analysis. 'Ideal-type' should not be considered as some kind of general methodology for the social sciences. As Burger argues, ideal-type concepts are particularly useful when we have a pure model, such as that of bureaucracy, against which actual organisations can be measured to determine the degree to which they are bureaucratic, at least in terms of the model. Even so, an 'ideal-type' concept of bureaucracy not articulated with a political economy of capitalism would certainly be unnecessarily autonomous and impoverished.

Both Weber and Althusser were anti-Hegelian and anti-essentialist, but in other respects they could hardly have been more different. While Weber's neo-Kantianism pushes the philosophy of the subject to an extreme, Althusser's structuralism largely purges the subject from philosophy. As I have previously argued, the Unoist political economy that I am advocating avoids both of these extremes, though it is closer to Althusser in believing that social science should seek to theorise the deep structures and explanatory mechanisms that operate in and through human history.

5 The Problematic Althusser

There has been a remarkable resurgence of interest in Althusser's work in recent years with the publication of a spate of books and articles by and about him. Most of the writing about Althusser treats his work as interesting for its historical influence on the development of poststructuralism and other schools of thought. Others extract certain concepts from the corpus of his work, for example 'overdetermination', and use them as a basis for postmodern Marxism.[1] Lehmann (1993) and Resch (1992) go the furthest in resurrecting Althusserian social science in opposition to poststructuralism, with Lehmann advocating a 'critical structuralism' and Resch a Bhaskarian critical realist interpretation. I intend neither to praise nor to bury Althusser. Instead I intend to engage with some of his perspectives in order to move beyond them without falling into the modish antiscience stance of postmodernism.

Althusser's work is important to the argument of this book, and this is because he asks so many of the right questions. In particular he focuses with great intensity upon the nature of the object of knowledge of the theory of capital. He asks about the specificity of capital as an object, the type of discourse needed to theorise capital, and the relation between this discourse and the object of knowledge that it theorises (Althusser and Balibar, 1970, p. 14). In my view these are precisely the questions that need to be asked; Althusser's answers, however, can be significantly improved upon.

Althusser's writings have contributed to our understanding of Marx's *Capital*, if only by providing us with a new set of questions to pose to the text. For example Althusser's critique of empiricism enables us better to understand the 'object of knowledge' and its problematic relation to the 'real object.' After reading Althusser we can no longer be sanguine about unproblematised objects that are assumed to be simply given, and from which pregiven subjects abstract knowledge that is then thought in some sense to reflect the real object.

With his conception 'epistemological break' Althusser enabled us to develop a sharp focus on the distinctions between classical political economy and Marxian political economy. He recognised that Marx's *Capital* is a theory of fully developed capitalism and not a theory of its genesis or of a move from simple commodity production to capitalism proper. He placed emphasis on the need to understand the theory as a thought-totality that establishes meaning through a system of internal relations amongst concepts. He urged us to read *Capital* volume I chapter 1 with the utmost attention, even though Althusser himself lacked the background in economics fully to understand the theory as an economic theory. And above all he urged us to appreciate *Capital* as the founding work of a new science, and in explicating this new science to question its object of knowledge.

Althusser's intensely anti-Hegelian structuralism inclined him to read Hegel as Marx's extreme other. While this served to underline the important differences between them, ironically, in his very determination to rid Marxism of all Hegelian influences he takes on some of the characteristics of his opponent.[2] Even more ironically, some of these characteristics are not always the ones that might prove most useful in advancing Marxian political economy. To some extent Althusser's 'othering' of Hegel defeats itself and points beyond Althusser's problematic towards a dialectical approach that recognises a different sort of Hegel in Marx's *Capital*.

It is my contention that the Uno–Sekine approach to political economy, whose Hegelianism may seem anathema to Althusserian Marxism, in fact shares at least some common interpretations. This commonality means that the Uno–Sekine approach can offer ways forward from Althusser's problematic that do not follow the usual path towards poststructuralism taken by so many of his disciples. It can also proceed further in solving many problems that are left hanging by Althusser without falling into the kinds of essentialism that would represent a pre-Althusserian regression. It also avoids the sorts of poststructuralism that in moving beyond Althusser fall into scepticism, with the result that many of Althusser's positive achievements are lost.[3] In a sense this critique of Althusser involves using Hegel to reinforce the modernist gains of Althusser that are worth preserving, while avoiding those forms of essentialism that are undesirable. At the same time I avoid postmodernist forms of thought that not only undermine Althusser's contributions, but also, in some cases, impoverish the possibilities for knowledge in general.

ALTHUSSER'S HEGEL AND SEKINE'S DIALECTIC

According to Althusser (1969, p. 189) with Hegel's dialectic the movement from abstract to concrete is simply the 'autogenesis of the concept', and furthermore he claims that '"conditions" do not really exist for Hegel since, under cover of simplicity developing into complexity, he always deals with a pure interiority whose exteriority is no more than its phenomenon' (ibid., p. 208).[4]

None of these claims are quite accurate when applied to the dialectic of capital (nor to Hegel's *Logic* for that matter) as simply one level of analysis within Marxian political economy. 'The autogenesis of the concept' does not capture the sort of conceptual work involved with the cunning of capital overcoming use-value obstacles in moving through the dialectic of capital from abstract-in-thought to concrete-in-thought, and it plays no role in the movement from the abstract level of theorising pure capitalism to the concrete level of theorising the course of capitalist history. In other words the concept can never capture the complexity of history such that the concept's pure interiority can never reduce exteriority to its phenomenon. To do so would produce the most flagrant and one-sided economic determinism. For example, in a purely capitalist society capital achieves an indifference to difference (use-value) in general. Hence in the abstract, capital simply exploits homogeneous human labour power and is indifferent to its colour, gender, religion, politics, age, ethnicity or sexual orientation. At the same time we know, for example, that in history women have generally been treated quite differently from men by capital, but this is for reasons that cannot be strictly derived from capital's logic alone. Hence if our understanding of history were reduced to being a direct function of capital's logic we would lack a full understanding of capital's patriarchy.

Indeed one of the most fundamental problems with Marxian political economy is how to move from the rigorous logic of the theory of pure capitalism (pure interiority) to the messiness of capitalist history, or in other words, how to use the logic to inform our understanding of that history without overstating or understating the role of capital's logic in particular historical outcomes. Since capital's reifying force is not powerful enough on its own to establish a transparent pure interiority at the level of history, it would be folly to assume at the historical level that exteriority would simply be the phenomenon of a pure interiority. In short, in order to theorise capital's logic, we *assume* a purely capitalist society governed entirely by a commodity-economic logic, or in other words by self-regulating markets containing the circulation of commodities, money and capital. This assumption, however, is not arbitrary because it is assisted by the 'real abstraction' that occurs in history as a result of the expansion of self-abstracting exchange processes and labour processes governed increasingly by purely quantitative considerations.[5]

The Hegelian dialectic, according to Althusser, 'is completely dependent on the radical presupposition of a simple original unity which develops within itself by virtue of its negativity, and throughout its development only ever restores the original simplicity and unity in an ever more "concrete" totality' (ibid., p. 197). In other words the Hegelian dialectic is an 'expressive totality' in the sense that the parts are not relatively autonomous, but are nothing more than the expression of a teleology of an original simple unity. There is no real externality in the dialectic as the original simple unity is always restored through a process of internalising negativity.[6]

The 'original simple unity' in the dialectic of capital is 'the commodity.' Among other things the commodity is an historically specific set of social relations that has become embedded in a thing. In history this embeddedness is manifest as a tendency that never reaches completion, but can serve to guide thought towards theoretical completion. Thus a certain work of theoretical production is needed to arrive at an understanding of 'the commodity' as 'an original simple unity', and as a result it may not be original, simple or unified.

The commodity form originates the dialectic of capital only in the sense that it is the logical cell form of capital, but this does not imply that it is necessarily the historically originating force of capital as in some sort of historical prime mover. Indeed the theoretically developed capitalistic commodity form is not an original in the historical sense, but is a result. It is the result not only of a long duration of historical economic practices, but also a relatively long duration of theoretical practices. Thus the commodity form is 'original' only in the sense that it locates the dialectic of capital. That, of course, is not saying much since any theory must have a first category or a starting point. The dialectic itself, as argued in Chapter 3, originates with the category 'value.'

Furthermore the materiality of 'value' means that it can never be simple in history, since as a material force it may always be resisted to varying extents. In theory, however, we can allow the motion of value successfully to subsume all use-value obstacles to the point where, through its own self-expansion, value can dynamically expand and reproduce the socioeconomic life of a purely capitalist society. While the self-abstracting character of capital aids our theory construction, we must complete the work of capital with the work of theoretical practice because the self-abstracting character of capital both reveals and hides aspects of its *modus operandi*.

'Value' is in a sense a unity, but perhaps more accurately it is a unifying and homogenising force that can maintain its unity in the dialectic of capital only insofar as a commodity-economic logic can by itself, without any outside aid, operate the economic life of a purely capitalist society. But we know that in history there are no purely capitalist societies and that a commodity-economic logic always has support, is always resisted and always subsumes only part of economic life. But if we know that social life in history always sprawls beyond capital's logic, then in an unproblematic sense we cannot consider history as a concretisation of capital's logic.

'Commodity' or 'value' is 'simple' only in the sense of being the most abstract category of capital; it is 'original' only in being the starting point of the theory; and it is a 'unity' only in the complex sense of being able to unify relatively autonomous economic variables under a commodity-economic logic. The dialectic of capital moves from the abstract-in-thought to the concrete-in-thought by way of negation. But Unoist political economy in its totality is not in any sense expressive in Althusser's sense, because at least three relatively autonomous levels of analysis are needed to articulate the relations between more abstract and more concrete levels of analysis.[7]

The dialectic of capital has a sort of teleology, but it is not the sort about of which Althusser writes. It is not a teleology that involves a necessary advance towards some set of ends in history. In the dialectic of capital temporality takes the form of logical time, not historical time; hence the 'end' of the dialectic of capital is simply the subsumption of all major economic variables to self-expanding value or to the logic of the commodity form. It is a theory that seeks to demonstrate the logical possibility in principle of a purely capitalist society that through logical time could reproduce itself, and by demonstrating this possibility reveals the inner logic of capital. The dialectic of capital would not be possible at all were capital not a very substantial force in history, but strictly speaking the theory of capital's inner logic says nothing at all about the specific effectiveness of the laws of motion of capital at the level of historical particularity, other than to suggest that the closer actual historical societies come to resembling a purely capitalist society the more likely the laws of motion of capital will prevail.

While there is no historical teleology in the dialectic of capital, it demonstrates that at least in logical time, capitalism must come to an end because ultimately a falling rate of profit will make it impossible for capital to reproduce itself. One might of course deduce from this that to the extent that historical societies are capitalist, then their capitalistic character must also come to an end. This of course leaves open the debate about the extent to which actual historical societies are capitalist.

CONTRADICTION

If we theorise the value/use-value contradiction dialectically in a purely capitalist society, it is apparent that

> the 'contradiction' is inseparable from the total structure of the social body in which it is found, inseparable from its formal *conditions* of existence, and even from the *instances* it governs; it is radically *affected by them*, determining, but also determined in one and the same movement, and determined by the various *levels* and *instances* of the social formation it animates; it might be called *overdetermined in its principle* (Althusser, 1969, p. 101).

This quotation from Althusser could apply entirely to the value/use-value contradiction in the dialectic of capital as long as we take 'social formation' to mean a purely capitalist society (Althusser clearly did not).[8]

Every major logical step in the unfolding of the dialectic of capital involves the resolution of some kind of contradiction between value and use-value. Whether the use-value obstacles are associated with commodities, money, capital, labour, variations in technique, fixed capital, merchant activities, land or moneylenders, each use-value obstacle forces value to adopt particular forms in order to exist as self-expanding value.

In the dialectic of capital we theorise how value operating through a commodity-economic logic can manage all the major inputs that are involved in capitalist production. Land, for example, is not capitalistically produced and can be monopolised by a landlord class. Land therefore constitutes a serious use-value obstacle to the self-expansion of value. It is not possible to turn land entirely into a capitalistically produced commodity, and yet it must have a value if it is to be managed commodity-economically. The category 'rent' is generated in the dialectic of capital to ensure that the surplus profits associated with land ownership will not permanently disrupt the regulating role of the average rate of profit, and 'rent' and 'interest' are utilised to commodify land and give it a capitalistic rational price.

This example illustrates that the value/use-value contradiction is 'inseparable from the total structure of the social body' of a purely capitalist society and from the 'formal conditions' of that body and 'the instances it governs' (ibid.). Landed property as part of the total structure of the social body and as an instance governed by the value/use-value contradiction is radically determined by the need for self-expanding value to be self-reliant, and at the same time it forces upon value the category 'rent', which establishes a *modus vivendi* between industrial capital and landed property. Does it follow that the value/use-value contradiction in the dialectic of capital is 'overdetermined in its principle'? I suspect not, but since Althusser explicates the concept in connection with the Russian Revolution and the concreteness of a social formation, it is not clear in what sense the value/use-value contradiction would be overdetermined for him.[9]

If capital's inner logic is dialectical in form, this implies the use of some notion of 'contradiction.' I have argued that the basic contradiction is between value and use-value, but this plays itself out differently in the doctrines of circulation, production and distribution. In the doctrine of circulation we move from the commodity form to the capital form, with value increasingly freeing itself from use-value constraints until with the capital form, $M–C–M'$, it can apparently subsume society's material economic life to its project of infinite expansion. At work is a logic of transition whereby use-value obstacles are overcome by generating one qualitatively distinct circulation form out of another. The kind of contradiction at work here generates new forms by overcoming use-value obstacles.

In the doctrine of production a logic of reflection is at work. Here the circulation forms at first appear as the mere outer reflection of inner essential production relations, but as we work through the dialectic this outer reflection becomes a necessary set of appearances with a certain dependence/independence *vis-à-vis* the labour and production process, and this necessary connection becomes schematised in the expanded reproduction of capital (reproduction schema).

In the doctrine of distribution the self-expansion of value must deal with certain heterogeneities, for example technical differences in different branches of production, the seeming external character of land,

and functional differences between industrial, merchant and banking capital. Here a logic of development overcomes certain forms of difference that value's identitarian logic must subsume. In other words, capital develops a certain heterogeneity that in each case is contained by self-expanding value.

It is beyond the scope of this book to analyse the precise nature and function of contradiction in each of these types of dialectical logic and in the transitions between them. But this brief summary will at least indicate that contradiction has a complex cognitive function in the dialectic of capital, and while the parallel with Hegel's *Logic* is pronounced, the materiality of the dialectic of capital forces the dialectic to do real work to achieve even the closure arrived at by assuming that all use-values are sufficiently docile to be internalised by self-expanding value.[10]

In his famous essay 'Contradiction and Overdetermination: Notes for an Investigation', Althusser begins by arguing that Marx's appropriation of Hegel's dialectic is not simply a process of extracting a rational kernel from a mystical shell, but rather is a process that involves a fundamental break that thoroughly transforms the dialectic. To illustrate this claim, Althusser (1969, p. 100) uses the example of the Russian Revolution, the unity of which cannot be adequately understood as the coming together of the pure phenomenon in the internal unity of a simple or general contradiction. Instead the Russian Revolution must be understood as a fusion of relatively autonomous practices, each with its specific modality of action. Let me return to an earlier quotation from Althusser. The revolutionary contradiction that is the condensation of many contradictions

> is inseparable from the total structure of the social body in which it is found, inseparable from its formal *conditions* of existence, and even from the *instances* it governs; it is radically *affected by them*, determining, but also determined in one and the same movement, and determined by the various *levels* and *instances* of the social formation it animates; it might be called *overdetermined in its principle* (ibid., p. 101).

Althusser goes on to argue that all Marxian contradictions are overdetermined, as opposed to Hegelian contradictions, which are cumulative internalisations that always start from a simple centre and end with an expressive totality that denies any real autonomy to its constituents.

What interests me here is that Althusser establishes his notion of overdetermined contradiction at the level of historical analysis, at the level of analysing historical class struggle and revolutions. At this level it is relatively easy to contrast materialist, overdetermined contradictions that are never pure, self-contained or unconditioned, but are attuned to the heterogeneity and complexity of social forces operating in history, with simple 'idealist' contradictions that tend to homogenise history in accordance with the most abstract and simple idea that infuses the whole with its spirit and unfolds in accordance with a preset teleology. Such a contrast would surely incline one towards the more complex and materialist Althusserian overdetermined contradiction.

The problem with Althusser's position as I see it, despite its claim to be complex, is that it is too simple! It is beyond the scope of this chapter to attempt anything like an analysis of all the various types and levels of contradiction in the writings of Marx and Engels, but it is clear to me that Althusser pays too little attention to the differences between the kinds of contradiction involved in the unfolding of the Russian Revolution and the kinds of contradiction involved in the unfolding of the law of value in Marx's *Capital*. *Capital* contains a considerable variety of contradictions, and they do not strike me as either having the qualities of Althusser's characterisations of Hegel's dialectic, or being the types of contradiction that he sees in the Russian Revolution.

By treating the Russian Revolution as the paradigm case for developing a specifically Marxist conception of contradiction, Althusser is taking one kind of historical event as the basis for a general theory of contradiction. While different kinds of historical event may exhibit different kinds of contradiction, it is possible to agree with some of what Althusser argues with regard to overdetermined contradiction at the level of historical analysis. At the level of historical analysis it is obviously true that 'the Capital–Labour contradiction is never simple, but always specified by the historically concrete forms and circumstances in which it is exercised' (ibid., p. 106). It seems similarly obvious that at the level of historical analysis 'the economic dialectic is never active in the pure state' (ibid., p. 113). But granting these points to Althusser at the level of historical analysis, where they seem perfectly appropriate and indeed obvious, does not take us towards clarifying the nature of contradiction in the theory of capital's inner logic or in the theory of the self-expansion of value. Is the theory of value, not as it is used to aid thinking about history, but in and of itself, overdetermined by imperialism, feudal survivals, ruling class divisions and Bolshevik organisational and strategic skills? If not, then in what sense are the contradictions internal to the theory of capital's logic overdetermined? Is the only alternative the simple expressive contradictions of Althusser's Hegel? It seems to me that these are not the only alternatives, and that by locating his paradigm case of overdetermined contradiction at the level of historical analysis, Althusser is using a complicated concept to say something rather obvious, and at the same time he also manages to make misleading suggestions about how historical forces can or should be studied. The contradictions in the theory of capital's inner logic do not seem particularly overdetermined because the political and ideological are reduced to passive background conditions at this level of analysis, so that contradictions only exist between or within economic categories. The materiality of these categories and their historical specificity makes the dialectic of capital different in important respects from Hegel's *Logic*. The most important difference is that contingency is essentially neutralised by Hegel's view that contingency is simply the externalisation of necessity, such that there is a more or less easy and direct movement from the most abstract level of Hegel's dialectic to various levels of more concrete contingency. In the case of the dialectic of capital, we have a theory of capital's inner logic, but we do not know how or in what forms this logic manifests itself at more concrete and contingent levels of analysis. Other realms of social life may be relatively autonomous, so that we do not know in advance just how these realms will articulate with capital's logic or to what degree this logic itself will become less of a logic as it is deflected by other social forces. This necessitates some conception of levels of analysis, where the levels inform one another while remaining relatively autonomous. To a large extent, what Althusser is attempting to accomplish with the concept 'overdetermination' (presumably causal complexity), the Uno–Sekine approach accomplishes much better with the idea of relatively autonomous levels of analysis.

In 'Is it Simple to be a Marxist in Philosophy'?, Althusser (1990, pp. 221–2) argues that

> contradiction, as you find it in *Capital,* presents the surprising characteristic of being *uneven*. ... Because the working class is not the opposite of the capitalist class, it is not the capitalist class negated. ... They do not share the same history, they do not share the same world, they do not lead the same class struggle, yet they do come into confrontation, and this certainly is a contradiction since the *relation of con-*

> *frontation reproduces the conditions of confrontation* instead of transcending them in a beautiful Hegelian exaltation and reconciliation.

The confusions in this argument indicate that indeed it is not simple to be a Marxist in philosophy.

In the theory of a purely capitalist society, the relation between capital and labour is first presented at the end of the doctrine of circulation (as a transition to the doctrine of production), when it becomes clear that only the commodification of labour power makes possible the subsumption of the labour and production process by *M–C–M′*, and it is with this subsumption that capital finds the secret of its self-expansion within itself. In the doctrine of production, it becomes clear that it is from the exploitation of this special commodity in the realm of production that all surplus value arises. In the logic of reflection characteristic of this doctrine, capital and labour are presented as relational categories necessitating each other. Thus the contradiction between them is not transformed into harmonious reconciliation, but is continually reproduced even in this 'pure' dialectic. In a purely capitalist society, we assume that labour remains docily in the commodity form, but this certainly does not suggest anything like a 'reconciliation' in real life or in history.

At the level of historical analysis it is obvious that 'they do not share the same history', but in a purely capitalist society labour is reduced to being capital as a self split into another, that both stands in stark opposition to capital and is totally dependent on capital. This relation of total dependence–total otherness is crucial to understanding the capital–labour relation, and is not helped in any way by Althusser's observation that 'they do not share the same world.' In the dialectic of capital, they not only share the same world, but also this world can reproduce itself, forcing labour to continue to 'share the same world.' In the theory of capital's inner logic, where persons are reduced to being bearers of economic categories, labour exists for and only for capital to exploit in order to expand itself. From the point of view of capital, labour is a commodity, the continued commodification of which requires periodic crises. The 'confrontation' always remains incipient in the sense that we assume that labour power always remains in its commodity form. In actual history the relation of confrontation may *not* 'reproduce the conditions of confrontation' in the sense that class struggle may transform them.

'Uneven development' and 'contradiction' are both Marxian concepts, but Althusser does not advance the cause of philosophical clarity by merging them together. As I understand Marxian political economy, 'contradiction' can occur at any of the three levels, but at levels more concrete than pure capitalism, contradiction lacks the strict necessity of dialectical contradiction. 'Uneven development', on the other hand, is a concept that can only be used effectively at the level of historical analysis, where indeed development is always uneven in the sense that different, relatively autonomous practices have distinctive developmental temporalities. In contrast, at the level of pure capitalism there is a homogeneous abstract temporality, and at the level of stage theory distinct temporalities are synchronised from the point of view of capital accumulation in order to arrive at a stage-specific type of capital accumulation.

Having said that a theory of capital's inner logic can by itself tell us nothing about the efficaciousness of this logic at more concrete levels, it would be a mistake to fail to recognise the very great cognitive gains that result from having a theory of capital's logic. Such a theory is a giant step forward in understanding what capital has been, is, and can be, and hence in analysing its ways of being in the world, including its articulation with other social forces. Indeed, given the obvious importance of capital in shaping modern history, the importance of such a theory can hardly be overstated.

CAPITAL'S OBJECT OF KNOWLEDGE

In the early pages of *Reading Capital*, Althusser (Althusser and Balibar, 1970, p. 14) declares his intention to pose Marx's *Capital* 'the question of its *relation to its object*, hence both the question of the specificity of its *object*, and the question of the specificity of its *relation* to that object'. It seems to me that these are absolutely crucial questions to pose, but Althusser's answers are not as strong as they might be. In what follows I shall criticise these answers both from within the assumptions of Althusser's own problematic and from within the Uno–Sekine approach, which I consider provides better answers.

In sorting out Althusser's claims about the specificity of *Capital's* object of knowledge, I have arrived at five propositions that seem most representative of his position:[11]

1. The object is 'contemporary bourgeois society, which is thought as an historical result' (ibid., p. 65).

2. The object is 'economic relations' in 'their articulated combination [*Gliederung*] within modern bourgeois society' (ibid., p. 64).
3. The object is 'the theory of a region which, as a region (level or instance) is an organic component of the object of the theory of history itself' (ibid., p. 117).
4. The object 'is the mechanism which makes the result of a history's production exist as a society ... and not as a heap of sand' (ibid., p. 65).
5. The object is the 'core form' (*Kerngestalt*) of the capitalist mode of production (ibid., p. 195).

Althusser's claim that the object of knowledge of *Capital* is 'contemporary bourgeois society, which is thought as a historical result' is an expression of his point, based on passages from the *1867 Introduction*, to the effect that Marx's theory is not an attempt to explain the genesis of bourgeois society, but a theory of bourgeois society as an historical result. While this point is well taken, using these concepts to express *Capital's* object of knowledge is infelicitous in a number of respects. First, there is the problem of the meaning of 'contemporary bourgeois society' as a whole and of each of its terms. Is contemporary bourgeois society a totality that can be the object of knowledge of a single theory? The problems here become clearer if we take each term in turn.

'Contemporary' raises the issue of temporality, and Althusser himself criticises the view that historical times of relatively autonomous practices such as those that make up the economic, political and ideological can be assumed to be contemporaneous with each other. Indeed the collapsing of the unevenness of times into a single 'essential section' or contemporaneity is, according to Althusser (ibid., p. 138), the typical Hegelian move that underlies most historicism. 'Contemporary', then, is a problematic concept not only because we do not know what span of historical time is to be included, but also because whatever span is included there may be different times embedded in different, relatively autonomous practices that are not contemporaneous with each other. Thus for Althusser the temporality (rhythms of development) of religion or of the family may not be the same as the mode of capital accumulation. In short the movement of developmental time in different practices and societies may be uneven.

'Bourgeois' raises issues of time, space and meaning. When and where do we find bourgeois society, and what is it exactly that makes certain societies 'bourgeois'? Are some societies more bourgeois than others, and if so, according to what criteria? If bourgeois society is an historical result, does this mean that it is an object given to us by history as though history simply dropped it in our laps. According to Althusser, objects of knowledge are constructed in accordance with a mode of production of knowledge, and in this case Marx's theory achieves an epistemological break that reorganises the object of knowledge. If the object of knowledge is a reconstruction produced by Marx's theory, then bourgeois society is not simply an historical result, but is a construction of Marx's theory. The tension here is between the object of knowledge as an historical given and the object of knowledge as a theoretical construction. If 'bourgeois' is a theoretical construct, by what mechanism do we determine its meaning, determine whether that meaning is adequate to the object of knowledge, and determine whether the object of knowledge is adequate to the real object? Further problems arise with the concept 'society', but these are best discussed under proposition four.

If, with Uno and Sekine, we take the object of knowledge of *Capital* to be primarily the inner logic of capital or a purely capitalist society, then the difficulties arising from Althusser's proposition can be largely resolved. The concept of a purely capitalist society is arrived at by letting the commodification of economic life complete itself in theory, such that all inputs and outputs of production are securely commodified. Since total commodification assumes that persons are reduced to being mere 'bearers' or 'personifications' of economic categories operating in harmony with a self-regulating commodity-economic logic, it follows that such a society is also totally reified. Total reification in this context does not imply that persons cannot act, only that their actions are always trumped by market forces so that it is self-expanding value and not their actions that determine social dynamics.[12]

In a society that is totally reified in this sense, there is no extra-economic force that intervenes to subvert the commodity-economic logic. This means that we are essentially theorising an economic society in which the political and ideological are reduced to mere 'passive reflexes' of the economic. This follows from the assumption that a purely capitalist society is governed not by persons but by the market and its commodity-economic logic. At this level of analysis politics and ideology are not relatively autonomous in the sense that they can be the source of independent agency or causality that would disrupt and therefore confuse the operation of the purely market-economic mechanisms that we wish to understand.

The concept of a purely capitalist society is in one sense an historical result since it cannot be considered until after capitalism has achieved a considerable degree of development in history, and until after political economy has reached a certain point in its process of purifying and interrelating concepts such as price, wage, profit, rent and interest, which initially arise out of the self-abstracting processes of actual economic exchange in daily life (Sohn-Rethel, 1978, pp. 30, 44, 53).

But a purely capitalist society is not 'contemporary bourgeois society'; as an idealisation it never exists as a concrete society in historical time and space. Hence in theorising a purely capitalist society we are not collapsing complex historical time into a simple contemporaneity because we are not dealing with historical time at all, but with abstract logical time. An example will illustrate what I mean by logical time.

In logical time we know that abstract tendencies towards centralisation could move capitalism increasingly towards monopoly, but we have no idea what degree of monopoly will occur in what length of time since numerous factors, such as the development of the corporation as a legal form or the development of certain kinds of financial institution, cannot be derived from the operation of the law of value and must therefore be dealt with at more concrete levels of analysis. The logical time that I am talking about refers to the abstract tendencies of the inner logic of capital itself. In the law of value we know, for example, how changes in the length of the working day affect value relations, but we do not know just what the length of the working day is, since this is determined by class struggle and other more concrete factors. Furthermore, we do not have the problem of spatial location in history since a purely capitalist society only exists in abstract logical space. In other words a purely capitalist society implies a single global (not planetary) society that is governed by a self-expanding commodity-economic logic. We would never expect such a state of affairs to occur in concrete historical space. Finally, the concept 'bourgeois' cannot be given the same precision as the concept 'capital' precisely because it is an historically variable class concept. The meaning of 'capital' is made very precise by the theory of capitalism's inner logic, but this precision can only be achieved by imagining an economic society in which capital's *modus operandi* is allowed to operate without interference in a logical time and space.

In Althusser's second formulation the key concepts are 'economic relations' and 'articulated combination' or 'Gliederung (the articulated, hierarchised, systematic combination)' (1970 p. 64). Here the problems stem from distinguishing 'economic relations' from other types of social relation, and having distinguished them, considering their 'articulated combination', which implies thinking about their systematic combination with each other and with other relatively autonomous practices within the social totality.

According to Althusser, 'At the economic level, strictly speaking, the *structure* constituting and determining economic objects is the *following*: the unity of the productive forces and the relations of production. The concept of this last *structure* cannot be defined without the concept of the global structure of the mode of production' (ibid., pp. 182–3). This is because, 'The relations of production cannot be thought in their concept while abstracting from their specific superstructural conditions of existence' (ibid., p. 177). It seems that for Althusser the relations of production are primary in determining the economic since he claims that 'the structure of the relations of production determines the *places* and *functions* occupied and adopted by the agents of production' (ibid., p. 180); indeed '*The true "subjects" are these definers and distributors: the relations of production*' (ibid.) It is perhaps apparent from what I have already argued that I consider the 'true subject' of the economic to be not the relations of production, but the totality of capital. Indeed, it is a little surprising that Althusser would even use such a concept as 'true subject', since for Althusser the economic cannot be considered without the political and the ideological, conceived as relatively autonomous practices that enter the conditions of existence of the economic. Thus the economic can only be conceptualised by conceiving it as a level within a mode of production that has a particular location and effectiveness *vis-à-vis* other levels (that is, 'determinant in the last instance' and the 'structure-in-dominance' in the capitalist mode of production). These formulations produce a prodigious knot of problems.

Exactly what is to be included in our concept of the structure of the relations of production? Are these primarily property relations, and if legality is integral to these relations, how do we distinguish the economic and the legal? Is 'legality' a political or ideological concept? Assuming that we have a determinant concept of relations of production, how are we to proceed from this to knowing what to include in the economic? What sorts of economic, political and ideological structures are we to theorise and at what level of abstraction? How do we even distinguish between these supposedly relatively autonomous practices? Furthermore, it can be argued that the 'relations of production' is one-sided in leaving out the highly important circulation forms and distribution relations that are specific to capitalism.

According to the Uno–Sekine approach, the theory of the capitalist mode of production at its most abstract level is the same thing as the theory of pure capitalism. It follows that their conception of mode of production has little in common with Althusser's. Instead of trying to theorise the 'capitalist mode of production' in accordance with abstract structural variables that are expected to yield all possible modes of production, an approach that has proved futile for all who have tried it, the Unoist theory of the capitalist mode of production is content to be nothing more nor less than the theory of capital's inner logic. Legality, at this level of theory, is simply a passive background condition that confirms private property. Because in most of their manifestations the political and the ideological are not characterised by total reification, little can be said about them at this level of pure economic theory except insofar as certain political and ideological forms are required as background conditions to the operation of a commodity-economic logic. This has the virtue of preventing us from conflating value theory with more contingent levels of analysis. After we have clearly specified the operation of the law of value, it is then appropriate to theorise its articulations with other instances of social life at more concrete levels of analysis, even as it becomes less law-like in the process.

It follows that the law of value is not simply a theory of a region within the capitalist mode of production that is continually interfered with by practices that are non-economic and relatively autonomous. To a large extent the political and ideological are absorbed into the economic in the theory of the law of value only to reemerge and disrupt its automaticity at more concrete levels of analysis. Perhaps we cannot ponder economic relations abstracted 'from their specific superstructural conditions of existence' (ibid., p. 177), but in the market-governed society of pure capitalism there is very little superstructure, and what does exist is a passive reflex of the economic.[13]

With the Uno–Sekine approach, the economic is not simply defined as some subjectively constructed ideal type or a dogmatically stipulated meaning that is declared adequate to its object; instead its concept is produced by theorising a society in which value expands itself without support or interference from outside. The economic relations of pure capitalism are an 'articulated combination' that achieves the rigor of a dialectical logic precisely because the political and ideological at this level provide no basis of independent determination. In some sense it may be true that the unity of productive forces and the relations of production determine economic objects in pure capitalism, depending on how these concepts are defined, but since 'productive forces' and 'relations of production' seem to have highly contested meanings, I would prefer to claim that economic objects in a purely capitalist society are determined by capital's inner logic, or perhaps by the dialectical ensemble of forms of circulation, relations of production and relations of distribution.

In his third formulation, Althusser suggests that the object of *Capital* is a theory of a region of the theory of history. This proposition rests upon the claim that it is useful to have a theory of history at the same level of abstraction as the theory of capital's logic, such that the latter can be thought of as simply a regional theory within the former. Here Althusser seems to deny any distinction between a theory of abstract economic laws and a structural theory of history. But this is a dubious position to take, to put it mildly.

There are no laws of motion of history (or dialectic of history) in the same sense as there are laws of motion of capital because history is not self-reifying in its totality, and is never governed in its totality by a self-regulating commodity-economic logic (or by an Althusserian 'structure of structures').[14] The theory of a purely capitalist society is a theory of structural dynamics and structural determinations only because in such a society social relations between things and material relations between humans objectify social life. Not even *capitalist* history can be considered successfully using such rigid structural and synchronic categories. Contrary to Althusser, the theory of capital's inner logic does not contain a theory of history, though it can provide indispensable categories to aid our analysis of history. Of course Marx's *Capital* contains a great deal of historical analysis, but this is ancillary and illustrative to the theory of capital's inner logic, which is formulated in logical time not historical time. *Capital* contains elements that an Unoist approach would place at the level of mid-range theory or at the level of historical analysis, but we should not let this confuse us about the primary object of knowledge of *Capital*, which is pure capitalism, even though Marx may lack the concept.

I will concede to Althusser that historical analysis should be theoretically informed, but I break with his contention that the law of value is simply a subregion of the theory of history. As usual Althusser does not shy away from stating his position:

> The only difference that can be established between the theory of political economy, of which *Capital* is an example, and the theory of

> history as a science, lies in the fact that the theory of political economy only considers one relatively autonomous component of the social totality, whereas the theory of history in principle takes the complex totality as such for its object. Other than this difference, there can be no distinction between the science of political economy and the science of history, from a theoretical viewpoint (Althusser and Balibar, 1970, p. 109).

Althusser (ibid., p. 173) even goes so far as to claim that it is the concept 'mode of production' that makes possible 'the construction of the concept of history'. It is beyond the scope of this chapter fully to analyse the deleterious impact this particular view has had on Marxism. Its effect has been to transfer to historical analysis a kind of structuralism that can only be consistent with the total reification of pure capitalism. Such transference can only produce a reductionist and mechanical kind of historical analysis that is completely alien to the kind of emphasis on process (as opposed to pure structure) that is required by thinking at this level of analysis. In an attempt to carry out the Althusserian research programme, thinkers such as Hindess and Hirst were led down a path that ultimately forced them to abandon Marxism, others engaged in a rather arid modes of production debate, and yet others dissolved Marxism into postmodernism. Moreover, most leading Marxist historians (for example Foster, Hill, Ingham, Hobsbawm and Thompson) continued to engage in effective Marxist historical writing by ignoring Althusser's problematic all together.

Althusser has, in my view, reversed the cognitive statuses of political economy and historical materialism. Historical materialism simply cannot be a science in the same sense as political economy is a science. The peculiar self-reifying character of capital is the necessary condition for constructing a rigorous dialectic of its inner logic, and once constructed, this theory can inform both more concrete levels of political economy and non-capitalist historical analysis. Historical materialism is nothing more than an approach to the study of history informed by political economy. Political economy is far from being a regional theory within historical materialism; rather historical materialism depends on the knowledge provided by the political economy of capitalism for any limited claim it makes to being scientific. Furthermore, Marxian political economy's claim that it is scientific rests upon the unique ontology of capital, which is the ground for a unique kind of science that is not fully applicable to other objects in the social sciences and requires distinct levels of analysis to avoid economic reductionism.

A book could be written about the incredible confusion that has resulted from equating Marxism with historical materialism and from taking historical materialism as the core of Marxism's scientificity. This way of conceptualising things completely conceals the ontological specificity of the economic under capitalism. By treating the economic, political and ideological as simply three different regions of the capitalist mode of production, the specific self-reifying and self-abstracting character of the economic tends to be overlooked. Such an approach also transfers to the study of history an inappropriate structuralism or economic determinism. While it is appropriate in the context of pure capitalism to theorise persons as bearers of economic categories, this kind of structuralism is out of place in theorising even the economic at the level of a mid-range theory of the stages of capitalism's historical development, not to mention more empirical studies of capitalism. It is certainly inappropriate for the study of non-capitalist societies. Althusser's historical materialism, with its category 'mode of production', infects politics and ideology with a reified structuralism that is appropriate only to the economic in pure capitalism, and infects the law of value with considerations about political and ideological structures that are only appropriate to more concrete levels of analysis. In the end, 'mode of production' becomes a rigid and mechanical structural-functional nightmare that is not appropriate to the rather pure structuralism of the law of value, nor to the much more agencied process approach that is appropriate to historical analysis.

The intellectual odyssey of Hindess and Hirst is representative of the fate of many who seriously tried to carry out Althusser's research programme of a Marxian science of history. When confronted with the complex processes of history, they were initially forced to abandon the concept 'mode of production' in favour of the more concrete 'social formation'. In the end Hindness and Hirst found that even 'social formation' proved too constricting for an effective analysis of historical change because it subsumed too many social practices to rigid structures. In order to escape the stultifying strictures of Althusser's abstract science of historical materialism, they eventually abandoned Marxism altogether.

Althusser's fourth proposition is that

> what Marx studies in *Capital* is the mechanism which makes the result of a history's production exist *as a society*; it is therefore the mechanism which gives this product of history, that is precisely

> the society-product he is studying, the property of producing the '*society effect*' which makes this result exist *as a society*, and not as a heap of sand, an ant-hill, a workshop or a mere collection of men (Althusser and Balibar, 1970, p. 65).

Here Althusser is getting very close to answering to the problem with which he is wrestling, but his deep commitment to a certain sort of anti-Hegelian structuralism prevents him from doing so.

Marx's object is most fruitfully conceptualised not as 'contemporary bourgeois society, which is thought as historical result' (ibid., p. 65), nor 'economic relations ... in their articulated combination' (ibid., p. 64) within such a society, rather it is the inner logic of capital. Now, that which gives capital a logic that is 'inner' is its self-reifying force, or in other words its historical tendency to purify economic relations and make them more autonomous by its own motion or capacity for self-regulation wherever and whenever it can. We can say, therefore, that the mechanism that makes capitalist society cohere insofar as it is specifically capitalist is capital's self-reifying force (the tendency for *M–C–M'* to subsume social life and make it more capitalist). Althusser cannot name this mechanism because it would cause him to break with his problematic in too many ways, and in particular to accept concepts that are presumably tainted by Hegelianism. But 'reification' and 'self-reification' are not necessarily wedded to an 'expressive problematic', even though in the hands of Lukács and others they often have been. In the present context they simply refer to 'total commodification' and the tendency in history for capital to expand and deepen the commodification of social life such that capitalist society moves at least to some extent and over some period of time in the direction of total commodification. Thus it is quite true that Marx studies the mechanisms of coherence in capitalist society and these mechanisms have to do with the reifying force of capital and not some sort of mysterious structure of structures, structured in the last instance by the structure of the economic.

In its enlarged form Althusser's fifth proposition reads:

> *Marx's theoretical object is not England but the capitalist mode of production in its* 'Kerngestalt' *and the determinations of that* 'Kerngestalt'. When Marx tells us that he is studying an 'ideal average', we must therefore understand that this ideality connotes not the unreal or the ideal norm, but the *concept* of the real; and that this 'average' is not an empiricist average, i.e., it does not

> connote the non-unique, but on the contrary, it connotes the concept of the specific difference of the mode of production concerned (ibid., p. 196).

Here, once again Althusser gets close to an effective answer. Indeed Marx is not simply studying England (though as the most advanced capitalist country of the time, England serves as the main source of empirical evidence and illustrations for his theory), nor an empiricist abstraction that averages the economic relations in England, but instead is studying the core forms of the capitalist mode of production, understood as a purely capitalist society. Unfortunately neither Marx nor Althusser take this last step (that is, conceptualise a purely capitalist society), though in Althusser's theory it becomes an extremely 'pregnant silence.' If the ideality in question is 'the *concept* of the real', which 'connotes the concept of the specific difference of the mode of production concerned', it is unclear just how it is that we are to know that this particular ideality is indeed 'the concept of the real'.

As I have already suggested, the concept of the real is not arrived at via a Weberian ideal-type (an ideal norm), but by understanding the sense in which the real can be self-reifying. The concept of the real is the concept of capital's reifying force, which operates as a tendency in historical capitalism and is allowed by the theorist to complete itself by eliminating those forms of use-value resistance that cannot be overcome by its own motion. It is not the concept of 'the specific difference of the mode of production', if by that we mean a concept to be arrived at by comparing the capitalist mode of production with the feudal mode of production. It is rather the internal structure of the capitalist mode of production, itself understood as capital's inner logic – as that logic that operates when the motion of value is confronted by use-values that do not resist commodity-economic management.

In the foregoing analysis I have taken seriously Althusser's project to define *Capital's* specific object of knowledge. I have argued that his formulations are sometimes inconsistent with his own problematic, sometimes creating more problems than answers, sometimes vague and imprecise, sometimes having unfortunate consequences for the development of Marxist theory, sometimes coming close to effective answers only to be blocked by anti-Hegelian biases, and generally far less effective in grasping the specificity of *Capital's* object or perhaps capital as an object of knowledge than the Uno–Sekine approach.

THE INTERNAL RELATIONS OF CONCEPTS

The next step is to analyse Althusser's understanding of the internal relations of concepts within the theory of capital. Exactly what determines the purity of the concepts and the sequence of categories in the theory of capital? In what way does the particular sequence of categories produce knowledge?

According to Althusser 'the mechanism of production of the knowledge effect lies in the mechanism which underlies the action of the forms of order in the scientific discourse of the proof' (Althusser and Balibar, 1970, p. 67). What is this 'mechanism' that 'underlies the action of the forms of order'? Althusser's answer is that 'the forms of order (forms of proof in scientific discourse) are the "diachrony" of a basic "synchrony"'. The mechanism then is the basic synchrony, which refers to 'the organisational structure of the concepts in the thought-totality or *system* (ibid., p. 68). In other words the sequence of concepts in the theory is determined by their relation to each other within the thought-totality. But as we have seen, Althusser is vague about what constitutes the thought-totality. If this totality is a 'system', it must manifest some degree of closure, but Althusser leaves us with no way of demarcating the inner from the outer in order to gain some sense of what it is that belongs to this 'thought-totality' or what determines the sequence of categories within the theory. For him the thought-totality is usually the capitalist mode of production, but as we have seen, this is a vague and controversial concept.

If our 'thought-totality' is the self-expansion of value through a commodity-economic logic operating in a purely capitalist society, then it becomes clear what belongs within the theory. Althusser is correct to claim that the synchrony is the basic mechanism that determines the forms of order in the theory, but given his anti-Hegelian commitment, he cannot understand the sense in which this synchrony is dialectical in ways that are Hegelian and yet supersede Hegel's idealism. Thus the mechanism that underlies the action of the forms of order is not some mystical synchrony of the capitalist mode of production, but is a rigorous dialectical logic that leads us through the theory of pure capitalism.

Now that we have a clear and precise answer to the generating mechanism behind the sequence of categories, we need once again to confront the question of the categories themselves: where do they come from and in what sense are they 'pure'? Let us start with Althusser's interpretation of a quotation from Marx's *Capital* where

Marx declares that his intention with regard to ground-rent is 'to study it in *its pure form* free from all distorting and obfuscating irrelevancies' (quoted in ibid., 1970, p. 192). Commenting on this quotation, Althusser writes: 'we abandon the empiricist idea of a purity which is thus only the result of an empirical *purge* (since it is a purge of the empirical) – we really think the purity as *the purity of the concept*, the purity of a knowledge adequate to its object' (ibid.). While I agree with his claim that the purity of the concepts are not the result of a knowing subject purifying away the dross by a kind of purge (or process of abstraction) that leaves a pure essence, as though concept formation were like panning for gold; yet insisting upon the purity of the concept adequate to its object does not seem to offer much of an alternative. Where does this pure concept come from and how do we know that it is adequate to its object?

Elsewhere Althusser (ibid., p. 82) writes: 'for Marx the concept of the law of value is in fact a concept perfectly adequate to its object, since it is the concept of the limits of its variation'. But I would argue that the law of value, as Marx left it, is not perfectly adequate to its object, but is only a rough first approximation. Furthermore Althusser does not specify what he means by 'the concept of the limits of its variation'. The law of value, for example, can specify the meaning of the category 'interest' in a purely capitalist society by showing its connection to profit and surplus value, and it can indicate the constraints limiting the range of the rate of interest; but it cannot determine a particular rate of interest, precisely because such a determination will always involve contingent factors outside the operation of a commodity-economic logic. Monopoly rent is also outside the law of value as are monopoly prices in general since they are not completely determined by the necessities of self-expanding value, but are instead partially determined by historically contingent phenomena. Hence to the extent that the law of value is adequate to its object, it is because it deals only with the necessities of self-expanding value and not with historically variable and contingent use-value configurations and resistances. The limits to the variation of the law of value are determined by that which a commodity-economic logic can by itself determine without relying on extra-economic force. The rate of interest is a good example of a concept that indicates the limits of variation of the law of value. The law of value can only determine a range for the rate of interest, it cannot determine a specific rate of interest. The Uno–Sekine approach can give determinate meaning to words that Althusser leaves vague.

Althusser takes another tack on the problem of the concepts of the theory of capital by favourably quoting from Lenin's reponse to Struve, which includes the following:

> we must remind him [Struve] that all the other laws of capitalism revealed by Marx, also depict only *the ideal of capitalism and not its reality.* ... The theory of capital assumes that the worker receives the full value of his labour-power. This is the ideal of capitalism, but by no means the reality. The theory of rent presupposes that the entire agrarian population has been completely divided into landowners, capitalists, and hired labourers. This is the ideal of capitalism, but by no means its reality (ibid., p. 195).

I have no objection to this as far as it goes, but where does the ideal of capitalism come from? And in what sense are the pure concepts of the theory 'ideal'? As we have seen from the work of Uno and Sekine, the ideal is neither an ideal-type (that is, a Weberian artificial construct) nor an 'ideal average' as an empirical average, but rather capital's ideal of itself, arrived at by letting capital unfold its laws of motion or logic in the ideal environment of a purely capitalist society.

TOTALITY AND TOTALISATION

The issue of totality is highly complicated and controversial. For Althusser, the Marxist totality consists of ever-pregiven, relatively autonomous practices that develop unevenly, are overdetermined by each other and the totality of which they are a part, and are in turn unified by a structure in dominance, which in the last instance is determined by the economic. It is my argument that these stipulations simply do not apply to some single totality called *the* Marxist totality.

Totalities can be relatively more open or closed, but the very concept 'totality' implies at least sufficient closure to be able to distinguish inside from outside. In Unoist political economy the most closed totality is the dialectic of capital. On the one hand it is closed in the sense that in the end the motion of value completes the dialectic by subsuming capital itself to the commodity form as interest-bearing capital. In other words the dialectic is closed because in theory, value, working through a commodity-economic logic, completely subsumes economic life in a purely capitalist society. On the other hand, because at many points the tenuousness of the dialectic of capital and the materiality of its categories point to the necessity for more concrete levels of analysis that are relatively autonomous, and as such are bound to disrupt capital's inner logic, the closure points beyond itself to more concrete levels of analysis. For example, as I have just pointed out, the law of value cannot by itself determine the rate of interest, only constrain it within a certain range. This indicates that it would be necessary for more contingent factors to enter the analysis at more concrete levels if we wanted to try to understand the determination of a particular rate of interest. Likewise the theory of rent assumes that landlords do not earn monopoly rents, but in reality they often do, hence implying more concrete levels of analysis where monopolistic practices can be taken into account.

At more concrete levels of analysis, such as the mid-range stage theory and historical analysis proposed by Uno and Sekine, the law of value does not govern a unified totality, but instead works its way through institutions that disrupt it to some extent so that its totalising force is unable to complete a unified totality. Thus, for example, the characteristic organisational forms of capital change from one stage to the next.

According to the Uno–Sekine approach, Marxian political economy includes several 'objects of knowledge' (distinct levels of analysis), and Marxism as a whole has perhaps quite a large number of objects of knowledge. Assuming this to be a fruitful approach, then, contrary to Althusser, there is no single Marxian 'problematic' that proposes a single way of posing and answering all questions to be contrasted with a single Hegelian problematic. If there is a distinctive problematic for Marxian political economy, included in its distinctiveness is a single dialectical logic that informs relatively autonomous logics and methodologies operating at more concrete levels of analysis.

Althusser contrasts a single Marxian problematic with a single Hegelian problematic, but this forces him into an overly totalising way of thinking. While he claims that Marx's philosophy is to be discovered by a close, symptomatic reading of *Capital*, he reads *Capital* one-sidedly as a philosopher carrying particular baggage and not as an economist attempting to make sense out of the laws of motion of capital.[15] One must have a strong understanding of capital's economic logic fully to consider the unique ontology of capital and produce a strong epistemology out of Marx's texts. Instead Althusser borrows concepts and perspectives from numerous French structuralist thinkers and produces a single general Marxian problematic in contrast to other problematics, particularly Hegel's. The problematic that he produces is an amalgam of Marxian concepts and structuralist concepts, and the result is a universal Marxist science of history with 'mode of production' as the basic unit of analysis.

According to Althusser, 'mode of production' is a theoretical social totality consisting of three relatively autonomous practices: economic, political and ideological. While such a concept may be defensible for other modes of production, it is not really appropriate to capitalism. As Marx (1976, p. 1014; 1963, p. 483) makes clear in numerous places, the law of value must be theorised in a context where no extra-economic forces of any kind interfere with the self-expansion of value. This means that in theorising a purely capitalist society where we assume total reification, politics and ideology can only be theorised as passive reflexes of the law of value. It follows that 'mode of production' in Althusser's sense cannot be the most abstract unit of analysis when it comes to theorising capitalism, rather it would have to be useful at the level of mid-range theory where it is possible to conceive of the above practices as relatively autonomous.

As I read Althusser, his 'mode of production' is part of a package that views historical materialism as Marxist science and treats the theory of capital as simply the theory of a region within one mode of production amongst others. I believe this approach is mistaken because other modes of production are not self-reifying the way that capitalism is, and hence there is not the same tendency for the economic to become both autonomous and hegemonic. There is not an inner logic of slavery or feudalism as there is of capitalism. If precapitalist modes of production have any logic at all it is a situational logic and not a logic associated with necessary commodity-economic laws. If I am right about this, it follows that treating capitalism as simply one mode of production amongst others may hide capitalism's unique ontology.

CONCLUSIONS

Althusser's influence on Marxism was mixed. On the one hand he introduced new questions and new levels of complexity into Marxist theory. On the other hand his extravagant claims for the scientific nature of Marxism could not be substantiated by his problematic, forcing many of his most earnest followers either to abandon Marxism or to reduce it to a mere shadow of its former self. Furthermore, his dogged anti-Hegelianism, instilled a highly negative interpretation of

Hegel in the minds of a generation of scholars influenced by his ideas, and as a result blocked the possibility of understanding Hegel's immense scientific importance to Marxian political economy. His anti-Hegelianism was advanced even further by his student, Foucault, and his friend, Derrida, as they converted his structuralism into poststructuralism.

In this chapter I have used the theory of the dialectic of capital as a corrective to some of Althusser's structuralist excesses, and as a basis for providing much stronger answers to many of Althusser's questions. Althusser lacked an adequate understanding of the economic theory put forward by Marx in *Capital* and its close correspondence to Hegel's *Logic*. His structuralist reading of *Capital*, therefore, not only failed to grasp capital's unique ontology, but also failed to improve upon the economic theory as Marx left it. His failure to understand capital's ontology made it possible for him to treat economics, politics and ideology as simply three ontologically homogeneous but relatively autonomous practices in his conception 'mode of production'. Furthermore, the capitalist mode of production was treated as ontologically similar to all other modes of production, reducing the theory of it to a regional theory within the general science 'historical materialism'. Finally, while he claimed that each science has an epistemology that is specific to its object of knowledge, he also claimed that all sciences are defined by developing an adequacy to their object relative to ideologies that they displace and break with. In the case of *Capital*, he does devote some attention to its breaks with previous political economy, thus saying what it is not, but he devotes nowhere near enough attention to what the logic of capital is – its ontology, epistemology and methodology. Thus his theories constitute a 'theoreticism', as Derrida claims, precisely because they are so full of theoretical posings that simply do not deliver anything like what we are led to expect.

The critique of Althusser from the point of view of the Uno–Sekine approach reveals ways in which reference to the thought of Hegel may help us to move beyond the limits of Althusser's problematic. But there are also ways in which in the very act of opposing himself to Hegel allows Hegelian influences to penetrate his thought. First, in opposing himself to a Hegelian totality, he seems compelled to construct or characterise a single Marxian totality, thus excluding the possibility that the very concept of totality may be very different in Marxism. Second, the paradigm case of 'overdetermined contradiction' is a conjunctural analysis of the Russian Revolution, which he then projects onto the most abstract level of analysis, as in 'mode of production', which results in an inadequate framework for theorising economic practice and its relation to political and ideological practice. Third, he universalises and reifies a concept of structure that is most appropriate to theorising the single case of a purely capitalist society conceived in accordance with a dialectical logic. Where there is total reification, there is total domination by structure over agency, but not necessarily elsewhere.

In Chapter 2 there is a critique of Althusser's distinction between reflection and production theories of knowledge, arguing that the dialectic of capital is in a very particular sense both 'reflected' and 'produced'. This implies that a distinction that poses such an alternative is itself problematic. Another indication that Althusser's problematic is itself problematic.

It is appropriate that a discussion of Derrida follows this chapter on Althusser, since Althusser's friend pushed many of his ideas much further. Derrida avoids with a vengeance a theoreticism that poses without delivering. Deconstruction avoids abstract theory and promises to deliver so little that even when it delivers the minute, one is inclined to give it a gold star. Derrida is interested in gifts that are either too small or too camouflaged to be recognised as gifts, for it is only in this fashion that he can be truly generous.

6 Deconstruction and Political Economy

> It is clear, moreover, that Hegel is not just one more philosopher in the range of philosophical and literary figures that Derrida treats in his work. Rather, one could argue that it is the task of deconstruction to come to terms with Hegel.... Hegel's work forms both the horizon and limit of deconstruction as well as its very condition of possibility.[1]

> Everything Althusser says about overdetermination satisfies me more than the rest...[2]

> One must distinguish between levels of analysis...[3]

'Deconstruction' is the most important and characteristic concept in Derrida's large and growing philosophical opus. Because it is a cluster concept that is capable of diverse forms, it has been picked up and widely disseminated throughout the corpus of postmodern thought, iterating indefinitely its protean potentials. In the process of usage, 'deconstruction's' coinage has inflated, cheapening its value without reserve. And yet, unlike economic coinage, philosophical concepts can always be directly deflated to get at their less dilute usages. It is my intention to map the areas of strength and of limitations to deconstructivism.

If it is true that 'the dialectical form of exposition is only correct when it knows its limits',[4] the same is doubly true of deconstruction. Deconstruction is at its best when disrupting certain binary oppositions that are characteristic of Western metaphysics and of capitalist or patriarchal ideology; it is totally out of its depth when it pretends to provide an adequate basis for social science as a whole. This is because social science, including Marxian political economy, is ultimately concerned with determining what is the case, how it became what it is, and how action might influence future change; whereas deconstruction is primarily concerned with disrupting thinking that has become rigid, smug and oppressive. Disrupting and knowing are not completely at odds, but knowing does require at least some settling of accounts and clarity about meaning so that truth claims can be made. Disrupting can actually help to advance knowledge when it limits itself to the unsettling of existing pieces of knowledge for the sake of their improvement. The problem is that deconstruction often disrupts radically and indiscriminately, as though disruption were an end in itself. It thereby becomes the imperialist project 'deconstructivism', undermining knowledge possibilities.

In *Specters of Marx* Derrida (1994) tries valiantly to effect some complementarity between deconstruction and Marxism, but the results are thin indeed. This is because Derrida's deconstructive proclivities completely blunt his razor-sharp mind when it comes to saying anything that would substantially advance political economy as the science of capitalism. This suggests a strong tension between Derrida's considerable aptitude for disruptive and deconstructive play with metaphors and any project whose fundamental aim is to advance knowledge of the world. The main focus of this chapter is on this tension and how it might be resolved.

Because the previous chapter dealt with Althusser and because some deconstructionists trace their roots more to Althusser than to Derrida, the natural progression of the argument may seem to point towards a detailed comparison of Althusser and Derrida. Indeed the influence of Althusser on Derrida is so pronounced that those who like to draw out Althusser in a Derridian direction refer to Althusser as a postmodern thinker, despite his modernist insistence that Marx was the founder of a new science.[5] Althusser and Derrida seem particularly close when one begins to add up what they mutually oppose: Hegel's 'expressive problematic', subject-centred problematics, centred totalities, mirror myths of knowledge, historicism, humanism, empiricism, metaphysics of origins and presents, mechanical causality, reductionism and teleology. With a little tolerance for oversimplification, one might say that Derrida simply pushes Althusser's decentring strategy further: particularly into the arena of language and linguistics. Derrida's decentring of language, however, radically undermines Althusser's modernism and structuralism.

Derrida has never commented extensively on his differences with Althusser, but he has explicitly rejected Althusser's arguments for determination in the last instance by the economic, his use of terms such as 'class' and 'class struggle', his use of 'epistemological break', his distinction between science and ideology, his structuralism, and his general 'scientism'. With regard to dialectics, Derrida states: 'I feel less 'anti-dialectical than Foucault, Deleuze, etc., but more so than Althusser' (Kaplan and Sprinker, 1993, p. 206).[6]

In the previous chapter I argued that Althusser's problematic was not so far removed from that of Uno–Sekine in certain respects. For example both focus sharply on capital as an object of knowledge in order to clarify the specific scientific nature that such an object is capable of possessing. Despite his criticism of Hegel's 'expressive problematic', more similarities can be found between Althusser's problematic and Althusser's interpretation of Hegel's problematic than some of his rhetoric might suggest. Although Derrida sees himself as more antidialectical than Althusser, I argue that even Derrida's deconstruction shares certain similarities with Hegelian dialectics, and that there is a role for deconstruction conceived as a sensitivity to difference within Marxian political economy. Once one accepts the possibility and desirability of theorising capital's inner logic, deconstruction is a potential source of arguments for levels of analysis. In the problematic that I am proposing, levels of analysis achieve many of the goals of deconstruction without radically undermining theory and hence the possibilities of the knowledge of capitalism.

DERRIDA AND DIALECTICS

Despite his many protestations to the contrary, Derrida's deconstruction has at least some commonalities with Hegel's dialectics. Both break down any sharp distinction between the conceptual and the real, though arguably Derrida goes further than Hegel in this direction. Both adopt an internal point of view in the sense that there is nothing outside the 'Idea', just as there is 'nothing outside the text'.[7] Both focus on the binary oppositions of Western metaphysics and utilise negativity to renegotiate these dualisms.[8] Both offer their particular approaches (dialectics and deconstruction) as universal thought strategies, thereby failing to consider the possibility that particular objects of knowledge may require particular thought strategies. To a large extent Derrida's philosophy is an attempt to subvert Hegel's dialectic from the inside, and since it is an immanent critique, it must necessarily accept certain ground rules associated with what it is critiquing. If this is true, then it must be an exaggeration to claim that deconstruction is 'allergic' to dialectics.[9]

Yet it is against Hegel that deconstruction takes shape since deconstruction is to a large extent offered as an alternative to *aufhebung* (supersession) as a way of dealing with binary oppositions. According to Derrida (1981, p. 40), 'If there were a definition of *différance*, it would be precisely the limit, the interruption, the destruction of the Hegelian *relève* wherever it operates.' Why such intensity from Derrida on this issue? Perhaps even more than Althusser, Derrida cannot abide the spiritualism and religiosity in Hegel's *aufhebung*, *relèver* or supersession. As Derrida (1978, p. 257) puts it: 'The notion of *Aufhebung* (the speculative concept par excellence...) is laughable in that it signifies the *busying* of a discourse losing its breath as it reappropriates all negativity for itself...' For Derrida it is laughable and absurd to treat negativity this way: to make death so neatly slide under life. The contradictions that Hegel always supersedes until the Absolute is reached are treated by Derrida as binary oppositions, to be reversed and permanently displaced and destabilised precisely to prevent that smug and harmonious Hegelian homecoming of reason as spirit.

Derrida (ibid., p. 256) certainly gives negativity more than equal play in his philosophy of language, which breaks decisively with Hegel's 'laughable ... *submission* to the self-evidence of meaning'.[10] But in viewing Hegel as 'the last philosopher of the book and the first thinker of writing' Derrida (1974, p. 26) displays a great respect for Hegel as a pivotal thinker in the history of philosophy.

> The Idea of the book is the idea of a totality, finite or infinite, of the signifier; this totality of the signifier cannot be a totality, unless a totality constituted by the signified preexists it, supervises its inscriptions and its signs, and is independent of it in its ideality. The idea of the book, which always refers to a natural totality, is profoundly alien to the sense of writing (ibid., p. 18).[11]

The preexisting 'totality constituted by the signified', Derrida refers to as the 'transcendental signified' because it is a totality that transcends all contexts and provides the ultimate guarantee of knowledge. In Hegel the transcendental signified is the divine reason or Absolute Idea that rules the universe.

This transcendental signified can be thought, according to Derrida, because Hegel models language on speech that seems immediate, transparent and fully present to itself. Derrida claims 'that the thought of being, as the thought of this transcendental signified, is manifested above all in the voice.... The voice *is heard* (understood) ... closest to the self as the absolute effacement of the signifier' (ibid., p. 20). In other words the contextual and disruptive potentials of the signifier, which cannot be denied in language as writing, are absolutely effaced when the voice speaks immediately of the signified. Hegel's dialectic begins with the thought of being as present and capable, through a dialectical logic, of completing a totality of signifiers that together constitute the deep structure of pure thought. But Hegel's project must be disrupted from the beginning if the signifier is given some free play – no transcendental signified is possible.

For Derrida the category 'Being', then, cannot be fully present as a transcendental signified, and it cannot be fully present as an origin. The impish signifier denies pure transcendence as much as pure origin. The origin 'was never constituted except reciprocally by a nonorigin, the trace, which thus becomes the origin of the origin' (ibid., p. 61). Thus for Derrida there cannot be 'any absolute simplicity' or pure origin, and hence no pure beginning to Hegel's dialectic. Derrida (1988, p. 93) claims that:

> The enterprise of returning 'strategically', ideally, to an origin or to a 'priority' held to be simple, intact, normal, pure, standard, self-identical, in order *then* to think in terms of deriviation, complication, deterioration, accident etc. All metaphysicians, from Plato to Rousseau, Descartes to Husseral, have proceeded this way, conceiving good before evil, the positive before the negative, the pure before the impure, the simple before the complex, the essential before the accidental, the imitated before the imitation, etc. And this is not just *one* metaphysical gesture among others, it is *the* metaphysical exigency, that which has been the most constant, most profound and most potent.[12]

Furthermore the categories of Hegel's dialectical logic are understood by Derrida as signs that constitute themselves 'by virtue of [their] iterability' (ibid., p. 10), which means among other things the possibility of '[breaking] with every given context, engendering an infinity of new contexts in a manner which is absolutely illimitable' (ibid., p. 12). Such a view of language would require an absolutely stable (transcendental?) context in order to render Hegel's dialectical logic possible, since the meaning of a sign is ultimately all the possible contexts of its use, which is illimitable.[13] According to Derrida (1974, p. 70) it is not possible to get rid of the trace in speech and thereby make it full:

> All dualisms, all theories of the immortality of the soul or of the spirit, as well as all monisms, spiritualist or materialist, dialectical or vulgar, are the unique theme of a metaphysics whose entire history

> was compelled to strive toward the reduction of the trace. The subordination of the trace to the full presence summed up in the logos, the humbling of writing beneath a speech dreaming its plenitude, such are the gestures required by an onto-theology determining the archeological and eschatological meaning of being as presence, as parousia, as life without difference: another name for death, historical metonymy where God's name holds death in check (ibid., p. 71).[14]

This is a very good summary of Derrida's philosophical perspective, which he iterates and reiterates as he finds new ways of saying nearly the same thing in dialoguing with text after text, including, as we shall see, some texts by Marx.

SPECTRES OF MARX

Derrida's metaphysics is above all an ethics of thought aimed at respecting the other without reserve; and hence it is perhaps to be expected that he might have little to say about Marxian political economy as a research programme aimed at gaining knowledge of capitalism. He is much more interested in showing the one-sidedness of bogus and oppressive knowledge claims than he is in charting new courses in epistemology. But even taking his ethical orientation into account, I feel that his gesture of friendship towards Marxism in *Specters of Marx* (1994) is, at least from the point of view of Marxian political economy, rather retrograde. In this work Derrida has interpreted a number of Marx's texts not in order to advance Marxian political economy, but to put a new spin on deconstruction by using some of Marx's metaphors ('spectre') to further explicate his metaphysics of non-presence/non-absence. This just goes to show that despite the radically high demands of his ethics of generosity (of the gift), even Derrida can in the name of friendship use another thinker as a means to his ends.

Derrida writes: 'Upon rereading the *Manifesto* and a few other great works of Marx, I said to myself that I know of few texts in the philosophical tradition, perhaps none, whose lesson seemed more urgent *today*, provided that one take into account ... their own possible "aging" and their intrinsically irreducible historicity' (ibid., p. 13). But Derrida has always been better at playing with trope concepts than relaying urgent lessons, and better at critiquing thinkers from

Rousseau to Fukuyama than drawing out the lasting cognitive benefits of theories. So what are the urgent lessons? What is important in the legacy?

Derrida gets a huge amount of mileage out of the concept 'hauntology': a cute and amusing play on ontology that not only represents a new spin on his presence–absence metaphysics, but also enables him to analyse interesting articulations and resonances between spirit, ghost, phantom and spectre. It is perhaps not an exaggeration to say that the main purpose of the book is to show that hauntology is 'larger and more powerful than an ontology or a thinking of Being' (ibid., p. 10). According to Derrida, Marx is to be criticised for his fundamental commitment to ontology, which leads him to make too sharp a distinction between the real and the unreal; yet in Marx's writings there is a good deal of grist for Derrida's hauntological mill. But Derrida seems less interested in really engaging with Marx than in selectively appropriating those Marxian grains that can be processed to leaven his hauntology, which, as usual is primarily ethical. For example, we need 'to learn to live *with* ghosts' (ibid., p. xviii) as those who dwell (or that which dwells) between life and death, positivity and negativity, presence and absence.

In interpreting Marx, we think about 'the radical and necessary *heterogeneity* of an inheritance ... a quasi-juxtaposition without dialectic (the very plural of what we will later call Marx's spirits)' (ibid., p. 16). This raises the question of which spirits we are to commune with, and as we shall see, Derrida does not go far beyond claiming that it is those spirits that support a hauntology.

The closest Derrida really comes to engaging with Marx is in Chapter 5, when he brings his hauntology to bear on *Capital*. Derrida points out that for Marx the commodity is 'very complicated' and 'perhaps undecidable'. (Derrida, 1994, p. 150) 'Undecidable' is a typical Derridean wrench to be thrown into the machinery of dialectics such that contradiction remains forever unresolved in any kind of neat synthesis. As I argued at some length in Chapter 3, the commodity is not ultimately undecidable in a purely capitalist society since its contradictions, though complex, can be ultimately resolved by the commodity-economic logic that governs the economic reproduction of a purely capitalist society. Within Unoist political economy as a whole (including all three levels), however, the commodity is not just 'perhaps undecidable', it is definitely undecidable. If for no other reason, this is the case because at the level of historical analysis commodity-economic logic has only a partial grip on economic life.

Derrida is his usual brilliant poetic self in the metaphors that he chooses to discuss the reification associated with value in the theory of capital's inner logic. As a value, Marx's famous table becomes 'a sensuously supersensible thing' (ibid., p. 151) – the becoming immaterial of matter' (ibid., p. 152)–'and *number* belongs to the movement itself, to the non-finite process of spectralization' (ibid., p. 154). Furthermore,

> The capital contradiction does not have to do simply with the incredible conjunction of the sensuous and the supersensible in the same Thing; it is the contradiction of *automatic autonomy*, mechanical freedom, technical life. Like every thing, from the moment it comes onto the stage of the market, the table resembles a prosthesis of itself. Autonomy *and* automatism, *but* automatism of this wooden table that spontaneously puts itself into motion, to be sure, and seems thus to animate, animalize, spiritualize, *spiritize* itself, but while remaining an artifactual body, a sort of automaton, a puppet, a stiff and mechanical doll whose dance obeys the technical rigidity of a program.... The autonomy lent to commodities corresponds to an anthropomorphic projection. The latter *inspires* the commodities, it breathes the spirit into them, a human spirit, the spirit of a *speech* and the spirit of a *will*' (ibid., pp. 153, 157).

These descriptions of 'value' in the theory of capital's inner logic are quite wonderful, and it is here that Derrida shows some sign of really engaging with Marx and of having a deep understanding of the nature of reification in capitalism.

It is in the next step of his argument that Derrida makes a false move. Instead of attempting to understand the general relation between value and use-value within the theory as whole, Derrida focuses on a particular passage and reads it to imply that 'use-value' is to be conceived as a pure origin, and of course nothing sounds the alarms of deconstruction faster than a 'pure origin'. As I have sketched it, the dialectic of capital begins with a contradiction between 'pure' value and 'pure' use-value. Here 'pure' refers to the abstractness that serves as a theoretical starting point, and not a kind of primal existential origin. In order to think clearly and dialectically, it is an enormous help to be able initially to ponder these categories in their least complicated opposition: value as quantitative sociality and use-value as qualitative materiality.

If, in the way Marx puts it, there is a suggestion of a pure beginning, a pure use-value outside of value, this is simply a loose or metaphorical usage on Marx's part in this passage.[15] In the dialectic of capital there is no value without use-value, and *vice versa*. Furthermore, as I have noted, the dialectic should begin with 'value' and not 'use-value', and to reverse the order not only goes against dialectical logic, it also undermines clear thinking about the historical specificity of capitalism. There is something to Derrida's argument in the suggestion that use-value is always haunted by value, but this is simply good dialectics. As Hegel argues throughout his dialectical logic, positivity is always haunted by negativity, and *vice versa*. Otherwise there would be no dialectic, simply a standoff.

In arguing that use-value is not a pure beginning in Marxian political economy (in the dialectic of capital there is no *pure* beginning since we are dealing with logical time that assumes the existence of a purely capitalist society), Derrida (1994, p. 160) asserts that use-value 'must be complicated in a general (in any case more general) theory of capital'. In some ways this little phrase – 'in any case more general' – is a kind of metonomy for all that haunts Derrida. Just how are we to theorise the commodity form and the opposition between use-value and value? Does a general theory of capital contain an 'inner' logic. Hardly any word could be more vague than 'general', but even such an empty word makes Derrida very nervous and forces him into a qualification. 'More general' than what, and less general than what? Given Derrida's epistemological commitments, it is unclear how he would formulate even a 'more general' theory of capital. In Unoist political economy, 'use-value' outside the dialectic of capital does indeed become more complicated, as for example in mid-range theory or historical analysis. The 'more complicated' comes not with the 'more general', however, but with the more concrete. It seems that Derrida would never consider the possibility that the 'more general' might be helped along by the fact that capital is self-abstracting, and that at the most abstract level use-value is the most docile and least complicated.

Like Althusser, Derrida is a philosopher with a philosopher's need to universalise. Just as Althusser universalised a structuralism that was specific to pure capitalism, so did Derrida universalise a hauntology. At some points in the argument Derrida seems to be developing a hauntology specific to capital, but this possible direction is betrayed in the end when he abruptly moves from his confused discussion of use-value to the claim that 'it is necessary to introduce haunting into the very construction of a concept. Of every concept, beginning with the concepts of being and time' (ibid., p. 161).[16] Even if we should agree that major theoretical concepts should never be thought of as exhaustively and fully present, the haunting (reification) associated with capital is radically distinct from that associated with, say, Derrida's grandfather.

In the dialectic of capital, value is in one sense 'fully present' only insofar as all other categories of the dialectic are fully present. This 'full presence', however, only exists within a pure capitalism that is never fully present at the levels of mid-range theory or historical analysis. At the level of historical analysis, capital has a peculiar presence/absence that in its reifying force is quite different from the presence/absence of Derrida's grandfather.

Derrida claims that 'Marx continues to want to ground his critique or his exorcism of the spectral simulacrum in an ontology. It is a – critical but pre-deconstructive – ontology of presence as actual reality and as objectivity' (ibid., p. 170). I am not sure what 'Marx continues to want' (how could Derrida know?), but Marxian political economy as I understand it eschews an 'ontology of presence' while striving to attain as much contact with reality and objectivity as possible. The dialectic of capital is the theory of the 'real' and 'objective' deep structure of capital, though the inner logic of capital can never exist in this unadulterated form at the level of historical analysis. Moreover Marx is less concerned to carry out an 'exorcism of the spectral simulacrum' than he is to replace capitalism with democratic socialism. Democratic socialism would mean an end to the reification (haunting?) specific to our surrender to commodity-economic logics, but as Althusser argues forcefully, it would not imply any general transparency or ending of all forms of reification, haunting or ideology.

Derrida shies away from theory, but his hauntology is loosely and vaguely disseminated in many directions. It is essential for thinking about disjointed and present/absent temporalities, spatialities and beings. It is crucial for thinking about all inheritances and legacies from the past and about all possibilities in the future. It helps us to break down rigid distinctions between the 'real' and the 'unreal'. It is the basis for all ethics, including thought about justice as the 'incalculability of the gift' (ibid., p. 23) and 'what must be rendered to the singularity of the other' (ibid., p. 28). It helps us to deconstruct totalising discourses (ibid., p. 30). It enables us to substitute messianic eschatology ('alterity that cannot be anticipated' (ibid., p. 65) for teleology (ibid., p. 37). 'Haunting belongs to the structure of every hegemony' (ibid.), and hence is essential to the analysis of power. It facilitates the presence/absence of a new international without organisation and without knowledge, which nonetheless will haunt the present. It promotes clear thinking about value, exchange value, money and capital, all of which have ghostly forms. Hauntology is particularly important for thinking about the spectralising power of the media (ibid., p. 50). 'It points toward a thinking of the event that necessarily exceeds a binary or dialectical logic' (ibid., p. 63). It encourages us to face up to responsibility by passing through the 'ordeal of undecideability' (ibid., p. 75). It helps us to avoid the perversions of communism, which 'are the effect of an *ontological* treatment of the spectrality of the ghost' (ibid., p. 91), and to radicalise Marxism (ibid., p. 92). Also, through hauntology we can avoid the 'autonomization of spirit, idea, or thought, as happens *par excellence* in Hegelian idealism' (ibid., p. 126).[17] 'The theory of ideology depends in many of its features, as we will emphasize, on this theory of the ghost' (ibid., p. 127). In a 'time out of joint' such as ours, a new thinking of borders is facilitated by hauntology. Finally, haunting is where we should begin, as Derrida makes very clear when he claims that 'If Marx, like Freud, like Heidegger, like everybody, did not begin where he ought to have … namely with haunting, before life *as such*, before death *as such*, it is doubtless not his fault' (ibid., p. 175). I could go on, but this should be enough to indicate that *Specters of Marx* is much more about using the concept 'hauntology' to put a new spin on deconstruction than it is about seriously engaging with Marx or even with 'one of the spirits of Marxism' (ibid., p. 75). Furthermore, what we have here is not a theory of hauntology that sets forth and analyses different types of haunting and their interconnections, but rather an indiscriminate and metaphorical spreading of spectral seeds in a typically Derridean promiscuous 'dissemination'.

The 'urgent lessons' come less from reading Marx and Marxism than from Derrida's highly selective appropriations from Marx to preach *his* urgent lessons. Besides using Marx to feed his hauntology, what other urgent lessons emerge for Derrida from Marx's legacy?

'We [Derrida] believe that this messianic remains an *ineffaceable mark* … of Marx's legacy' (ibid., p. 28). 'Messianic' is not a religious concept for Derrida. It is 'the coming of the other, the absolute and unpredictable singularity of the *arrivant as justice*' (ibid.) This way of writing is in some ways reminiscent of Sorel (1961), who in *Reflections on Violence* put forward the general strike as a way of giving oneself without knowledge to the future in order to inaugurate the ineffable coming of the other as justice. Sorel's general strike, however, at least had the benefit of being a determinate act carried out by determinate actors. In contrast Derrida (1999 p. 29) calls for a 'new international' in which we come together 'without effacing the heterogeneity of the other', and without knowledge or organisation 'turn *ourselves* over to the future'. Ah, what generosity of spirit!

Derrida (ibid., p. 63) writes of a 'new world disorder', the analysis of which will require a 'problematics coming from the Marxian tradition.' But what is this problematics? First, as should be obvious from the above, it is based not on an ontology but a hauntology. Second, we must think the three apparatuses of culture: the political, mass media, and scholarly as they are intertwined in propagating a hegemonic discourse (ibid., pp. 52–3). Third, we must avoid the concepts 'social class' and 'class struggle' in favour of a 'hierarchized conflictual field' (ibid., p. 55). Fourth, the future of Marxism is highly dependent on what happens in the Middle East, particularly the struggle for Jerusalem. Fifth, we need to analyse the ten plagues of the new world order, which Derrida simply lists without theorising, though he prioritises the present inadequacy of international law and claims that the New International would be primarily 'a profound transformation … of international law' (ibid., p. 84). Sixth, we need to criticise the gap between the ideal of liberalism and its reality as well as criticising the ideal itself. Seventh, foreign debt 'holds a mass of humanity under its yoke and in a new form of slavery', and to treat this problem we will need 'critique of the market, of the multiple logics of capital, and of that which links the State and international law to this market' (ibid., p. 94). This is about as much as Derrida has to offer in the way of a new Marxist problematic, and the above is offered quite assertively and dogmatically without theoretical support. Such embarrassing paucity is not unusual when deconstruction wanders away from textual criticism and attempts to advance the cause of substantive knowledge of the world.

When deconstructivists make statements or claims about the world, these tend to be dogmatic, and this is because they have no epistemological or theoretical grounds upon which to make such claims.[18] One should note that Derrida does not write '*knowledge* of the multiple logics of capital', but '*critique* of the multiple logics of capital'. This is because deconstructivism is basically a critical stance and not a cognitive one. But how are we to carry out an effective critique of the multiple logics of capital if we do not have clear knowledge about how they operate and with what consequences?

Throughout this study I have claimed that capital has a logic and that numerous theorists from Marx to Sekine have attempted to theorise this logic, and yet many poststructuralists, including Derrida, would feel uncomfortable about such a claim. The main reason is the economic and class reductionism that have generally been associated with utilising the theory of capital's logic. Indeed this reductionism has been like a nightmare weighing upon our thought and from which we have tried desperately to escape, even if it means denying that capital has any logic at all. Such strategies of escape and denial are not necessary once we fully realise that no reductionism whatsoever follows necessarily from theorising capital's logic. The problem has lain not in the construction of such theories, but in their use. For example, when the law of value is applied directly to historical analysis, economic reductionism inevitably follows. But once we problematise the relation between the logical and the historical, it is possible to treat capital's logic as a particularly strong and peculiarly self-reifying social force operating amongst other social forces, and as a result the role of capital's logic in any particular historical outcome can never be determined *a priori*. The outcome depends on the ensemble of social forces at work.

Deconstructionists such as Derrida find themselves caught up in a series of dilemmas because on the one hand they still want to refer to things such as the 'logic' or 'logics of capital', but on the other hand their radically contextual epistemological commitment makes it difficult to see how a capital logic could be theorised and not be inconsistent with such commitment. Indeed one might say that Derrida's appropriation of Marx is haunted by the spectre of capital's logic. He wants to criticise the multiple logics of capital, while denying that capital has a logic. He wants to criticise a new capitalist world order without any theory that could clarify just what is capitalist about this world order.

Derrida's mission is 'to do everything we can so as to avoid the neutralizing anesthesia of a new theoreticism' (ibid., p. 32). The problem is that the struggle against a 'new theoreticism' often undermines theory *per se*, even given Derrida's commitment to avoid 'anti-scientific or obscurantist temptations', and to carry out a radical critique 'in the name of a new Enlightenment for the century to come' (ibid., p. 90). Is his New International without knowledge or organisation characteristic of the 'new Enlightenment'? Just what kind of social science is he proposing?

Derrida claims that 'a problematics coming from the Marxian tradition will be indispensable for a long time yet' (ibid., p. 63), and yet he has precious little to say about how one might go about constructing such a problematics. He is deeply concerned about the global structure of debt, but it is not clear why he singles this out as his primary focus other than a moral outrage that it has triggered in him. In referring to this debt, he writes: 'we are pointing to the *interest* and first of all the interest of capital in general' (ibid., p. 94).

What exactly does Derrida mean by 'capital in general'? 'Capital in general' is a concept that I would locate only in the context of the theory of pure capitalism. It is surprising that Derrida would choose a way of writing that so radically reifies capital, when he espouses the correctness of a radically contextual process-thinking in his methodological texts. This is followed by generalisations that link '*the* order of the world today' and '*the* world-wide market' [my emphasis]. But does the world today have a single order, is there such a thing as a single worldwide market? Is it not more accurate to say that the world is a complex of multiple orders with distinct temporalities and that one important causal factor in this complexity is a complex of different types of interacting markets?

Apparently for Derrida we can critique 'the multiple logics of capital', but we cannot theorise capital's inner logic even though such a theory would be a tremendous aid in understanding such logics. Indeed, just how are we supposed to go about understanding capitalism's multiple or local logics? Which logics are capital's, and, assuming that we can identify them, can we try to understand them through any method other than an empirical analysis of each logic? If Marx's theory of capital's logic and Sekine's dialectic of capital are of any use, how do we use them? Derrida does not even begin to attempt to answer any of these absolutely crucial questions.

Nearly everything Derrida writes concerning spectrality in relation to the commodity and capital is just using different language to write about reification. Reification is the tendency for capital as an object to take on subject-like characteristics, or in other words to be inhabited by spirits such that capital takes on a 'life' of its own. To claim as Derrida does that exchange values have a will of their own, speak to each other and engage in commerce among themselves is also a way of expressing the reality of reification in pure capitalism.

Like Althusser's initial paradigm of 'overdetermination', Derrida always seems to critique an abstract metaphysics of presence from the point of view of a concrete metaphysics of presence/absence. He never seems to consider the possibility of an abstract metaphysics of presence/absence. As you will recall, Althusser's paradigm case of overdetermination is the Russian Revolution and not the theory of the economic in the capitalist mode of production. It is easy to criticise abstract theory from a contextual standpoint, but in doing so, one is always prone to undermine theory itself, when it is precisely theory that helps us to find our way through the dense undergrowth of context. Thus Derrida has discarded the theory of capital's deep structure, but it is not clear where he will now go for criteria of identity with which to distinguish the multiple logics of capital from other social logics.

In a sense the dialectic of capital is an abstract metaphysics of presence/absence, because its closure is achieved by an idealisation of materiality that makes use-values docile to the management of value. In other words, even at the moment of closure it is 'haunted' by use-value and materiality considered more concretely. And it is this haunting that necessitates more concrete levels of analysis if what we want to understand is not simply capital's deep structure, but also world-historic phases of its development and its impact on historical change. In other words, in the problematic that I am proposing Marxian political economy must consist of more than the dialectic of capital. At more concrete levels of analysis the logic of capital is both present and absent.

According to Derrida (ibid., p. 59), '...there is no longer, there never was just capital, nor capitalism in the singular, but capitalisms plural – whether State or private, real or symbolic, always linked to spectral forces – or rather capitalizations whose antagonisms are irreducible'. This quotation illustrates Derrida's tendency to think of capital only at the level of the event or of history. It is rather obvious that at the level of history there has always been 'capitalisms plural', but this does not obviate the need to theorise capital's inner logic.[19] And instead of the rather mystical and vague need to connect this inner logic to 'spectral forces' conceived as some sort of antagonistic historical process, is it not better to consider these connections rather more systematically through distinct levels of analysis? Indeed the more 'capitalisms' there are, the greater the need for a theory of capital's logic to make sense of this plurality, and in particular to understand the interconnections between the types and forms of capitalism. Indeed the plurality can only be recognised as such by at least an implied reference to a notion of capital's logic. If this is the case, why not make the theory of capital's logic explicit?

Elsewhere Derrida (ibid., p. 63) contrasts the 'logic of the ghost' with dialectical logic, which he sees as a logic of presence in which the ideal becomes concretised into the real. But, as I have argued, the dialectical logic of the theory of capital's logic is not like this. The dialectical logic of capital is both real and ideal. The inner logic of capital is real, but it can be theorised in the ideal environment of a purely capitalist society with its assumption of ideal use-values. At the level of the historical event it is both present and absent in the sense that it is active even if partially refracted and blocked, and further more it may be partially counteracted or rendered partially ineffective by other social forces and use-value resistance. At the level of event, the inner logic of capital is never fully present in its pure, unadulterated form. It follows that Derrida's 'logic of the ghost' is quite compatible with capital having a dialectical logic as long as it is theorised within the framework of levels of analysis.

MARXISM AND DECONSTRUCTION

One of the most ambitious attempts to synthesise deconstruction with Marxism is Ryan's text, appropriately entitled *Marxism and Deconstruction*. According to Ryan (1982, p. 13) 'All of the conceptual oppositions of metaphysics which deconstruction undoes can be said to hang on the frame of the interiority/exteriority binary. What is inside, according to metaphysics, is "own," proper, good, primary, original, unadulterated; what is outside is other, improper, bad, secondary, derivative, degraded.' Does the theory of capital's inner logic represent the sort of interiority–exteriority binary to which Ryan is referring to here?

To begin with, the inside in the dialectic of capital is not in any sense 'superior' to what is outside; that which is 'inside' is simply those aspects of social life which take the commodity form and which value must deal with in order to expand itself. Above all, capital as self-expanding value is oriented towards profit maximisation, and it is absolutely indifferent to social relations that are not commodified and do not figure in profit. Capital in its inner logic has no concern whatsoever with many things that may concern us. For example it has no concern with the environment, with gender relations, with human suffering, with poverty, with sexuality, with extra-economic coercion or with oppression and violence. In a purely capitalist society it is assumed that all commodities are secured in their commodity form, so that the motion of value does not have to rely upon extra-economic force. Among other things this assumes that there are classes, but that the resistance of working-class individuals and groups is contained by the market. Indeed 'exploitation' is a fundamental and crucial concept to the dialectic of capital, but at this level of analysis it must be theorised under the assumption that collectivities, like persons, are mere bearers of economic categories. Such are the implications of total reification, an assumption that is essential to thinking about capital's logic independently from human intervention that might alter it. It follows that what is inside capital's logic is not determined by some metaphysician, but by capital's logic itself, or perhaps more accurately by capital's logic as it manifests itself through theoretical conceptualisation.

Theorising capital's inner logic is important not only for the insight it gives us about capital's economic dynamics, but also for its bringing into sharp relief what is excluded. For example, from the point of view of capital as self-expanding value, some forms of labour are of no value because they do not form part of the commodity-economic logic of profit maximisation. In a purely capitalist society self-employed labour and forced labour do not exist, domestic labour is ignored and not valued, while voluntary labour or cooperative self-organised labour is totally ignored as though it were non-existent.

In order to break down the identitarian and exclusionary logic of capital, we must break down capitalism itself. It is a delusion to think that this is helped in any way by a theory that 'deconstructs' the economic by denying the need for an abstract economic theory, or by undermining any possibility for such a theory by breaking down the very distinction between the economic and the political.

The dialectic of capital achieves closure, but unlike Hegel's *Logic* it does so without any illusion that it includes everything. For Hegel the contingent is simply the concretion or externalisation of the idea; for the dialectic of capital, the 'outside' represents relatively autonomous practices at more concrete levels of analysis that cannot be brushed aside as secondary, derivative or supplementary. The character of this 'outside', forces upon Marxian political economy levels of analysis that attempt to explore the articulations between capital's logic and other social forces without any *a priori* privileging of capital's logic in terms of historical causality. Capital's logic is a particularly powerful social force and it differs from other social forces in its peculiarity as a reifying and self-reifying force, but it does not follow that this logic is the cause of all modern historical outcomes.

The outside is not purely derivative and it is not purely 'outside'. As argued earlier, the inner logic of capital is haunted by or points to an outside that in a sense is suppressed by the assumption of total reification, an outside that capital itself marginalises and whose silence is leaden within the dialectic of capital, a silence that cries out to be broken by more concrete levels of analysis.

Ryan's attempt to break down the inside–outside binary is directed primarily at breaking down the distinction between the economic and the political in the theory of capital. But as I shall argue later, this leads him into serious contradictions. On the one hand he wants to preserve something called 'the law of value', but on the other he denies the conditions that make it possible both to theorise the motion of value and to theorise such a motion as being law-like.

Poststructuralists' principal strategy for deconstructing abstract economic law is to argue that the economic is directly and thoroughly political and ideological. In an interview with Michael Sprinker, Derrida (1993, p. 205) says: 'Each time I have discussed economy, I did so by bringing in all sorts of elements that were not simply forces of production or effects of ownership or appropriation.' But Derrida nearly always discusses the economy at the level of historical analysis where obviously one would want to discuss more than forces and relations of production. Derrida apparently sees no need for a distinctively Marxian economic theory that would theorise capital by letting its real self-abstracting tendencies complete themselves in theory. But then it is also unclear just what kind of Marxian political economy he would support and how he would go about theorising capital.

Ryan's (1982, p. 15) account of these issues is even more confused and contradictory because he sticks his neck out far more than Derrida. On the one hand he seems to believe in something called 'the law of value', but gives us no clue about how thought that is committed to being 'radically historical' can theorise 'the law of value'. He argues that the law of value is thoroughly political, and even goes so far as to claim that '"The political" and "the economic" cannot even be considered as separate categories for the sake of theoretical exposition' (ibid., p. 99). Thus there is no difference between an economic law and political force (ibid., p. 92).

The kernel of truth in this is that the law of value is coercive in history, and as a result it is always resisted to varying degrees and in various ways.[20] In a purely capitalist society, however, we assume that the historical coercion of the law of value has been so successful that all collective resistance is temporarily quelled and reification is total. This means that consideration of extra-economic force is excluded from the theory of capital's logic, and that the force of a self-regulating commodity-economic logic has subdued all opposition.

The only forces that are exercised in a purely capitalist society are the impersonal structural economic forces of the market. Thus periodic crises in a purely capitalist society cause massive unemployment, but there is no political force involved, rather there is the operation of economic force only as impersonal laws. This assumption is essential to arrive at a clear and consistent theory of the law of value. In a theory of the law of value we do not theorise powerful monopolists who use their power to distort value relations, or highly organised and powerful workers who use their power to reduce profits and take partial control away from capital. Such considerations are of a contingent and historical nature, whereas the law of value reveals the necessary inner connections of capital in the abstract and in general.

Ryan's confusion about the logical and historical is manifold. According to Ryan the economistic reading of *Capital* privileges necessary economic development, while the voluntarist side of Marxism highlights contingent political force. Ryan proposes to deconstruct this binary opposition by taking the position that the two sides are 'undecidably intertwined'. Thus 'Economic development (in the capitalist mode of production) cannot occur independently of political force, and capitalist political force is never exercised for its own sake, but for economic reasons' (ibid., p. 84). It is perhaps a truism to state that economic development cannot occur independently of political force, but what does this have to do with the theory of capital's logic? The problem here is that the theory of capital's logic is not, as I understand it, a theory of economic development in the historical sense at all. It is a theory of an inner logic and says nothing directly about how that logic mixes with configurations of use-value resistance (including human resistance) at the level of history. Thus the binary opposition between economism and voluntarism is not overcome by stating the obvious fact that in history the economic and political are intertwined, but by problematising the relation between the theoretical and the historical in a way that does not *a priori* privilege the causal primacy of the economic.[21] Clearly, then, we are not limited to the choice presented by Ryan between a binary opposition and a collapsing together of categories.

According to Ryan (ibid., p. 97), 'The law of value is not a description of an objective mechanism, beyond human control; it is something that can be either obeyed or disobeyed, heeded or displaced.' Contrary to this formulation, by which it seems that Ryan himself falls into voluntarism, I would argue that the law of value is an objective mechanism that can be modified, resisted and ultimately displaced.

Since the law of value plays a major role in structuring our society, our identity, and our daily lives, it is not simply a question of obeying or disobeying as one might the command of a sergeant, rather it is a matter of a long-term, collective project of working our way out of a series of complex structural and relational determinations.

Again, Ryan refers to 'modern economic ideologies ... which claim that the economy is governed by objective and natural economic laws, next to which the strata of social relations is [sic] secondary, derivative, and accidental' (ibid., p. 61). Marx's alternative to this was not to collapse the economic into an undifferentiated social totality, but rather to understand the economic as reified social relations. According to Marx the economic absorbs social relations into reified economic categories that interact in ways that are, unfortunately for us, to some extent not unlike natural laws. That the economic achieves a certain objectivity at the level of pure capitalism does not of course solve the problem of considering the relation between economic social relations and non-economic social relations at more concrete levels of analysis, but it does avoid facile formulations about overcoming binary oppositions by collapsing distinctions into an overcooked social soup where the economic is immediately political, the political is immediately economic, and everything is immediately ideological, with no sense of the relative autonomy or strength of factors.

Ryan often recognises the reifying force of capital, but does not connect this with any recognition of the need for a theory of capital's logic. For example he writes: 'Capitalism, therefore, requires an idealizing operation that abstracts from inequality, identifies difference, and resolves seriality into a paradigm' (ibid., p. 85). He then goes on to claim that Marx was less interested in the homogenising aspects of the law of value than the heterogeneity that disrupts the logic of capital. But the point is that one must first have a law of value before one can discuss disruptions, and there is no doubt that Marx was centrally concerned in *Capital* with theorising the law of value, and not all possible heterogeneities at the level of history that the law of value may have trouble pacifying and might remain permanently outside the purview of the law of value. Ryan himself writes: 'In its very structure, value unifies by homogenizing difference' (ibid., p. 89). But how do we theorise value 'in its very structure'? The law of value is simply a law that subsumes difference to identity. It therefore cannot help when theorising such a law to side with difference against identity. A few pages later, when referring to the wage struggle, Ryan writes: 'Capital wins through the medium of the law of value' (ibid., p. 88). But this is not always true at the level of historical analysis, and if we let capital win throughout the theory of a purely capitalist society, what we get in the end is the law of value in its entirety. Indeed a purely capitalist society is simply a society in which it is assumed that capital wins totally.

Having taken a radical deconstructionist stance that breaks down all distinctions between the economic and the political and between abstract theory and historical analysis, it is somewhat surprising for Ryan to claim that 'In order to survive, capitalism must remain the same, be self-identical, continuous, absolutely adequate to itself' (ibid., p. 181). But surely this is a confusion of temporalities. On the one hand, in logical time where capital is adequate to itself, there is no question of survival.[22] On the other hand, in historical time capital only has a partial grip on economic reality, is never self-identical, and yet displays considerable longevity.

J. K GIBSON–GRAHAM'S PERFORMATIVISM

While Gibson–Graham identify with postmodernism, unlike Ryan, their primary deconstructive move is not to collapse the economic into the political. And given the strength of their insistence that by representing capital as possessing an internal logic we are inevitably contributing to capital's continued hegemony, one might conclude that the approach being advocated here would have nothing in common with that of Gibson–Graham.[23] But such a conclusion would be mistaken, for although our positive prescriptions for Marxian political economy are quite at odds, there is considerable overlap in our diagnosis of the difficulties with orthodox Marxism. Furthermore, while they would reject the theory of pure capitalism, Unoist historical analysis is potentially consistent with at least some of their perspective. This is because Unoists argue that capital at the level of historical analysis is always plural and that it only ever has a partial grip on history, a grip that can only be estimated by analysing the causal efficacy of various capitalisms as they articulate with non-capitalist economic forces and non-economic social forces.

In their review of Derrida's Specters of Marx, Gibson–Graham outline, five ghosts that haunt capitalism. First they call up 'the specter of economic difference that haunts the capitalist hegemon' (Gibson–Graham, 1996, pp. 243–4). The dialectic of capital is indeed haunted by 'economic difference' since the unassisted operation of a governing commodity-economic logic requires the theoretical neutralisation of use-value obstacles and recalcitrant materialities. It is the reactivation of economic difference at the level of mid-range theory that produces distinct stage-specific capitalisms, and it is its further reactivation at the level of historical analysis that makes it so difficult to determine the precise role of capitalism in various historical outcomes.

Ghost number two further specifies economic difference: 'haunting the commodity and the market are noncommodity production and nonmarket exchange' (ibid., pp. 244). If we take 'commodity' in its strict meaning as a capitalistically produced commodity, then it is likely that the majority of the world's production is non-commodity production given that the majority of the world's producers are petty bourgeois producers (peasants, farmers, shopkeepers, craftspeople and so on). Again in its strict meaning, most service sector labour is non-commodity production. Finally most domestic and voluntary labour is even more clearly non-commodity production. Some of these 'non-capitalist' forms of labour are more easily integrated with capitalist forms than others, and this is something that Gibson–Graham seem to ignore. Furthermore, non-market exchange can take many forms, including barter, gift-giving, emotional exchanges, verbal exchanges, gestural exchanges, power exchanges, recognition exchanges, sexual exchanges and so on, and once again, some of these exchanges are more economic than others and some have greater potential to move beyond the market than others.

Ghost number three refers to non-capitalist commodity production (ibid., p. 245). In my framework 'commodity' would have to be used loosely here, since the dialectic of capital makes it clear that the commodity only comes fully into its own within capitalism. But if we use it loosely to mean any product exchanged for money in markets with some regularity, then there can be slave-produced commodities, feudal commodities, family-based commodities, communal commodities, cooperative commodities, prisoner-produced commodities, petty bourgeois commodities and so on. What is of interest, of course, is not simply listing all the differences, but strategic theorising that explores those forms of non-capitalist commodity production that provide the strongest basis for moving towards democratic socialism.

According to the fourth spectre, 'The concept of capitalism itself is haunted by heterogeneity, by the historicity and singularity of each form of economy that might be called capitalist. Each capitalist site is constituted within a social and political context, and that contextualization is itself contaminating of any pure or essential and invariant attribute associated with the concept' (ibid., pp. 246–7). I agree that 'the concept of capitalism itself is haunted by heterogeneity', but in order to have this haunting one must first have a concept of capitalism, a concept that seems to lack any clear determinacy in the work of Gibson–Graham. For them capitalism may not exist, or if it does, it is only because we believe that it does.[24] Furthermore, while I agree that 'each capitalist site is constituted within a social and political context' and that this must 'contaminate' capital's logic, accepting these propositions does not prevent us from theorising capital's deep structure. What does follow is a radical problematising of the relation between the theory of capital's logic and the contamination of that logic as it works through various social and political contexts. Unlike Gibson–Graham's approach, the Unoist approach can be quite specific about degrees of 'contamination' because of its clarity about the nature of capital.

The fifth and final spectre is that 'capitalism is haunted by its discursivity' (ibid., p. 247). Here Gibson–Graham have little to say about the precise sense in which capitalism is discursive, other than to claim that this fact 'situates the concepts of capital and capitalism ... as targets of deconstruction. If the means of deconstruction are not readily apparent, they nevertheless are available both within Marx's and within Derrida's text' (ibid., p. 248). These are large claims to leave so vague, particularly given Derrida's claim that 'What I call "text" implies all the structures called "real", "economic", "historical", socio-institutional, in short: all possible referents' (Derrida, 1988, p. 148). It follows that deconstructing the text of capitalism implies ending its hegemony, and while 'the means ... are not ... apparent' we are to have faith that they are 'available'. 'Rewriting' the 'text of capitalism' presumably implies transforming those structures that put profits first, encourage exploitation, create class domination, create economic insecurity and so on. The 'rewriting' that Gibson–Graham carry out contributes to the celebration of the plurality of capitalism as an end in itself and not to the structural transformation of capitalism.

The means of deconstruction offered by Gibson–Graham all flow from their deep commitment to 'performativity'. As they put it:

> Writing about social existence and change we inevitably face the problem of how to represent a particular social configuration, which for us has become less a question of accuracy or fidelity (to the 'truth' of what we describe or seek to understand) than one of 'performativity.' When we tell a story and represent a social practice or

> site, what kind of social world do we construct and endow with the force of representation? (Gibson–Graham, 1996, p. 206)

They do not have a theory of the 'force of representation', but they assume that it is very great, and that since it has been neglected in the past, it is a good idea to 'bend the stick'. But if the force of representation is given too much emphasis, a number of difficulties are created. First, we might be led to deny the existence of a reality that is independent from our representations of it, and while language and reality are no doubt to varying extents embedded in each other, they are also in part distinct. Second, we might fail to consider different ways that language and reality relate in different regions of social life. For example I have argued for a peculiar relation between them in the theorising of capitalism. Third, we might overestimate the extent to which changing our way of representing something will help to change the thing being represented. Fourth, we might lose touch with what actually exists as opposed to what we would like to exist, as adumbrated by our means of representation. Fifth, it can give intellectuals the delusion that they have the power to transform capitalism by simply 'rewriting it' in words. The indiscriminate emphasis on performative force that gets into these difficulties and makes the force of representation imperialistic over other social forces, I call 'performativism'.

Unfortunately much of Gibson–Graham's refreshing and exciting prose is overshadowed by excessive performativism. If society is a temporary, unstable, 'complex disunity' (ibid., p. 58) of discursive processes, then it is very difficult to explain how it is that capitalism has lasted so long despite Herculean efforts to overthrow it. I cannot see how Gibson–Graham can, within their framework, theorise the continuity through difference of capitalism.

While there has been some tendency for Marxian political economists to overemphasise the monolithic hegemony of capitalism, I believe that in recent years there has been a strong move away from this. Nearly everyone from E. P. Thompson to Althusser have been attacking economism for a long time, and as a result there is now much more sensitivity to the complexity and decentredness of capitalism, and to difference in general.

It is no doubt true that 'Representations of capitalism are a potent constituent of the anticapitalist imagination, providing images of what is to be resisted and changed' (ibid., p. 3), and this is one reason why I have trouble with Gibson–Graham's perspective. They completely ignore the reifying force that has made capitalism so enduring, and vastly overestimate the 'performative force of economic representation' (ibid., p. 7), as though it is simply thinking that makes it so. What is capitalism? If a capitalist site is simply 'an irreducible specificity' such that we cannot 'assume that a capitalist firm is interested in maximizing profits', then it is not clear what might make a firm capitalist. Individual capitalist firms may have all sorts of short-term interests connected to representation, market share, 'satisficing', beating competitors, maintaining labour relations and so on, but surely in the long term a capitalist firm must have some interest in profits. Gibson-Graham refer to 'capitalism's provisional and unstable dominance (if indeed such dominance is understood to exist.)' (ibid., p. 15) Is capitalism dominant or not? If it is not, there is little point in organising anticapitalist strategies.

Although Gibson–Graham are vague about what the economic is, what capitalism is, and whether or not they exist, they insist that the economic should not be ignored, as in much postmodern thought. 'Unless the economy is explicitly written out, or until it is deconstructively or positively rewritten, it will write itself into every text of social theory' (ibid., p. 39). But how can the capitalist economy write itself into every text if it does not have any logic of its own, but is simply another 'complex disunity' that may not exist? That it is possible to construct a dialectical logic of pure capitalism is precisely due to the fact that in a sense capital can and does 'write itself' into the social text.

Gibson–Graham lament the fact that in capitalcentric theory 'Complex processes of social development – commodification, industrialization, proletarianism, internationalization – become legible as the signatures of capitalism rather than as unique and decentered determinations' (ibid., p. 43). But as a matter of fact these complex processes, when viewed at the level of historical analysis, are not a simple function of capital's logic, but neither are they 'unique determinations'; instead they develop unevenly but in connection with each other and with capitalism as a whole. Really to understand these developments, it is essential to have a theory of capital's logic as well as a thorough analysis of the specific context within which this logic is partially refracted.

Gibson–Graham place a lot of emphasis on 'overdetermination' as a concept that gets rid of all 'essentialism', which they see as something that should be rejected. Following the work of Resnick and Wolff, they claim that the basic premise of 'overdetermination involves an understanding of identities as continually and differentially constituted rather than as pre-existing their contexts or as having an invariant core' (ibid., p. 16). But are these the only alternatives? At the level of historical analysis identities are 'continually and differentially constituted' as the complex dynamic core of capital is partially refracted in the process of negotiating with or compromising with these identities. The core is not invariant, it is dynamic, and the identities are relational within the context of a purely capitalist society. The core only partially determines identities at the level of historical analysis, but it informs our understanding of how a partially refracted logic articulates with identities in process.

Lacking a determinate theory of capitalism or socialism, Gibson–Graham tend to advocate difference as an end in itself. Many capitalisms are better than one capitalism, and the proliferation of non-capitalist economic differences is viewed as the key to 'rewriting capitalism'. Begging in the street, a good deal of petty crime and forced labour are all non-capitalist economic differences, but how do they contribute to the rewriting of capitalism? Is 'creating alternative economic futures in which class diversity can flourish' (ibid., p. 52) an important goal of their performatist strategy? Do we simply want a greater diversity of capitalists and more diverse forms of exploitation? Is globalisation a good thing if it helps to produce a more diverse class of small capitalists in third world countries as Gibson–Graham suggest (ibid., p. 138)?

Gibson–Graham claim that their performativist vision of capitalism is informed by feminist retheorisations of sexual identity, without even considering the possibility that differences between sexual identity and the identity of capitalism might make the analogy extremely problematic. Sexual identities are straightjacketed by stereotypes that are particularly vulernable to parody and other kinds of performative attack. Furthermore, with sexual identity there is a strong case to be made for difference as an end in itself. If capitalism does have an inner logic that is a self-reifying force, this makes the 'identity' of capitalism rather different from sexual identity, in which ideology plays such a crucial role. Parody may in some circumstances dislodge or weaken gender stereotypes, whereas the parody of capitalism is likely simply to strengthen it, as strategically directed anger is diffused by polymorphous laughter turned into an entertainment buck. If, as I suspect, the ontology of sex/gender is different from the ontology of capital, then uncritical borrowings and analogies will only confuse, not enlighten.

CONCLUSIONS

Derrida's philosophy is essentially an immanent critique of Hegel, the last philosopher of the book and the first of writing. We learn from Derrida that the dialectic of capital cannot internalise all materiality within itself under the sign of value, just as Hegel's dialectic of thought cannot internalise all negativity or difference under the sign of the Absolute. The dialectic of capital assumes an abstract and docile materiality, and it is this that demonstrates the partial grip of capital's logic on history. Marxian political economy must therefore come to grips with a reactivation of materiality that at least partially refracts capital's logic as we think about it articulated with relatively autonomous forms of materiality at more concrete levels of analysis. Even as the dialectic of capital achieves closure, it is haunted by the necessity for distinct non-dialectical levels of analysis that are more concrete. As we move towards the concrete, materiality, difference, negativity and use-value are freed up in a theoretically controlled way.

At the still rather abstract level of mid-range theory, the inner logic of capital is converted into stage-specific capitalisms that explore the articulations between a dominant mode of capital accumulation and other relatively autonomous social forces. At the level of historical analysis, difference becomes more prominent the more we focus on specific, unique and local temporal and spatial contexts, but even in these cases the two more abstract levels inform our analysis.

Deconstruction offers some useful critical tools, but it needs the discipline of a social science such as Unoist political economy because of its penchant for pushing deconstruction, difference and performativity too far. Ryan's work is a good example of the incoherence that follows from indiscriminately deconstructing the economic, essentially by merging it with the political. This move is quite common, and can be seen in the work of Laclau and Mouffe and many others. The result is total inability to philosophise the economic or to think the automaticity that capital continually displays. This move is also often made in the name of a radical chic that would politicise everything, totally failing in the process to understand the ontological specificity of distinct social realms.

Gibson–Graham do not make this move, and instead call for 'rewriting' the economic in the name of difference. This is a more constructive use of deconstruction, as they demonstrate that capital at the level of historical analysis is not monolithic, but is rent with difference in all sorts of ways. And while some of their critique of regulation theory and others is quite good, difference appears to be an end in itself and the force of representation knows no bounds. In part this follows from overplaying the analogy between sexual identity and the identity of capital. Their intention to open up our thought about capital is well taken, but in pushing difference too far they close off the possibilities for knowledge of capital or for thinking through effective strategies of change. Effective strategies of change need to know *which* differences can be most effective as arenas for organising to transform capitalism into democratic socialism. And socialism must be more than and different from the maximisation and intensification of difference. Gibson–Graham's approach does not enable us to attain knowledge of where we are coming from, and in the light of this knowledge, where we might go.

The best antidote to Althusser's universalising and totalising structuralism is not to adopt a poststructuralism that proposes opposite universalisms, such as a universal privileging of anti-essentialism against essentialism, of fiction against reality, of process against structure, of rhetoric against science, of context against abstract theory or of difference against identity. I believe a more fruitful approach for Marxian political economy is really to come to grips with Marx's texts, the kinds of object he was trying to understand, and particularly his hitherto unparalleled understanding of the unique ontology of capital. At the same time it would seem worthwhile to avoid all simple dualisms such as those mentioned above in favour of considering the specificity of each kind of object of knowledge and the specificity of the concepts, methods, logics and theories that need to be put to work to advance knowledge in each case. Above all this means considering the possibility that different objects of knowledge may possess different kinds of ontology and different kinds of epistemology.

This chapter has attempted to demonstrate that deconstruction needs to be limited by dialectics, and that this can be achieved in Unoist political economy. Unlimited dialectics is totalitarian and unlimited deconstruction is chaotic. But dialectics clearly has the dominant role in Unoist political economy, where the role of deconstruction is primarily to sensitise us to difference and to the other. From the point of view of Uno–Sekine political economy, poststructuralism in its anti-Hegelian fetishism has totally failed to grasp the important structural parallels between Hegel's *Logic* and the dialectic of capital. The poststructuralist conversion of capital into something so protean and polymorphous as to be indecipherable, of course, plays into the hands of capital. Despite Herculean acrobatics, poststructuralists have escaped neither Hegel nor capital. As Foucault put it so well:

> But to truly escape Hegel involves an exact appreciation of the price we have to pay to detach ourselves from him. It assumes that we are aware of the extent to which Hegel, insidiously perhaps, is close to us; it implies a knowledge, in that which permits us to think against Hegel, of that which remains Hegelian. We have to determine the extent to which our anti-Hegelianism is possibly one of his tricks directed against us, at the end of which he stands, motionless, waiting for us.[25]

7 Conclusions

Marxist theorists interested in developing the Hegel–Marx nexus have usually done so to bolster the ethical–revolutionary praxis side of Marxism in opposition to a mechanical or scientistic interpretation. Lukács is perhaps the paradigm case of this kind of appropriation of Hegel, an appropriation that combines Weber's culturalist 'rationalisation', Hegel's 'alienation' and Marx's 'fetishism of commodities' to form the concept 'reification'. I call this type of Marx–Hegel synthesis 'Hegelian Marxism'. This book is the most extensive attempt so far to appropriate Hegel in a way that is completely different from Hegelian Marxism. In doing so it leaves behind the stale opposition between scientific socialism and revolutionary socialism.

The favourite Hegelian text of Hegelian Marxists tends to be *The Phenomenology of Spirit* for its master–slave dialectic and its use of the concept 'alienation'. Little attention is focused on *The Science of Logic*, and hence on Hegel's profound contribution to scientific thought. But it is precisely in this latter work that the dialectical method works best and is most appropriate for advancing the scientific aspects of Marxian political economy in ways that break completely with the mechanical Marxism of much of the theory produced by the Second and Third Internationals.

My central aim has been to show that the theory of the dialectic of capital achieves a knowledge of the deep structure of capital that is unprecedented in the social sciences. It is this theory which grounds Marxian political economy and gives it the potential for such great explanatory power. But if Marxian political economy is potentially the most scientific of the social sciences, it is so in ways that are utterly different from the positivism that is characteristic of mainstream economic science.

By theorising a purely capitalist society, the dialectic of capital theorises the deep structure of capital as a whole as it governs the expanded reproduction of social life. This immediately problematises the relation between abstract theory and more concrete levels of analysis since the economic is never artificially separated from the social, so that as we move towards the concrete, capital's logic must be rethought in connection with relatively autonomous social practices.

Furthermore, unlike positivism, the dialectic of capital does not artificially separate science from criticism. It is economic reification that makes a dialectic of capital possible, and at the same time economic reification is something that democratic socialism would want to work its way out of. This does not imply a transparent society of fully self-actualised human beings, as in the end of all alienation and all reification, but it does imply that we increasingly democratise economic life in order drastically to reduce the immense human costs associated with existing inequalities, insecurities and rampant environmental destruction, generated in large part by the reifying forces of capitalism.

The capitalist epoch will come to be seen as one in which we relied on incredibly crude economic mechanisms called 'markets.' Markets are like machines for coordinating and relaying information, but they are only effective in relaying limited kinds of information in very circuitous ways. Markets are often thought to be highly efficient, but in the future they will be seen as highly inefficient and costly. Markets not only fail to take account of social and environmental costs, but they also generate instability, insecurity, inequality, antisocial egotism, frenetic life styles, cultural impoverishment, beggar-thy-neighbour greed, and oppression of difference.

Deconstruction must have a strong appeal in a world where homogenising forces establish narrow and oppressive normatives that either ignore the other or label it as inferior. Deconstruction offers a kind of tool kit to combat oppressive ideologies that fail to recognise, respect or appreciate otherness. In a world where the homogenising forces are so great, it must seem as though difference is something of which we could never have enough.

Even Derrida, however, advocates a 'new enlightenment' for the twenty-first century. If 'enlightenment' means anything, it means the use of human reason to ameliorate the human condition. If the world were simply a flux of difference, reason would be at a total loss. As I have argued, *in Specters of Marx*, Derrida (1994) presents not a new enlightenment, but a new dogmatism. This is because he is so immersed in difference that when it comes to making substantive claims about the world he has no theoretical basis for doing so. As a result these claims come out as dogmatic assertions, backed up only by the authority of Derrida's name. I take this as strong evidence that while deconstruction can act as an underlabourer to science in the sense that it can induce some humility in the face of difference, by itself it can offer no positive basis for knowledge of the world.

A new enlightenment must not shy away from using abstract theory to make sense of the world, but it must do so with a new sensibility to difference and otherness and a new responsibility for the power embedded in theory itself. This is precisely what I have set out to do in this book.

Notes and References

1 Introduction

1. Henceforth 'capital' refers to an abstract logic while 'capitalism' refers to an historical reality.
2. Here I would particularly emphasise the work of neo-Sraffians such as Steedman (1977).
3. Examples would include Althusser (Althusser and Balibar, 1970), who extracts a structuralist epistemology from *Capital*, and Postone (1996), who extracts a telos that involves the radical transformation of the capitalist labour process.
4. For example see Freeman and Carchedi (1996) for a rendering of Marxian economics that goes to extreme lengths to remove 'equilibrium' from Marxian economics, despite Marx's explict use of the concept, because 'In a world out of balance the principle of equilibrium is neither a valid foundation nor a real result' (ibid., p. viii). They seem oblivious to the fact that Marx's *Capital* is basically a theory of the deep structure of capital in the abstract and not directly of an empirical 'world out of balance'. Further, in their radical revisions of Marx's theory of capital's inner logic, the category of money is used magically to solve nearly every problem of value and price.
5. In their work the economic side is more fully and explicitly developed, but strength on this side is absolutely crucial for the effective development of the philosophical side. This book is largely a development of the philosophical implications of their largely economic theories. To place primary emphasis on the philosophical side, as with Althusser, has led to deeply problematic results.
6. By 'political economic critique of philosophy' I do not in any sense mean a sociology of knowledge, but rather a critique of general ontology from the point of view of the ontology of capital.
7. In today's international monetary system, the IMF plays the disciplinary role that the gold standard played in earlier systems.
8. I realise that claims of objectivity are rare these days, but I hope to convince the reader that the theory of capital's inner logic has the potential to be objectively true.
9. Some mention of levels of analysis can be found in Weber, Althusser, Bhaskar, Jameson, Mandel, Postone, Adorno, regulation theory, social structure of accumulation theory and many other theoretical approaches to international political economy. Indeed at least some mention of levels of analysis is the rule in most general approaches to political economy.
10. Sekine (1997), for example, thinks that capitalism ends with the stage of imperialism, and that since the 1920s we have been in a phase of transition away from capitalism.

2 The Unique Ontology of Capital

1. This is a substantially revised version of an article by the same name that appeared in *Poznan Studies in the Philosophy of Science and Humanities*, volume 60.
2. As Marx (1963, p. 483) puts it: 'In this quite alienated form of profit and in the same measure as the form of profit hides its inner core, capital more and more acquires a material form, is transformed more and more from a relationship into a thing, but a thing which embodies, which has absorbed, the social relationship, a thing which has acquired a fictitious life and independent existence in relation to itself, a natural-supernatural entity...' This expresses exactly what I mean by 'reification.' In a purely capitalist society where reification is total, economic categories refer to things that *embody* and *absorb* the social relationship. In other words, economic categories refer not simply to things or interpersonal relations, but to reified social relations, to social relations mediated by commodities.
3. I understand 'ontology' to refer to the fundamental properties or the being of objects of knowledge. 'Epistemology' refers to the possibility of gaining knowledge with varying degrees of validity of such objects. 'Methodology' refers to the techniques or logic used to gain knowledge or back up knowledge claims. It should be clear from what follows that I agree with Bhaskar (1978) about giving priority to ontology since it is the fundamental nature of objects of knowledge that constrains the sorts of knowledge and methodologies that are possible.
4. Basing himself on Bachelard, Lecourt (1975) argues that there is no unitary epistemology. Althusser (Althusser and Balibar, 1970) argues that criteria of validity are internal to each science, and Suchting (1992) claims there is 'no single social science', and that methodological discussions divorced from the specificities of particular sciences are bound to be defective. While I agree with these emphases, there have not been enough studies focusing on the differences between objects of knowledge in the social sciences. While Althusser wrote about the uniqueness of Marx's scientific breakthrough, I do not think he got it right. Also, too much emphasis on the internality of criteria of validity (internal to each science) does not account sufficiently for the similarities between sciences.
5. In this chapter I shall only develop bits and pieces of the theory of capital's inner logic. For a complete and rigorous reconstruction of Marx's *Capital*, I strongly recommend Sekine's *An Outline of the Dialectic of Capital* (1997).
6. Paradoxically an ontology that emphasises difference can end up homogenising and flattening the social by its one-sided single-mindedness.
7. 'Things' is placed in quotation marks because the commodity and money are very peculiar things that embody social relations.
8. Reification implies that capital has an 'independent existence', as Marx makes clear in the following quotation: 'Capital as self-expanding value embraces not only class relations, a society of a definite character

resting on the existence of labour in the form of wage-labour.... Those who regard the gaining by value of independent existence as a mere abstraction forget that the movement of industrial capital is this abstraction *in actu* .... value as capital acquires independent existence, which it maintains and accentuates through its movement' (*Capital*, vol. II, 1967, pp. 108–9).

9. While all production of commodities is assumed to be capitalist, not all commodities are produced. For example labour power and land are converted into commodities and are capitalistically managed, but they are not capitalistically produced.
10. There may be other objects of social knowledge with their own distinctive forms of reification. Thus in some sense the Lacanian subject may display reified characteristics, or Foucault's disciplinary society. I would argue, however, that it is in a purely capitalist society that reification is most clearly manifest, and that thinkers such as Lacan at times project onto psychic phenomena and onto language degrees of reification that are only appropriate to pure capitalism.
11. For me, 'total reification' does not mean that persons are totally converted into things, rather that economic outcomes are totally determined by the motion of capital and that human agency is simply used by capital for its own self-expansion.
12. See Burawoy (1985) for an interesting theory of factory regimes.
13. Sometimes thinkers contrast the 'visible hand' of bureaucracy with the 'invisible hand' of the market. Here, I just want to indicate a basic difference between bureaucracy and economic reification without carrying out a full analysis of all the differences.
14. In *One-Dimensional Man*, Marcuse (1964) argues that reification has become so complete in history that any hope of liberation must be abandoned.
15. Rosenthal (1993) refers to basic concepts that result from commodity exchange as 'practical concepts'.
16. I agree with Postone's (1996) critique of Sohn-Rethel's one-sided emphasis on exchange as opposed to production.
17. Real abstractions are helped along by theoretical ones in the sense that theorists such as Smith and Ricardo have a real impact on economic practice in the sense of actually fostering policies that make social life more capitalist (or more *laissez faire*).
18. In a purely capitalist society we are always considering subjects only insofar as they are *economic* subjects.
19. Even in the production process, the theory of pure capitalism assumes that the labour of supervision is minimised in a system of machines of which workers are mere appendages. The imperatives are built into the machinery rather than being the commands of a superior. And in a purely capitalist society, we assume that workers do not resist the machinery of production.
20. 'Interpellation' comes from Althusser (1971).
21. Since in my view the theory of pure capitalism is strictly a theory of *capital's* commodity-economic logic, and capital in its inner logic is totally indifferent to persons and their arrangements for biological

reproduction, all but the most abstract and formal discussion of the family, domestic labour and reproduction must take place at more concrete levels of analysis than that of the theory of capital's inner logic.

22. I use 'ontology' here because a purely capitalist society is a different kind of object from a stage-specific abstract type, which in turn is a different kind of object from capital as a unique social force articulated with other social forces in processes of change. Political economy or the science of capitalism, then, must be a layered object of knowledge.
23. Necessity here is not like the axiomatic necessity of a formal econometric system, but is instead the necessity of social relations totally shaped by capital's logic, a logic that Sekine (1986) has shown can be formulated as a dialectic that starts with the contradiction between value and use-value inherent in the commodity form. See also John Bell, 'Dialectics and Economic Theory', in Albritton and Sekine (1995).
24. For a substantive presentation of a theory of stages see Albritton (1991).
25. I generally agree with Brenner that changes in British agriculture played a crucial role in the incubation of capitalism, but I strongly disagree with his use of the term 'agrarian capitalism' because it suggests that this early incubation was far more capitalist than it actually was. See Albritton (1993b).
26. For a full discussion of the stage of mercantilism see Albritton (1991, ch. 5).
27. There are few substantive works using this approach that deal with the historical analysis of capitalism, hence it is not yet possible to be very specific about the epistemology appropriate to this level. For some discussion of the level of historical analysis see Albritton (1991), and for the importance of being clear about 'capital' for the analysis of history see Albritton (1993b).
28. See Albritton (1993a). Bhaskar (1978) uses 'generative mechanism' to refer to the deep structure of scientific theories. Bhaskar has also developed conceptions of levels of analysis, which in his latest work (1993) have become both important and complex.
29. This is Nowak's (1980) term, which has interesting overlaps with Uno's 'a purely capitalist society'.
30. For an extended critique of the logical-historical method see Albritton (1986).
31. 'Global' does not refer to this world but to the possible (ideal) world of a purely capitalist society.
32. Empirically we cannot foretell when or how it must come to an end – only that capital's inner logic must gradually lose its partial grip on history. Sekine (1997), in fact, argues that this has already occured.
33. In the short term the falling rate of profit simply forces capital periodically to reconstitute its value relation through crises, but the rate of profit cannot fall for ever. Even a relatively low rate of profit would indicate stagnation and probably unacceptable levels of unemployment.
34. See Albritton (1991, pp. 106–9).
35. 'It is not to be expected that a man who drudges on all his life in a laborious trade, should be more knowing in the variety of things done

in the world than a pack horse' (Locke, 1959, vol. II, p. 443). '...there is greater distance between some men and others ... than between some men and some beasts.' (ibid., p. 446).

36. See Cranston (1957, pp. 424–5).
37. In the *Second Treatise*, Locke (1963) argues that Africans could be justifiably enslaved because they were aggressors in an unjust war.
38. Throughout Locke's writings 'idleness' is used as a condemnatory metaphor.
39. Marx writes: 'One can see that though Ricardo is accused of being too abstract, one would be justified in accusing him of the opposite: the lack of the power of abstraction, inability, when dealing with the values of commodities, to forget profits, a factor which confronts him as a result of competition (1968, p. 191). Also, Nowak (1980, p. 9) makes this point forcefully.
40. This metaphor may seem farfetched, but when we assume a purely capitalist society reproducing itself entirely through a commodity-economic logic, we remove all those interferences that would inhibit capital from showing itself as it is.
41. Collier (1994, p. 43) writes: 'For a law to be true, it must hold when the mechanism it designates works unimpeded in a closed system. And for the law to be useful, it must contribute to explaining events in open systems in which the mechanism is operating alongside others'. Unfortunately Marxists have not fully realised that for the law of value to be true it must be theorised in the closed system of a purely capitalist society, but that having done this, the real work has just begun. For capital's logic not only works alongside other mechanisms in open systems but also articulates with many social forces at the level of 'events' that may have no underlying deep structures or generative mechanism that unilaterally determine their causal efficacy.
42. My aim here is not to belittle the important contributions made by Marxian political economy heretofore, rather it is to emphasise the great potential of the approach being outlined here.
43. I am in general agreement with Nowak (1980) that Marx's *Capital* is an idealisation theory aimed at tracing the internal structure of capital. Where Nowak's aim is to stress the importance of idealisation as a strategy in all sciences, my aim is to stress the peculiarities of one science: Marxian political economy.
44. In a democratic socialist society 'economic value' as a relatively autonomous reifying force would no longer exist.

3 Hegel's Dialectic and the Dialectic of Capital

1. Marx, *A Contribution to the Critique of Political Economy*, cited in Althusser (1990, p. 205).
2. Derrida (1981, p. 7).
3. The earlier two-volume work is longer and deals explicitly with some of the parallels with Hegel's *Logic*, while the more recent two-volume work contains improvements in some of the economic formulations.

4. For a discussion of some of the problems that Hegel had with 'contingency' see Inwood (1992, pp. 60, 199). For an argument that Hegel gave 'contingency' more autonomy in his thought than is usually recognised see Zizek (1993, pp. 125–64).
5. The mistake is often made because the first three categories – 'commodity', 'money', 'capital' – do appear in history in that order. If, however, the sequence in capital's logic were always to parallel history, then the first category would probably be 'land' and the second 'labour'. In the dialectic of capital, however, 'land' is one of the last categories to be dealt with, and 'labour' is not dealt with until the doctrine of production.
6. This contradiction is strongly emphasised by Postone (1996).
7. Johnson (1988, pp. 5–7) argues that Hegel's concepts of pure thought 'have a being which is neither mental nor physical' and that his position on this is close to Bertram Russell's; however Russell 'regards universals as mere abstractions and particulars as independent concrete existences', whereas Hegel conceives of universals as 'permeating' particulars 'and acting as the universal ground of their existence'. Furthermore Johnson (ibid., 230) argues that for Hegel 'True analysis has as its products, not mere ideas, but concept-determinations immediately contained in the object.' According to Inwood (1992, pp. 57–60), for Hegel concepts are not sharply distinct from subjects (the I), objects or other concepts.
8. Hegel (1991, p. 55) writes: 'thinking is only genuine with respect to its content insofar as it is immersed in the *matter* … that consciousness conducts itself as an abstract 'I', as *freed* from *all particularity* … allowing the *matter* [itself] to hold sway over us'.
9. 'All that is necessary to achieve scientific progress … is the recognition of the logical principle that the negative is just as much positive, or that what is self-contradictory does not resolve itself into nullity' (Hegel, 1969, p. 54).
10. For example see Derrida (1982), 'White Mythology: Metaphor in the Text of Philosophy'.
11. For example in *Capital,* volume I (1976) Marx assumes phenomena to be in their pure form in numerous contexts (pp. 203, 260, 261, 710, 793, 798), in volume II (1967, pp. 25, 108, 505) and volume III (1971b, pp. 175, 268, 281, 287, 314, 614, 624, 885). Similarly there are many examples that illustrate his view that he is essentially theorising capital's 'inner logic', 'immanent laws', 'necessary inner connections', 'basic structure', 'general nature', 'inner mechanism' or 'general and necessary tendencies': volume I (1976, pp. 260, 381, 433, 710, 739) and volume III (1971b, pp. 110, 195, 267, 791, 880).
12. For a good discussion of this see Postone (1996).
13. Besides studying the relevant part of Sekine's work (1997), see Bell's 'Dialectics and Economic Theory' in Albritton and Sekine (1995).
14. In the category 'price', value and use-value are 'vanishing terms', much as in the category 'becoming', being and nothing are 'vanishing terms' (Hegel, 1991, p. 145).
15. The doctrine of circulation roughly parallels *Capital*, vol. I, Parts I & II. The doctrine of production parallels the remainder of volume I and all

of volume II, and the doctrine of distribution parallels volume III of *Capital*.

16. According to Hegel (1969, pp. 329–30), 'The Idea of essence, namely to be self-identical in the immediacy of its determined being, is already immanent in measure.... This nature of quantity as a return-into-self in which it is qualitative constitutes that being-in-and-for-itself which is essence.'
17. In contrast, according to Johnson (1988, p. 143), for Hegel 'The connectedness of things is, the primary fact, and their separation the work of the senses and the intellect.'
18. Hegel believes that 'reciprocity' is a richer concept than 'causality'. As Johnson (1988, p. 151) puts it: 'This is because causality and action and reaction are external to substances, whereas in reciprocity, things are what they are only in accordance with the relations they enter into....'
19. Johnson (1988, p. 95) has a good explanation of what Hegel means by 'reflection': 'Essence shows itself in two ways, first in the fleeting glimpses we are given of it in immediate experience, and secondly, in the fact that they only present it from a single perspective, and that they pass away. In the sphere of essence, we are witness to a constant movement proceeding from the inner side of a thing outward, and then from the outer appearance back inward: this movement whereby essence is revealed is reflection.'
20. Thinkers such as G. A. Cohen (1988) would have a great deal more difficulty refuting Sekine's labour theory of value than the crude interpretation of Marx's theory that Cohen refutes.
21. I see no significant difference between Marcuse's 'one-dimensional' thought and Adorno's 'identitarian' thought.
22. Both Jameson (1990) and Dews (1987) see promise in Adorno in opposition to poststructuralism. If I thought that the main alternative to poststructuralism were Adorno's negative dialectics, then I too would join with Jameson and Dews.
23. Marx's entire theory assumes continual pressure towards equilibrium even if a general equilibrium is never achieved. If capital moves from sectors with lower profits to those with higher profits, at a limit (equilibrium) this movement will stop even if this limit is never reached. Understood in this sense, a tendency towards equilibrium is absolutely central to the laws of motion of capital. According to Marx (1971a, p. 336): 'The different spheres of production, it is true, constantly tend to an equilibrium ... the law of value of commodities ultimately determines how much of its disposable working-time society can expend on each particular class of commodities .... But this constant tendency to equilibrium, of the various spheres of production, is exercised, only in the shape of a reaction against the constant upsetting of this equilibrium.' In volume III (1981, p. 289) Marx writes: 'The exchange or sale of commodities at their value is the rational, natural law of equilibrium between them; this is the basis on which divergences have to be explained, and not the converse, i.e. the law of equilibrium should not be derived from contemplating the divergences.' Besides these explicit uses of the concept 'equilibrium' throughout the theory, Marx clearly

assumes the operation of tendencies towards equilibrium. However it is also important to realise that just as capital approaches most closely to a state of equilibrium, periodic crises disrupt the equilibrium tendencies (but not totally), forcing new value relations upon capital that will again tend towards equilibrium.

24. Elsewhere Postone (1996, p. 217) claims that 'Geist, in its unfolding, constitutes objective reality as a determinate objectification of self...'

4 The Anti-Essentialism of Max Weber

1. While Weber is relatively non-essentialist, thoroughgoing anti-essentialists would probably find his approach prone to creeping essentialism and would probably also find aspects of his particular mix of methodological individualism and empiricism objectionable.
2. For emphasis on Nietzschean strands in his thought see Lash and Whimster (1987) and Hennis (1988). For similarities with Foucault see Dreyfus and Rabinow (1986) and Lash and Whimster (1987).
3. On Weber's commitment to marginal utility theory see Simon Clarke (1982), Gören Therborn (1976) and Albritton (1991).
4. It should be clear from what I have written that I do not consider the theory of capital's inner logic a Weberian ideal-type.
5. In capitalism the economic tends in the long run to shape other social forces more than they shape it ,and this is because of the reifying force peculiar to the economic that enables it to reproduce itself and reinforce that reproduction.
6. The listing of dominant characteristics of something is fundamentally different from a dialectic that grasps its inner logic. Compared with a dialectic, a list appears to be dogmatic and not very informative about the interrelations among the key elements.
7. Burger (1987) only sees two levels: sociology and history, but he does not consider Weber's specific analysis of the economic. Cohen (Weber, 1987, p. xx) also distinguishes two levels: no specific reference to time and place versus such references. Roth (1976) refers to configurational, developmental and situational levels. Others see a synchronic level and a diachronic level.
8. The 'logical-historical method' in Marxian political economy refers to the tendency for Marxists to apply the theory of capital's inner logic directly to modern history as if that history were a direct function of the logic. For an extended critique of the unfortunate consequences of this method see Albritton (1986, ch. 2).
9. Contrast with Weber's position the sense in which the categories of the dialectic of capital are 'real.'
10. Although Weber uses the term 'preliminary step', it is not a step he ever takes. He never focuses on abstract economic theory itself, although he borrows concepts from it.
11. It is this aspect of Weber's thought that so influences the Frankfurt School.

12. Bhaskar's (1978) defence of ontological realism makes it very clear that a theory of an 'inner mechanism' cannot by itself predict concrete happenings since its causal effectiveness at the level of the concrete may be blocked or deflected by other forces.
13. Throughout the three volumes of *Capital* Marx continually utilises the analogy between capital's immanent laws and natural processes. For example: 'The more acute and frequent such revolutions in value become, the more does the automatic movement of the now independent value operate with the elemental force of a natural process' (1967, pp. 108–9).
14. See Wolin's (1960) *Politics and Vision* for strong arguments about how the social has suppressed our ability to think about the political as a distinct sphere with its own concepts and modes of action.

5 The Problematic Althusser

1. Particularly the work of Resnick and Wolff and a large number of followers.
2. Of course I am not the only one to argue this. For example see Derrida (1993, p. 206).
3. For example see Resnick and Wolff (1987a, 1987b), Cutler *et al.* (1977) and Laclau and Mouffe (1985).
4. It seems to me that Althusser's interpretation of Hegel is rather one-sided, certainly controversial and possibly wrong, but it is beyond the scope of this chapter systematically to analyse Althusser's version of Hegel.
5. The notion of 'real abstraction' was particularly developed by Sohn-Rethel (1978).
6. I do not think that this is an accurate characterisation of Hegel's *Logic*. In particular it does not seem entirely accurate to consider 'Being' an 'original simple unity'. 'Being' is a highly abstract and unstable category, whose negativity is hardly simple. Indeed, if it were really an original simple unity, then it would never move forward.
7. Postone (1996) is in many ways takes a similar position. He argues that the theory of capital can be viewed as a dialectical logic. He also argues for distinct levels of analysis. He is not so clear, however, on the actual construction and content of the dialectical logic of capital, or on precisely how it relates to more concrete levels of analysis.
8. In Althusser's problematic 'mode of production' is the most abstract unit of analysis, whereas 'social formation' is a more concrete unit of analysis where more that one mode of production may articulate with another. Presumably Althusser uses 'social formation' here because he is considering the concrete example of the Russian Revolution, and not because he thinks the concept is only applicable in concrete analyses of social formations.
9. 'Overdetermination' for Althusser essentially means that contradictions are never simple but always are articulated with other contradictions and the whole that encompasses them.

10. Suchting (1986) discusses four different uses of 'contradiction' in Marx, but I expect there are many more. Certainly the possible meanings of the term are not exhausted by Althusser's binary simple versus overdetermined contradiction.
11. Most of these propositions come directly from Marx. But it is the particular use of them by Althusser interests me here.
12. As Marx puts it: 'In this quite alienated form of profit and in the same measure as the form of profit hides its inner core, capital more and more acquires a material form, is transformed more and more from a reltionship into a thing, but a thing which embodies, which has absorbed, the social relationship, a thing which has acquired a fictitious life and independent existence in relation to itself, a natural-supernatural entity …'
13. See Albritton (1986, ch. 6) for an example of how to theorise the 'superstructure' as a set of passive background conditions in a purely capitalist society.
14. Althusser (Althusser and Balibar, 1970, p. 17) writes: 'the text of history is not a text in which a voice (the Logos) speaks, but the inaudible and illegible notation of the effects of a structure of structures'. This no doubt represents Althusser at his most hyperstructuralist.
15. In fairness to Althusser (Althusser and Balibar, 1970, p. 14), he does explicitly state: 'We did not pose *Capital* the question of its economic or historical content, nor of its mere interal 'logic.' We read *Capital* as philosophers, and therefore posed it a different question.' The question remains, however, can this 'different question' be adequately posed without combining it with a thorough understanding of capital's 'economic … content'?

6 Deconstruction and Political Economy

1. Barnett (1998, p. 26)
2. Derrida in Kaplan and Sprinker (1993, p. 204).
3. Derrida in ibid., p. 212.
4. Cited in Althusser (1990, p. 205).
5. Others such as Resch (1992) argue vehemently that Althusser is a modernist thinker in his insistance on the scientificness of Marxism.
6. See Barnett (1998, pp. 23–5) for a strong argument that even Foucault is Hegelian in important respects.
7. See for example Derrida (1974, p. 158).
8. Hegel always understands the 'other' to be the other within the self and hence reconcilable, while Derrida thinks of the 'other' as outside the self and always containing differences that prevent dialectical synthesis.
9. 'If I knew anything about deconstruction it was, I thought, its allergy to dialectics' (Parker, 1996, p. 4).
10. This strikes me as an unfair criticism of Hegel, whose penetrating analysis of basic philosophical categories such as 'necessity' and 'contingency' or 'identity' and 'difference' arguably make him the philosopher who up to the time of his writing submitted least to the 'self-evidence of meaning'. Furthermore, Hegel in creating theory created new meaning,

whereas Derrida can only break with commonsense meanings by playing with metaphor in ways that leave meaning undecidable.

11. It is inaccurate to argue that for Hegel the totality of the signified 'pre-exists' the totality of the signifier. Also, it is not at all clear what Derrida means by 'natural totality'.
12. Hegel did not start this way, since 'Being' is not fully present, but is the starting point precisely because of its emptiness and interpenetration with 'Nothing'.
13. 'Being' has no context, or is perhaps all contexts, but eventually becomes part of the dialectic of pure thought in the abstract and in general (is this a 'context'?)
14. 'Being' is not fully present, and initially is only an infinite bundle of traces yet to be unravelled.
15. Sometimes the dialectical category 'use-value' is used metaphorically to refer to products that are not produced for exchange. But this usage can be confusing, as we see in Derrida's analysis.
16. In a sense Hegel does just this. 'Being' is from the beginning haunted by its total emptiness.
17. What about the autonomatisation of capital?
18. Laclau and Mouffe (1985) are also an example of this. They simply borrow uncritically and dogmatically from regulation theory when it comes time to say something substantive about the world.
19. The plurality of capitalism at the level of historical analysis is an odd plurality because capital is an homogenising force that always strives to reduce plurality. Thus the plurality that exists is plurality against capital or despite capital. To speak of 'capitalisms' can mean many different things, and as usual Derrida does not explain what he means.
20. At the level of historical analysis the law of value is refracted through social institutions and partially disrupted, and yet, insofar as it is accepted and not resisted, it is not experienced as coercive even at this level. Hence though coercive, it is so in a special sense.
21. Not privileging the economic simply means that we cannot in advance of actual research determine its role in particular historical outcomes. Given my understanding of modern history, however, I would expect that the economic plays the main role in many of the major historical trends.
22. The declining rate of profit points towards the mortality of capital, but can give us no clue as to its actual historical lifespan.
23. Gibson–Graham are strongly influenced by Resnick and Wolff in their approach to political economy.
24. For example they ask us to theorise capitalism 'as having … no coherent identity' (1996, p. 15) and to think of 'every entity' as 'the nexus of a bewildering complexity of natural and social processes' (ibid., p. 29), as well as and to think of the 'Complex processes of social development … as unique and decentered determinations' (ibid., p.43). Taking any of these seriously would surely get in the way of arriving at a concept of capitalism.
25. Cited in Barnett (1998, pp. 2–3). Hegel may stand 'motionless, waiting for us', but capital in contrast, draws us into a frenzy of accelerated production and consumption.

Bibliography

Adorno, Theodor (1987) *Negative Dialectics* (New York: Continuum).
Aglietta, Michel (1979) *A Theory of Capitalist Regulation* (London: New Left Books).
Albritton, Robert (1984) 'The Dialectic of Capital: A Japanese Contribution', *Capital and Class*, vol. 22.
Albritton, Robert (1986) *A Japanese Reconstruction of Marxist Theory* (London: Macmillan).
Albritton, Robert (1991) *A Japanese Approach to Stages of Capitalist Development* (London: Macmillan).
Albritton, Robert (1992) 'Levels of Analysis in Marxian Political Economy: An Unoist Approach', *Radical Philosophy*, no. 60.
Albritton, Robert (1993a) 'Marxian Political Economy for an Age of Postmodern Excess', *Rethinking Marxism*, vol. 6, no. 1 (Spring).
Albritton, Robert (1993b) 'Did Agrarian Capitalism Exist?', *The Journal of Peasant Studies*, vol. 20, no. 3 (April).
Albritton, Robert (1995) 'The De(con)struction of Marx's Capital', *Transformation*, no. 1.
Albritton, Robert (1998) 'The Unique Ontology of Capital', *Poznan Studies in the Philosophy of the Sciences and the Humanities*, no. 60.
Albritton, Robert and Thomas Sekine, (1995) *A Japanese Approach to Political Economy: Unoist Variations* (London: Macmillan).
Althusser, Louis (1969) *For Marx* (New York: Vintage).
Althusser, Louis (1971) *Lenin and Philosophy and Other Essays* (London: New Left Books).
Althusser, Louis (1990) *Philosophy and the Spontaneous Philosophy of the Scientists* (London: Verso).
Althusser, Louis (1997) *The Spectre of Hegel* (London: Verso).
Althusser, Louis and Etienne Balibar (1970) *Reading Capital* (London: New Left Books).
Amariglio, Jack, Stephen Resnick and Richard Wolff (1990) 'Division and Difference in the "Discipline" of Economics', *Critical Inquiry*, Fall.
Andreski, Stanilav (1983) *Max Weber on Capitalism, Bureaucracy and Religion* (London: George Allen & Unwin).
Antonio, R. and R. Glassman (1985) *A Weber–Marx Dialogue* (Lawrence, Kansas: University of Kansas Press).
Barnett, Stuart (1998) *Hegel After Derrida* (London: Routledge).
Baudrillard, Jean (1975) *The Mirror of Production* (St. Louis: Telos Press).
Bhaskar, Roy (1978) *A Realist Theory of Science* (Brighton: Harvester Press).
Bhaskar, Roy (1979) *The Possibility of Naturalism* (New Jersey: Humanities Press).
Bhaskar, Roy (1989) *Reclaiming Reality* (London: Verso).
Bhaskar, Roy (1993) *Dialectic: The Pulse of Freedom* (London: Verso).

Brenner, Robert (1977) 'The Origins of Capitalist Development', *New Left Review*, no. 104 (July–August).

Burawoy, Michael (1985) *The Politics of Production* (London: Verso).

Burbidge, John (1981) *On Hegel's Logic* (New Jersey: Humanities Press).

Burger, Thomas (1987) *Max Weber's Theory of Concept Formation* (Durham, North Carolina: Duke University Press).

Callari, Antonio and David Ruccio (1996) *Postmodern Materialism and the Future of Marxist Theory* (Hanover, New Hampshire: Wesleyan University Press).

Cassidy, John (1996) 'The Decline of Economics', *New Yorker*, 2 December 1996.

Castree, Noel (1996) 'Invisible Leviathan: Speculations on Marx, Spivak, and the Question of Value', *Rethinking Marxism*, vol. 9, no. 2.

Clarke, Simon (1982) *Marx, Marginalism, and Modern Sociology* (London: Macmillan).

Cohen, G. A. (1988) *History, Labour and Freedom* (New York: Oxford University Press).

Collier, Andrew (1994) *Critical Realism* (London: Verso).

Collins, R. (1986) *Weberian Sociological Theory* (Cambridge: Cambridge University Press).

Colletti, Lucio (1975) 'Contradiction and Contrariety', *New Left Review*, no. 93.

Cranston, Maurice (1957) *John Locke: A Biography* (London: Longmans).

Cutler, Anthony, Barry, Hindness, Paul, Hirst, and Athar Hussain (1977) *Marx's Capital and Capitalism Today* (London: Routledge and Kegan Paul).

Derrida, Jacques (1974) *Of Grammatology* (Baltimore, MD: The Johns Hopkins University Presss).

Derrida, Jacques, (1978) *Writing and Difference* (Chicago, Ill.: University of Chicago Press).

Derrida, Jacques (1981) *Positions* (Chicago, Ill.: University of Chicago Press).

Derrida, Jacques (1982) *Margins of Philosophy* (Chicago, Ill.: University of Chicago Press).

Derrida, Jacques (1988) *Limited Inc.* (Evanston: Northwestern University Press).

Derrida, Jacques (1993) 'Politics and Friendship: An Interview with Jacques Derrida', in E. Ann Kaplan and Michael Sprinker, *The Althusserian Legacy* (London: Verso).

Derrida, Jacques (1994) *Specters of Marx* (London: Routledge).

Dews, Peter (1987) *Logics of Disintegration* (London: Verso).

Dreyfus, Hubert and Paul Rabinow (1986) *Foucault: Beyond Structuralism and Hermeneutics* (Brighton, Susse: Harvester Press).

Ferber, Marianne and Julie Nelson, (1993) *Beyond Economic Man* (Chicago, Ill.: University of Chicago Press).

Freeman, Alan and Goglielmo Carchedi (1996) *Marx and Non-Equilibrium Economics* (Cheltenham, UK: Edward Elgar).

Garnett, Robert (1995) 'Marx's Value Theory: Modern or Postmodern?', *Rethinking Marxism*, vol. 8 no. 4.

Gibson–Graham, J. K. (1995) 'Haunting Capitalism ... in the Spirit of Marx and Derrida', *Rethinking Marxism*, vol. 8, no. 4.

Gibson–Graham, J. K. (1996) *The End of Capitalism (as we knew it)* (Oxford: Blackwell).

Gramsci, Antonio (1971) *Selections From the Prison Notebooks*, ed. and trans. G. Hoare and G. Nowell-Smith (New York: International Publishers).

Hegel, G. W. F. (1956) *The Philosophy of History*, trans. J. Sibree (New York: Dover).

Hegel, G. W. F. (1969) *Hegel's Science of Logic, trans*. A. V. Miller (London: Allen & Unwin).

Hegel, G. W. F. (1970) *The Philosophy of Nature*, trans. A. V. Miller (Oxford: Oxford University Press).

Hegel, G. W. F. (1971) *Philosophy of Right*, trans. T. M. Knox (Oxford: Oxford University Press)

Hegel, G. W. F. (1975) *Hegel's Logic*, trans. William Wallace (London: Oxford University Press).

Hegel, G. W. F. (1991) *The Encyclopaedia Logic*, trans. T. F. Gereats, W. A. Suchting and H. S. Harris (Indianapolis: Hackett Publishing).

Hekman, Susan (1983) *Weber, the Ideal Type, and Contemporary Social Theory*, (Notre Dame, IA: University of Notre Dame Press).

Hennis, W. (1988) *Max Weber: Essays in Reconstruction* (London: Allen & Unwin).

Hindess, Barry (1977a) *Philosophy and Methodology in the Social Sciences* (Brighton: Harvester Press).

Hindess, Barry (1977b) *Sociological Theories of the Economy* (London: Macmillan).

Holton, R. and B. Turner (1989) *Max Weber on Economy and Society* (London: Routledge).

Huff, T. E (1984) *Max Weber and the Methodology of the Social Sciences* (New Brunswick: Transaction Books).

Inwood, Michael (1992) *A Hegel Dictionary* (Oxford: Blackwell).

Itoh, Makoto (1988) *The Basic Theory of Capitalism* (London: Macmillan).

Jameson, Fredric (1990) *Late Marxism* (London: Verso).

Jessop, Bob (1990) 'Regulation Theories in Retrospect and Prospect', *Economy and Society*, vol. 19, no. 2.

Johnson, Paul Owen (1988) *The Critique of Thought: A Re-examination of Hegel's Science of Logic* (Aldershot: Avebury).

Kalberg, Stephen (1994) *Max Weber's Comparative-Historical Sociology* (Cambridge: Polity Press).

Kaplan, E. Ann and Michael Sprinker (1993) *The Althusserian Legacy* (London: Verso).

Lacan, Jacques (1977) *Ecrits* (New York: W. W. Norton).

Laclau, Ernesto and Chantal Mouffe (1985) *Hegemony and Socialist Strategy: Towards a Radical Democratic Politics* (London: Verso).

Lash, S. and S. Whimster (1987) *Max Weber, Rationality and Modernity* (London: Allen & Unwin).

Lawson, Tony (1997) *Economics and Reality* (London: Routledge).

Lecourt, Dominique (1975) *Marxism and Epistemology: Bachelard, Canquilhem, Foucault* (London: New Left Books).

Lehmann, Jennifer (1993) 'The Undecidability of Derrida/The Premature Demise of Althusser', *Current Perspectives in Social Theory*, no. 13.

Lewis, Tom (1996) 'The Politics of "Hauntology" in Derrida's *Specters of Marx*', *Rethinking Marxism*, vol. 9, no. 3.
Locke, John (1959) *An Essay Concerning Human Understanding*, 2 vols (New York: Dover).
Locke, John (1963) *Two Treatises of Government* (Cambridge: Cambridge University Press)
Lukács, Georg (1971) *History and Class Consciousness* (London: Merlin).
Marcuse, Herbert (1964) *One-Dimensional Man* (Boston, Mass: Beacon Press).
Martin, Bill (1992) *Matrix and Line* (Albany: SUNY Press).
Marx, Karl (1963) *Theories of Surplus Value*, vol. III (Moscow: Progress).
Marx, Karl (1967) *Capital*, vol. II (Moscow: Progress).
Marx, Karl (1968) *Theories of Surplus Value*, vol. II (Moscow: Progress).
Marx, Karl (1971a) *Capital*, vol. I (Moscow: Progress).
Marx, Karl (1971b) *Capital*, vol. III (Moscow: Progress).
Marx, Karl (1973) *Grundrisse* (London: Penguin).
Marx, Karl (1976) *Capital*, vol. I (London: New Left Review).
Marx, Karl (1978a) 'The Eighteenth Brumaire of Louis Bonaparte', *The Marx–Engels Reader*, ed. R. Tucker (London: Norton).
Marx, Karl (1978b) 'The Communist Manifesto', *The Marx-Engels Reader*, ed. R. Tucker (London: Norton).
Marx, Karl (1981) *Capital*, vol. III (New York: Vintage Books).
Merton, Robert K. (1957) *Social Theory and Social Structure* (New York: Free Press).
Nowak, Leszek (1980) *The Structure of Idealization* (Dordrecht, Holland: D. Reidel).
Ormerod, Paul (1994) *The Death of Economics* (London: Faber & Faber).
Parker, Andrew (1996) 'Re-Marx: Prehistory', *Rethinking Marxism*, vol. 9, no. 4.
Polanyi, Karl (1944) *The Great Transformation* (Boston, Mass.: Beacon).
Postone, Moishe (1996) *Time, Labor, and Social Domination* (Cambridge: Cambridge University Press).
Resch, Robert Paul (1992) *Althusser and the Renewal of Marxist Social Theory* (Berkeley, CA: University of California Press).
Resnick, Stephen and Richard Wolff (1987a) *Economics: Marxian versus Neoclassical* (Baltimore, MD: The Johns Hopkins Press).
Resnick, Stephen and Richard Wolff (1987b) *Knowledge and Class* (Chicago, Ill.: University of Chicago Press).
Resnick, Stephen and Richard Wolff (1988) 'Marxian Theory and the Rhetorics of Economics', in A. Klamer, D. McCloskey and R. Solow (eds), *The Consequences of Economic Rhetoric* (Cambridge: Cambridge University Press).
Rosenthal, John (1993) 'The Objectivity of the Economic: An Essay on the Transformation of Philosophy in the Discourse of Marx's "Capital"', PhD Thesis, New School for Social Research, New York.
Roth, Guenther (1976) 'History and Sociology in the Work of Max Weber', *British Journal of Sociology*, vol. XXVII, no. 3.
Ryan, Michael (1982) *Marxism and Deconstruction* (Baltimore, MD: Johns Hopkins Press).
Sayer, Derek (1991) *Capitalism and Modernity: An Excursus on Marx and Weber* (London: Routledge).

Sekine, Tom (1986) *The Dialectic of Capital*, 2 vols (Tokyo: Toshindo Press).
Sekine, Tom (1997) *An Outline of The Dialectic of Capital*, 2 vols (London: Macmillan).
Shin, Jo-Young (1995) 'Althusser's Contribution to a Postmodern (Overdeterminist) Marxism', *Rethinking Marxism*, vol. 8, No. 2.
Sohn-Rethel, Alfred (1978) *Intellectual and Manual Labour* (London: Macmillan).
Sorel, Georges (1961) *Reflections on Violence* (New York: Collier Books).
Steedman, Ian (1977) *Marx After Sraffa* (London: New Left Books).
Suchting, W. A. (1986) *Marx and Philosophy* (London: Macmillan).
Suchting, W. A. (1991) 'On Some Unsettled Questions Touching the Character of Marxism, especially as Philosophy', *Graduate Faculty Philosophy Journal*, vol. 14, no. 1.
Suchting, W. A. (1992) 'Reflections Upon Roy Bhaskar's "Critical Realism"', *Radical Philosophy* no. 61.
Therborn, Göran (1976) *Science, Class and Society* (London: New Left Books).
Thompson, E. P. (1978) *The Poverty of Theory and Other Essays* (New York: Monthly Review Press).
Uno, Kozo (1980) *Principles of Political Economy*, trans. T. Sekine (Sussex: Harvester Press).
Warren, Mark (1992) 'Max Weber's Nietzschean Conception of Power', *History of the Human Sciences*, vol. 5, no. 3.
Weber, M. (1947) *Max Weber: The Theory of Social and Economic Organization*, trans. A. M. Henderson and T. Parsons (New York: Oxford University Press).
Weber, M. (1949) *The Methodology of the Social Sciences* (New York: The Free Press).
Weber, M. (1958) *The Protestant Ethic and the Spirit of Capitalism*, trans. T. Parsons (New York: Charles Scribner's Sons).
Weber. M. (1964) *The Sociology of Religion* (Boston: Beacon Press)
Weber, M. (1975a) 'Marginal Utility Theory and the So-Called Fundamental Law of Psychodynamics', trans. and ed., Louis Schneider, *Social Science Quarterly*, vol. 56: no. 1.
Weber, M. (1975b) *Roscher and Knies: The Logical Problems of Historical Economics* (New York: The Free Press).
Weber, M. (1977) *Critique of Stammler*, trans. Guy Oakes (New York: The Free Press).
Weber, M. (1978a) *Economy and Society*, 2 vols. (Berkeley, CA: University of California Press).
Weber, M. (1978b) *Weber: Selections in Translation*, ed. W.G. Runciman (Cambridge: Cambridge University Press).
Weber, M. (1987) *General Economic History* (New Brunswick, NJ: Transaction Books)
Winch, Peter (1958) *The Idea of a Social Science and Its Relation to Philosophy* (London: Routledge).
Wolin, Sheldon (1960) *Politics and Vision* (Boston: Little, Brown & Company)

Zaret, David (1980) 'From Weber to Parsons and Schutz: the Eclipse of History in Modern Social Theory', *American Journal of Sociology*, vol. 85, no. 3.

Zizek, Slavoj (1993) *Tarrying with the Negative* (Durham, North Carolina: Duke University Press).

Index